Media, Technology, and Society

DIGITALCULTUREBOOKS is an imprint of the University of Michigan Press and the Scholarly Publishing Office of the University of Michigan Library dedicated to publishing innovative and accessible work exploring new media and their impact on society, culture, and scholarly communication.

Media, Technology, and Society:
Theories of Media Evolution

W. RUSSELL NEUMAN, *editor*

The University of Michigan Press AND *The University of Michigan Library*
ANN ARBOR

Copyright © by W. Russell Neuman 2010
All rights reserved
Published in the United States of America by
The University of Michigan Press and
The University of Michigan Library
Manufactured in the United States of America
∞ Printed on acid-free paper

2013   2012   2011   2010   4   3   2   1

A CIP catalog record for this book is available from the British Library.

Library of Congress Cataloging-in-Publication Data

Media, technology, and society : theories of media evolution /
    W. Russell Neuman, editor.
        p.   cm.
    Includes bibliographical references and index.
    ISBN 978-0-472-07082-4 (cloth : alk. paper)—ISBN 978-0-472-
05082-6 (pbk. : alk. paper)
    1. Mass media—Technological innovations. 2. Digital media—
Technological innovations. 3. Mass media—Social aspects. I.
Neuman, W. Russell.

P96.T42M425 2010
302.23–dc22   2010004473

Acknowledgments

First of all we would like to express our appreciation to John D. Evans, whose support of communication research and practice at his alma mater, the University of Michigan, has been critically important and valued by the community at the University for many years. Professor Neuman occupies the Evans Chair of Media Technology, and the John D. Evans Fund for Media and Technology supported the production of this volume and the organizing conference in 2006. In addition this book has had contributions, commentary, and administrative help from the following friends and colleagues: Francois Bar, Sandra Braman, Scott Campbell, Susan Douglas, Robert Frost, Krysha Gregorowicz, Lauren Guggenheim, Steve Jackson, John King, Andy Lippman, Amanda Lotz, Alison Mackeen, Yong Jin Park, Roberta Saling, Marvin Sirbu, Chip Steinfield, Dawn Viau, and Steve Wildman.

Contents

Theories of Media Evolution

W. RUSSELL NEUMAN

Those who ignore history are doomed to repeat it.
—George Santayana

History does not repeat, but it does rhyme.
—Mark Twain

Our muse for this volume might well be the two-faced god Janus of the Roman pantheon who famously looked both forward and backward, the patron of beginnings, transitions, and new plantings. His name is the linguistic root for the month we call January. We will make the case here that the ongoing digital revolution in present-day media technology represents an important new beginning in public life and is likely to have a fundamental influence on how individuals, social groups, and societies define themselves, how individuals come to know the world around them, and whether further generations succeed in sustaining an energetic public sphere and open marketplace of ideas. If these technical transitions offer us an opportunity to collectively construct institutions and digital systems that best serve our shared (although frequently contested) ideals of the public good, how might we proceed most thoughtfully, realistically, and successfully? Our muse suggests a very careful look at the recent past. If we want to understand how the Internet is likely to evolve, perhaps we should take a long, hard look at the bizarre evolution of the infrastructures and institutions of the past century—newspapers, telephony, movies, radio, television, satellite-based cable TV, early digital networks.

Bizarre? That is a rather strong descriptive term to try to capture the essence of entire century of technical, economic, institutional, and cultural history. The term implies a notion of something freakishly out of the ordinary, unexpected, weird, not according to plan. At first glance, such a characterization would seem to be a poor match for what we know of newspapers, radio, and TV—humdrum, predictable, taken-for-granted elements of our daily lives. The last two centuries trace a now celebrated succession of genius inventors. Samuel F. B. Morse invented the telegraph, Alexander Graham Bell the telephone, Edison movies, Marconi radio, Farnsworth TV. These heroic visionaries knew what they were doing and their visions changed our lives. Yes?

Well, not exactly. As we will see in the pages ahead, most of those we now find it convenient to celebrate as genius inventors had notions about what they were building that turned out to be at some variance from what eventually evolved into working technologies and institutions of mass communication. When we take the time to look back carefully, we come to understand that it could have been otherwise, sometimes dramatically so. What we assume to be an inevitable technical progression is actually the result of accidental sequences of events and diverse political battles won and lost. In other words—bizarre happenstance.

It could have been otherwise. What we know as newspapers, radio, and television were socially constructed, not technologically determined by the nature of printing and of electromagnetic transmission through the air. That lesson will become a key element of our look forward to a world defined by ubiquitous digital broadband nodes and networks. The general term for our approach to these curiously repeating patterns is the *social construction of technology* (frequently abbreviated SCOT), a model of historical analysis popularized by Bijker, Hughes, and Pinch in their influential 1987 volume on the technological innovation. SCOT is a theoretical perspective, an overarching label for a series of more focused theories about the interaction of cultural presumptions, the radical new ideas of innovators and the constraints exerted by entrenched interests and political economy of technical change. We will introduce each of these theories briefly in this introductory chapter and then they will be put to work in the chapters that follow.

Bijker and colleagues reviewed a broad array of technologies and historical transitions. Here we will focus on seven dominant modes of communication, primarily mass communication that have in many ways come to define the character of American industrial society over the last two centuries, as summarized in figure 1. We have assigned each of

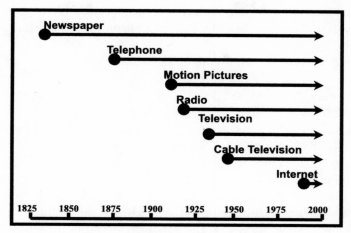

Fig. 1. Timeline of American Media

these media an official birthday, although as we will see shortly there is typically ambiguity, controversy, and a delay of varying numbers of years between technical invention and social utilization. We shall see that the history of innovation brings to light many examples of considerable confusion, false starts, and conflict.

A Succession of the New Media of Their Time

The steam-driven cylindrical rotary press made the modern mass-circulation newspaper possible. So although we celebrate Gutenberg's innovations of the fifteenth century, we will designate 1833 as the historical birth year of the modern newspaper because of Richard Hoe's invention of the modern rotary press and Benjamin Day's dramatic decision to sell the *New York Sun* for only a penny, making it economically available to a mass readership. For telephony we use 1876, the year of Alexander Graham Bell's patent application. In the early days of telephony many anticipated its use as a broadcast public-address style technology for concerts and speeches, a social definition that would strike most modern telephone customers as quaint. It would take three-quarters of a century before in-home telephony started to reach near universal penetration. The technology of motion picture photography and projection was developed by the Lumière brothers and Thomas Edison in the 1890s, but to signal the birth of commercial motion pictures we point to the year 1913, when the first commercial motion picture venue opened in the United States and movies moved from the nickelodeon arcade to the theater.

KDKA operated by Westinghouse in Pittsburgh is credited with being the first commercial radio station with regularly scheduled broadcasts in 1920. The corresponding date for commercial television was 1941, when NBC and CBS commenced limited wartime television broadcasts in New York. Cable, born originally as CATV, for *community antenna TV,* was first tested in the mountains near Philadelphia in 1948. It would take almost thirty years for cable to move from retransmitting a few regional TV stations to multiple channels of independent television programming. And finally, we mark the birth of the modern Web with the release of the first user-friendly web browser at the University of Illinois in 1993. The Mosaic browser built on the recent ideas of Tim Berners-Lee and, of course, the fundamental technologies of the Internet Protocol invented three decades earlier for military purposes. The seven chapters following this introduction look through a variety of theoretical lenses to review the overlapping histories and futures of these media, and the two subsequent chapters address public policy questions that arise as each of these media confront an increasingly digital world.

Figure 1 arrays each of these media in a straightforward timeline from their designated birth years. It is an uncomplicated diagram because for the time span of each medium, the basic technology, the stylized content, and the social definition of appropriate media use was a largely unchanged and consistent historical arc. Newspapers shifted from a flirtation with dramatically yellow journalism to the modern principles of professional journalistic practice at the turn of the century. Broadcast telephony never took off. Movies added sound in 1926. Radio migrated from the living room to the bedroom, kitchen, and car in response to competition from television in the 1950s. But the basic social definition of reading a newspaper or listening to radio or watching television remained unchanged.

When Old Technologies Meet New

Figure 1 depicts each medium as an arrow moving forward into the twenty-first century, but therein lies a central puzzle and a principal motivation for this volume. Many observers are predicting that these historically defined media will converge into a single digital medium—the medium we now refer to as the Internet or simply the Web. We see the outlines of this process in the multipurpose portable devices like the iPhone or Blackberry that function as telephones, cameras, web browsers, and audio and video players. Skeptics have raised doubts about this convergence, pointing out that newspapers survived the advent of radio news in the 1920s and movies survived competition from television. But this technological revolution may represent a different historical case because the Internet does not simply compete with its predecessors, it subsumes them. Is such a process really under way? Will it represent a collective opportunity for us to review the architecture of public communication to ensure that it best serves the public interest? The tradition of American mass communication is famously an intersection of the civil public commons and the realm of advertising and private enterprise. Will Internet radio and Internet newspapers simply mimic their commercial predecessors or develop new voices and functions perhaps derived from social networking web sites? Our strategy to assess these important questions is to draw on the recent past and exploit the best standing hypotheses and theories of technological evolution the literature provides us.

This first chapter will introduce the toolkit of concepts and theories the authors in this volume variously put to work. Toynbee famously chastised historiography as just the documentation of "one damned thing after another." We aspire to a somewhat higher level of organization. A frequent strategy in organizing these compelling tales is the thematic of human initiative pitted against powerful forces perceiving novelty as threat. Another strategic approach to theorizing is to focus on structural factors and systemic dynamics. All of the chapters confront the issue of technology, especially critical points in technical evolution. These are studies of coevolving media institutions, human initiative, technological capacities, and a changing society. I hasten to point out that none of the authors subscribes to any variant of technological determinism. Unfortunately, this specter of ill-considered causal attribution continues to plague this field of scholarly inquiry. Those of us who study changing technologies in historical context have grown accustomed to addressing this unfortunate and nearly inevitable epithet in most scholarly forums. None of the authors here succumb to such technological monism. None diminish the importance of human agency or the dynamic two-way interaction of technical design and cultural perspective. Most would agree with Castells's dictum: "Of course, technology does not determine society" (1996, 3).

The physical properties of alternative technical systems, however, do make a difference. They prove to be variously constraining and empowering of diverse human activities. Centralized printing and publishing is by its nature prone to one-way communication and is subject to censorship. Communication via the Internet is inherently bidirectional, decentralized, and less easily monitored and censored. But to constrain or facilitate is not to determine. Ignoring the character of technological systems is as shortsighted as unthinking deterministic attribution. The pages ahead will address the interaction of technical capacity and cultural initiative at length, not as a deterministic process but rather as a form of coevolution (Durham 1991; Garud and Karnøe 2001). As appropriate, authors use such terminologies as a *technological affordance* or *socially constructed use* to capture this technological-cultural interaction (Hutchby 2001; Bijker, Hughes, and Pinch 1987). In some more philosophically oriented analyses of technical history, the character and directionality of constraining forces is more central to the analysis. One such tradition of scholarship is *actor network theory,* frequently abbreviated ANT (Latour 1987). Latour and colleagues Michel Callon and John Law may have been reacting in part to the technological determinism critique and wanted to bring technical properties "back in" to theorizing without ignoring the critically important elements of social construction. Another tradition follows from Anthony Giddens's concept of *structuration* (1984). Giddens draws attention to the ironic fact that individual agents are both constrained by social structures and, through their routine behavior, powerfully reconstitute these structures. Accordingly, we come to understand that the power of the traditional mass media relies on the fact of massive public habitual reliance more than any fundamental technical capacities. As it turns out, none of our authors use Latour's or Giddens's work formally and explicitly, but the perspectives they have advocated and their concern about interactive causal connections inform the work in each of these chapters.

Heroes and Villains

The heroes of these stories of media evolution as they are most often told are those who support innovation, competition, a vibrant and inclusive public sphere, and an open marketplace of ideas. These include inventors, innovators, investors, insightful public servants, policy advocates, academic researchers, philosophers, and risk-taking entrepreneurs. The requisite villains, as these accounts progress, are the skeptical conservative forces, energetically protecting their profit margins, threatened by and resistant to the prospect of change in traditional patterns of public communication. The distinction, however, is far from clear-cut. The leading actors seldom conveniently identify themselves with white or black hats. Some established (and profitable) institutions provide important functions very much worth sustaining. One thinks of the importance of competitive and self-sustaining independent journalism, what we have come to label the "fourth estate" in modern liberal industrial democracies (Hallin and Mancini 2004). It is far from clear how independent professional journalism will sustain itself if the advertising-driven ink-on-paper news business model fails. One thinks also of numerous institutions associated with sustaining community arts and indigenous and classical arts and literatures. And some innovators have designs on constraining diversity, exploiting stereotypes and extracting oligopolistic profits.

We often confront, as well, two other forms of potentially self-serving villainy that may transcend the behavior of individual actors. The questions these behaviors raise are fundamental to the field of political economy—the study of the border between political and economic institutions. The first is the prospect of the excesses of an unconstrained and ill-behaved marketplace. The second is the prospect of an equivalently unconstrained and repressive political regime. Public communication and active mass media lie at the core of a successful polity. Governments regulate spectrum, rules for intellectual property protection, limitations on public speech, electoral processes, media ownership, and guidelines for individual privacy. The media marketplace, much more than the market for, say, golf balls or cardboard boxes, is wholly permeated with political and regulatory involvement. Historically, it might be modeled as a "tipping" or "slippery slope" problem—once big business or big government becomes all-powerful, the prospect of using that power to preclude any challenge to dominance is irresistibly seductive. Totalitarian state systems that deflect criticism from citizens and confine the potential of an adversarial and independent press represent one troubling exemplar (Pool 1973). Correspondingly dominant capitalist ideology and unchallenged manipulation of political institutions represents another, one that continues to attract a great deal of attention in the tradition of critical theory (Habermas 1989; Schiller 1989; Bagdikian 2004).

A Working Toolkit of Theoretical Constructs: First the Heroic Innovators

Stories require heroes. Histories too. In the many thousands of generations before the invention of the ultimate medium of communication—

the written word—generations passed their accumulated wisdom to their successors in an easily remembered format, the narrative. Stories of heroes and dragons and maidens would elevate the accomplishments of the protagonist rallying against difficult odds as a socially desired model for behavior, with partially remembered facts and useful fictions inevitably intertwined. Why, then, should we be surprised that one prominent approach to recording media history and understanding innovation could be characterized as the *heroic school?*

Behind every successful innovation in human endeavor is likely a champion, an articulate visionary, an inventor perhaps at the margins of the social institutions of the day, or contrastingly, a powerful player who seizes upon on an innovation as a means to a self-serving end. Most analysts in the tradition of such historiography do not actually use the word *hero*. Christensen (1997), among others, draws attention to the *innovation champion model*. Garud and Karnøe (2001) label heroic innovation as *mindful deviation,* but the analytic meaning is fundamentally the same. Both theories celebrate the willful capacity of socially situated individuals who have each in their own way been hit on the head by a falling apple and have responded appropriately, thoughtfully, and probably creatively. Garud and Karnøe's reading of the literature leads them to critique *path dependency* models as unnecessarily deterministic and incomplete. They prefer to emphasize *path creation,* noting that, of course, directions of innovation are limited by historical circumstances, by current technical capacities, and indeed by the previous choices that bias later ones. But the key observation is that mindful innovators think about and actively respond to these constraints. Their behavior represents an interesting twist on random mutation in the Darwinian tradition. Traditionally the mutation either enhances or diminishes survival odds of the organism in a given ecological niche. In Garud and Karnøe's model, the mindful observer reacts to potential of the mutation by working to change the character of the ecological niche itself or proactively finding a new niche for which the mutation is especially useful.

A variation of the heroic model that draws the attention of our chapter authors is the notion of a *founding myth,* the post hoc creation of a heroic narrative to explain the success of a technology or company. David Sarnoff, RCA's famous and charismatic CEO, for example, tells the story of how he foresaw radio as a magic music box in every household rather than the applications in marine telegraphy that occupied its early developers at the Marconi Company. There is some controversy about whether he actually authored—as he claimed—the famous 1916 music box memorandum that imagined radio in every home, but one can understand why such a memo is useful to the heroic narrative. A variant of founding mythology is *visionary rhetoric,* the use of slogans and catchphrases to capture the promise of various innovations.

Theorizing the Counterpoint to Heroism

And heroes require dragons. How could a satisfying narrative be complete without the requisite counterpoint to innovative heroism—the establishment, the status quo, those interests perhaps threatened by new ways of doing things? Sarnoff, who had worked his way up the chain of command from telegraph operator and visionary to leader of RCA and NBC, became himself the counterpoint to visionary inventor Philo Farnsworth, whose television technology threatened the RCA radio empire, whose leaders had plans of their own for television. Perhaps the most formalized model of counterpoint dynamics is Brian Winston's *law of the suppression of radical potential* (1986, 1998). In his analysis, established institutions alternatively delay the diffusion of competitive technologies or influence how new technologies are structured so they are less threatening to established institutions and social norms.

A close theoretical relation to Winston's suppression law is the idea, already noted, of path dependency. In the broadest sense, this perspective is simply a restatement of the less than controversial observation that "history matters." But in the tradition of technological historical analysis it has special meaning in the sense of technical "lock in" associated with processes of standardization and technical interoperability (Schmidt and Werle 1998; Shapiro and Varian 1998). Returns to scale often reward early technological initiatives with a competitive advantage not easily overcome. The classic example, of course, is the QWERTY keyboard, originally designed to prevent adjacent typewriter keys from jamming, which now provides a standard that precludes layouts more efficient and appropriate for the computer age (David 1985). Hughes (1987) and colleagues in the SCOT tradition sometimes use the analytic term *closure* to characterize largely the same phenomenon—the stage of technical development when the system architecture of technology and socially accepted common use become fixed and resistant to further development. One element of closure that draws more on cultural rather than technical factors is the *resilience of interpretive schemes,* the taken-for-granted and self-reinforcing patterns of professional practice and social definition Bourdieu often referred to as *habitus* (1991, 1993).

Notions of path dependency in the domain of media institutions have a somewhat different emphasis, focusing on the accumulation of political and economic power rather than technical lock-in, although both phenomena are in evidence. My personal favorite in historical examples of path dependency in communication history is one of the very oldest. It turns out that the spoken language of ancient Egypt was naturally amendable to a phonetic alphabet. Each of the twenty-two consonant sounds in use was represented by a unique hieroglyphic. The scribal hierarchy realized this and successfully resisted the spread of literacy in the general population by insisting on a much more complex all-hieroglyphic system for each word (akin to modern Mandarin, Japanese, and Korean). The professional scribes retained their power and unique position in Egyptian society for another millennium, until the Phoenicians and Greeks developed more accessible alphabetic writing systems (Saggs 1989, 74). Notably, what benefited the scribal status did not necessarily benefit progress in Egyptian culture and economics.

Michels's (1962) *iron law of oligarchy* adds a special sociopolitical dimension to the analysis of path-dependent media evolution. Michels's own work focused on political parties and labor unions, but the dynamic applies more broadly. He notes that in the historical evolution of complex organizations (in our case necessary to support complex network technologies) the bureaucracy increasingly restructures decision processes to serve bureaucratic ends, rather than the goals for which the organization was originally put in place, in effect hijacking control of the institutional structure. One example in modern media debates is intellectual property law: lawyers and industry lobbyists find it in their interest to continue litigation rather than develop new processes for technically sophisticated intellectual property remuneration that may benefit cultural creators and audiences, rather than litigators (Litman 2000).

Another conceptual instrument to add to our toolkit is *constitutive choice*, developed by sociologist Paul Starr. It bridges the notions of historical and technical constraint and of mindful deviation and in many ways, I will argue, characterizes the current historical threshold. His history of American media institutions centers on critical constitutive moments, historical windows of opportunity when

> ideas and culture come into play, as do constellations of power, preexisting institutional legacies and models from other countries. Although the people directly involved in the decisions may not be aware of their long-term implications, institutions and systems once

established often either resist change or invite it in a particular direction. . . . Early choices bias later ones and may lead institutions along a distinctive path of development. (2004, 1–2)

Starr narrates the evolution of American media institutions through the nineteenth and twentieth centuries with a careful eye for the conditions that promoted or resisted change. He notes, for example, that one might attribute the American decision to leave telegraphy and telephony to private industry—rather than government ownership and management, as in Europe and much of the rest of the world—to the characteristic American predilection toward free enterprise. Not so fast, he warns, explaining that the dramatic success of public section investment in canals and direct and indirect investment in railroad infrastructure had generated a very strong wave of support for a federally managed electronic communication system. Indeed the first telegraphic link between Washington and Baltimore was indeed a federally sponsored prototype system, and Samuel Morse himself favored federal ownership. It could easily have been otherwise, but the political winds blowing north and south in the decades prior to the Civil War, and particularly the election of 1844 and the ascendancy of President Polk, tipped the balance toward private ownership (Starr 2004, 163).

Systemic Theories

Several of our authors are less interested in various models of heroic and suppressive initiatives and focus on what might be labeled systemic factors. The historical actors, of course, are no less important, but the analyst's attention focuses on a particular progression of technical developments, especially uneven technical development. This is a central notion in the SCOT tradition organized around the notion of a *reverse salient,* that is, an element or problem in a complex system that appears to be holding progress back. Hughes's (1987) classic example of a reverse salient was Edison's concern that the price of copper would hold back the development of electric lighting. The ultimate solution was high-resistance lightbulb filaments that reduced power demands and accordingly the amount of copper required for the electrical grid to function. This is distinctly not an exemplar of technical determinism, far from it. The model requires a socially defined perception that an element within the system is a problem and a socially defined notion of the functionality of the system itself that is being held back. Beniger's (1986) "crisis of control" in nineteenth-century industrialization was another example of a reverse salient, as railroad and manufacturing systems outstripped the capacity of human control with their growing speed and complexity and required the innovation of electronic communication and control systems.

A related notion that will be put to work in the pages ahead is *excess capacity*—a salient rather than a reverse salient, a system element that is ahead of others in technical development and accordingly is underutilized (Johanson 1968). When a particular capacity is socially defined as "underutilized," that too becomes a problem that draws institutional attention and innovation.

Perhaps the most prominent systemic model of the history of technical succession is simply the notion of improved *technical and industrial efficiency*. Variations on a mechanical apparatus replace human labor. The steam-driven roll press replaces the hand-operated screw press. Radio replaces the town crier, and incidentally the newspaper extra edition. Brian Winston's fulsome turn of phrase for this phenomenon is *supervening social necessity;* he describes how some prototypes but not others are implemented as industrial standards, but core explanations usually boil down to simple physical and economic efficiency.

Media Evolution

So far we have reviewed a variety of conceptual lenses for understanding the dynamics of innovation and structural change broadly used in the fields of science and technology history. They represent relatively well-developed models that are applicable over a wide range of historical circumstance. Of special interest here are institutions of mass communication, which draw our attention to several communication-specific theoretical traditions.

The *principle of relative constancy* is drawn from the observation that American consumers appeared to have kept their spending on communication media as a relatively constant percentage of total income in the latter half of the twentieth century (McCombs 1972; McCombs and Eyal 1980; McCombs and Nolan 1992). As the theory was refined in the literature, analysts drew attention to the notion of *functional equivalence,* the mechanism predicting that as new media come along that better serve a particular function, the use of the previously dominant medium that served that function declines. Thus television replaced radio as a primary home family entertainment medium in the evening and radio moved to the bedroom, kitchen, and car. And the cellular phone displaces the wireline phone, especially among the young (Dupagne 1997; Dupagne and Green 1996).

Following the expansion of communication flows through increasingly broadband digital networks, we confront the *communication flow paradox,* observed by Ithiel de Sola Pool and associates in the 1980s: although the flow of information may continue apace with Moore's law of computer computational capacity, the twenty-four-hour day and physiological limits of multitasking must put a practical limit on media consumption (Pool 1983; Neuman and Pool 1986). The flow paradox may be seen as a distant theoretical cousin of the relative constancy finding, because both draw attention to gating functions and fundamental limits to media use—a temporal constraint in flow and a financial one in relative constancy.

If the quantity of information flow increases as a function of the efficiencies and increasing bandwidth of digital media, an intriguing question arises—will the diversity of available information and entertainment increase as well? The notion of commercial mass communication has long been associated with highly formulaic, mass-produced, common denominator fair. The cluster of theories here focus on the economic sustainability of targeted special-interest content and narrowcasting. The most widely cited model is that of the *long tail* developed by Christopher Anderson (2006). The thesis posits that companies like Amazon and Netflix with their national markets and computerized inventory not only have a greater capacity to service backlist books and videos outside the best-sellers and box office hits, they have strong economic incentives to promote the sales of a more diverse "product mix." Anderson focuses primarily on the diversity of content sustainably offered by an individual firm. Previous to this work, the emphasis was less on diverse offerings than on the diversity of competing firms and of ownership under the theoretical banner of *media diversity* (Bagdikian 2004; Schiller 1989). Media diversity is a key analytic concept of media economics and media regulation and is based on the notion that a diverse marketplace of ideas is best served by a structurally diverse pattern of media ownership, including nonchain local ownership, and ownership by individuals of diverse backgrounds, particularly gender and ethnicity. Although the evidence that diverse or local ownership leads to diverse programming is mixed (given the profit-maximizing constraints of the commercial media environment), the concept remains at the forefront of policy and economic analysis (Einstein 2004; Napoli 2006; Noam 2009).

The Structure of This Volume

Our contributors are diverse. They draw on backgrounds in law, economics, history, communication, sociology, journalism, and political science. Although conference organizers managed to get them into the same room several years ago, they are far from being on the same page, philosophically, politically, and historically. They share an aversion to reductive technological determinism and a strong inclination to take technology seriously as they study evolving cultural norms, economic institutions, and public opinion. None would claim to have a complete picture of how the digital revolution will resolve, or whether resolution is even an appropriate descriptor for the near future. But all of these authors have much to contribute to a better understanding of where we stand and where we are headed because they have been at pains to examine carefully where we have been.

As an editor introducing a volume of studies diverse in analytic focus, disciplinary roots, and style of exposition, I have resisted an attempt at discipline and enforced orthodoxy not just because it would have little chance of success (one is drawn to the metaphor of the herding of cats) but because it would diminish what I believe is a real strength of the enterprise—the prospect of intellectual convergence from diverse starting points. Given that we stand at the beginning of the process, true theoretical convergence is in the hands of the active readers who are challenged to compare and contrast narratives and analyses collected here.

To assist in that process, let me briefly review the chapters in this volume to assess which elements of the theoretical toolkit previously outlined the authors put to use. Table 1 highlights some of the key references. All of the contributors draw informally or explicitly on the social construction tradition pioneered by Bijker and colleagues (1987) in studying the coevolution of communication technologies and social-cultural definitions of their appropriate use. Following the usage in this introduction, when theoretical traditions are introduced for the first time in each chapter, they are italicized.

Pablo J. Boczkowski's essay on the culture of the newspaper industry contrasts the *visionary rhetoric* of senior newspaper executives as they confront the challenge of the Internet with the *resilient interpretive schemes* and newsroom norms evolved from journalism's storied history in the nineteenth century. As a result the *championship of innovation* is haltingly reactive, defensive, and pragmatic, permitting new competitors to gain an upper hand. Surprisingly, by experimenting with electronic news-

TABLE 1. THEORIES, THEORISTS, AND MEDIA: A PARTIAL LIST

Thematic	Theories	Authors	Media
Heroic	Visionary rhetoric	Boczkowski	Newspapers
Heroic	Visionary rhetoric	Ling	Telephony, radio
Heroic	Innovation champion	Carey	Radio
Heroic	Innovation champion	Schwartz	Television
Heroic	Innovation champion	Sawhney	Cable television
Heroic	Path dependency	Edwards	Internet
Heroic	Founding myth	Edwards	Internet
Counterpoint	Resilience of interpretive schemes	Boczkowski	Newspapers
Counterpoint	Law of suppression	Schwartz	Television
Counterpoint	Constitutive choice	Etzioni	Internet, telephony
Counterpoint	Law of suppression	Sohn/Schneider	Internet
Counterpoint	Resilience of interpretive schemes	Sohn/Schneider	Internet
Systemic	Reverse salient	Sawhney	Cable television
Systemic	Excess capacity	Sawhney	Cable television
Systemic	Efficiency	Noam	Motion pictures, Internet
Media Evolution	Relative constancy	Carey	Radio
Media Evolution	Functional equivalence	Carey	Radio
Media Evolution	Media diversity	Carey	Radio

paper delivery via videotex and teletext in the 1980s, newspapers were technically ahead of the still evolving Internet. But a defensive posture based on a closed and proprietary system turned out to be an inadequate model for technical leadership and "moving with their readers" to the digital age.

In the next chapter Rich Ling tracks the use of *visionary rhetoric* from the early days of the commercialization of electricity and telegraphy to the widely cited "Negroponte switch" as the wireless broadcast media (television) move to wireline delivery (cable TV and Internet) and the previously wired medium of the telephone is increasingly wireless as the cell phone moves to dominate personal voice and text messaging.

The next chapter, "Hollywood 2.0," turns our attention to the evolving economics of the motion picture industry as Eli Noam ponders whether Hollywood will wither away in a struggle with low-cost global competition. The fundamental technology of the 35mm motion picture camera and projector has been stable and unchallenged for eighty years. Digital video, computer-based editing, and Internet distribution, however, present new challenges to the traditional business model of celluloid celebrity. Noam's surprising conclusion is that Hollywood will not only survive but probably thrive in the new environment, primarily because of its capacity for *industrial efficiency.* It seems counterintuitive— big studios, high overhead, old ways of doing business. Noam explains that the iconic cigar-chomping Hollywood mogul leading an inefficient studio system unchanging since the 1930s is an image perhaps frequently found on the screen but it is not an accurate representation of the modern industry behind the screen.

Radio has survived television; will it survive the Internet? John Carey begins by looking forward but quickly concludes that the future of radio is rooted in its past. He traces the role of innovation champions from the earliest days of crystal radio sets to the rebirth of innovation in satellite and Internet radio eighty years later. He introduces the Steiner Paradox, which posits that true content diversity may be served best by monopolists rather than competitive ownership in the traditional media diversity model.

Evan I. Schwartz narrates the epic battle between independent inventor and *innovation champion* Philo Farnsworth and RCA founder and CEO David Sarnoff. It resonates with many of the counterpoint theories including *the Suppression of radical potential, closure,* and *the iron law of oligarchy.* It is a story so compelling it found its way to Broadway in 2007–8 as *The Farnsworth Invention.* In this case it was less a battle to suppress an invention than a battle to control it commercially. Unlike the early days of radio recounted by John Carey, when few had a sense of what radio could do, by the 1930s and 1940s people had come to expect some form of television and had a rough idea of its character and function—a commercial entertainment medium, basically radio with pictures.

Cable television started as minor footnote in the early days of television, primarily a shared cable connected to large television antenna for remote suburban and rural communities. These smaller markets were largely ignored by the television industry and constituted what systems analysts call a *reverse salient,* an unappreciated component of system development, a systemic blind spot. In time cable would come to be the primary medium for accessing television, leaving only 14 percent of television viewers still viewing a broadcast signal through rabbit ears (SNL Kagan 2008). What explains its growth and dominance? The answer is a systemic dynamic, Harmeet Sawhney argues, based on the commercial instinct to exploit *excess capacity.* Cable system operators realized they had the capacity to carry more than just local channels, and a truly diverse multichannel video medium was born in 1975 as satellite dishes made multichannel signal transmission possible to evolving and increasingly popular cable television systems. Sawhney concludes in drawing on Agre's amplification concept, a variant of SCOT and coevolutionary theory.

Paul N. Edwards's chapter turns to the most recent development in media technology—the Internet. The particularly curious characteristic of this new digital network is that its evolution was fundamentally a series of fortuitous accidents. The early developers of what was then known as the ARPANET (for the U.S. Department of Defense's Advanced Research Projects Agency) were experimenting with highly specialized military communication that would not be subject to disruption by opposing military forces. A public global digital network may have been the farthest thing from their minds. They designed a digital network that would get the message through despite military challenge and basically ignored developing any scheme for charging users and controlling the use of the network. The task was to design a network that could not be easily controlled (by the enemy), and as a curious and unintended result, commercial vendors and authoritarian governments find it frustratingly difficult to manage and manipulate the modern Internet. Thus from the perspective of commercial or governmental control, as Edwards suggests, the Internet should never have happened. Its developers, of course, are now heroic celebrities and genius inventors of the first rank, and Edwards pauses to examine these *founding myths* and the remarkable robustness of the technology, a notable exemplar of *path dependency*.

In the final two chapters of this volume we turn to overarching questions of policy that span the historical trajectories of individual technologies. Amitai Etzioni has developed an enviable reputation as a thoughtful student of public policy and has in recent years turned to the parallel issues of security and privacy in the digital age. His conclusion is both counterintuitive and provocative. He argues that the digital revolution provides the concerned individual a greater capacity for privacy, rather than less. Etzioni is far from a *technological determinist,* but his analysis points to a clear case of the capacity of technological affordances, the interaction of cultural and technical change. Indeed, he traces a particularly troubling cycle of imbalance and overcorrection in American political history between security and privacy in which technology plays an important but hardly a leading role. The security-privacy dynamic is often seen as a straightforward trade-off. Not necessarily so, Eztioni argues—consider it a *constitutive choice.*

Our final chapter, by legal scholars and activists Gigi Sohn and Timothy Schneider, draws us into the thorny legal realm of copyright and digital rights management. Sohn and Schneider make a powerful case that the historical trajectory of the one-way media of publishing and broadcasting we have been reviewing has collided awkwardly with a digital revolution that makes copying, sharing, and collaboratively producing culture as easy as consuming it. It is a classic case of youthful and perhaps heroic rebellion against established interests and traditional business models. From the innovators' point of view it is a classic case of the *suppression of radical potential* and (among established interests) the *resilience of interpretive schemes.*

An Eye to the Future

Historians take great pride in getting it right. They spend long hours with original sources, poring over dusty files to set the factual record straight in the disciplined Teutonic spirit of nineteenth-century German historian Leopold von Ranke (the very first honorary member of the American Historical Society). Speculating about what the past augurs for the future, according to this school of thought, should be eschewed. Such speculation would seem to threaten the sanctity of historiography, distract historians from their important work, and perhaps taint them with current disputes about the nature of politics and power.

Alas, our authors are tainted, one and all. They are not, strictly speaking, historians. They are communication scholars, sociologists, lawyers, and technologists. For this community, drawing lessons for the future is the very much the point of poring over the past. Our contributors' chapters are historically incomplete and selective in emphasis. These authors have a point of view as they write and usually a theory or two in hand. This is thick historical description in the spirit of anthropologist Clifford Geertz (1973). Thus in this introductory chapter we have reviewed theories and mechanisms and generalizations about how technical and social change interact—how we can draw lessons from the past to better understand the future—our patron Janus again.

It is widely noted that predictions about the digital future tend toward either utopian (e.g., Negroponte 1995) or dystopian visions (e.g., Zittrain 2008). For the most part, our authors steer away from both hang-wringing and arm-waving. The picture is mixed.

Proceed, esteemed reader. The stories are engaging and the issues they raise about innovation and political control are important. Our authors will not claim that history is doomed to repeat itself; that would be folly. But the historical patterns unfolding have a curious familiarity—as Twain would have it: If history doesn't repeat itself, it does seem to rhyme.

REFERENCES

Anderson, Chris. 2006. *The Long Tail: Why the Future of Business Is Selling Less of More.* New York: Hyperion.

Bagdikian, Ben H. 2004. *The New Media Monopoly.* Boston: Beacon Press.

Beniger, James R. 1986. *The Control Revolution: Technological and Economic Origins of the Information Society.* Cambridge: Harvard University Press.

Bijker, Wiebe E., Thomas P. Hughes, and Trevor Pinch, eds. 1987. *The Social Construction of Technological Systems.* Cambridge: MIT Press.

Bourdieu, Pierre. 1991. *Language and Symbolic Power.* Ed. John B. Thompson. Trans. Gino Raymond and Matthew Adamson. Cambridge: Harvard University Press.

Bourdieu, Pierre. 1993. *The Field of Cultural Production: Essays on Art and Literature.* Ed. Randal Johnson. New York: Columbia University Press.

Carlyle, Thomas. 2008. *On Heroes and Hero Worship and the Heroic in History.* Charleston, SC: Bibliobizaar.

Castells, Manuel. 1996. *The Rise of the Network Society.* Malden, MA: Blackwell.

Christensen, Clayton M. 1997. *The Innovator's Dilemma: When New Technologies Cause Great Firms to Fail.* Boston: Harvard Business School Press.

Comstock, George, Steven Chaffee, Natan Katzman, Maxwell E. McCombs, and Donald Roberts. 1978. *Television and Human Behavior.* New York: Columbia University Press.

David, Paul A. 1985. "Clio and the Economics of Qwerty." *American Economic Review* 75:332–37.

Dupagne, Michel. 1997. "A Theoretical and Methodological Critique of the Principle of Relative Constancy." *Communication Theory* 7 (1): 53–76.

Dupagne, Michel, and R. Jeffery Green. 1996. "Revisiting the Principle of Relative Constancy: Consumer Mass Media Expenditures in Belgium." *Communication Research* 23:612–35.

Durham, William H. 1991. *Coevolution: Genes, Culture, and Human Destiny.* Stanford: Stanford University Press.

Einstein, Mara. 2004. *Media Diversity: Economics, Ownership, and the FCC.* Mahwah, NJ: Erlbaum.

Garud, Raghu, and Peter Karnøe, eds. 2001. *Path Dependence and Creation.* Mahwah, NJ: Erlbaum.

Geertz, Clifford. 1973. *The Interpretation of Cultures.* New York: Basic Books.

Gersick, Connie J. G. 1991. "Revolutionary Change Theories: A Multilevel Exploration of the Punctuated Equilibrium Paradigm." *Academy of Management Review* 16 (1): 10–36.

Giddens, Anthony, ed. 1984. *The Constitution of Society.* Berkeley and Los Angeles: University of California Press.

Habermas, Jürgen. 1989. *The Structural Transformation of the Public Sphere: An Inquiry into a Category of Bourgeois Society.* Trans. Thomas Burger with Frederick Lawrence. Cambridge: MIT Press.

Hallin, Daniel C., and Paolo Mancini. 2004. *Comparing Media Systems: Three Models of Media and Politics.* New York: Cambridge University Press.

Hellman, Hal. 2004. *Great Feuds in Technology.* Cambridge: MIT Press.

Hughes, Thomas. 1987. "The Evolution of Large Technological Systems." In *The Social Construction of Technological Systems,* ed. Wiebe E. Bijker, Thomas P. Hughes, and Trevor Pinch, 51–82. Cambridge: MIT Press.

Hutchby, Ian. 2001. "Technologies, Texts and Affordances." *Sociology* 35:441–56.

Johanson, Leif. 1968. "Production Functions and the Concept of Capacity." *Collection Economie et Mathematique et Econometrie* 2:46–72.

Latour, Bruno. 1987. *Science in Action: How to Follow Scientists and Engineers through Society.* Milton Keynes: Open University Press.

Litman, Jessica. 2000. *Digital Copyright: Protecting Intellectual Property on the Internet.* Amherst NY: Prometheus Books.

McCombs, Maxwell E. 1972. "Mass Media in the Marketplace." *Journalism Monographs* 24(August).

McCombs, Maxwell E., and Chaim H. Eyal. 1980. "Spending on Mass Media." *Journal of Communication* 30 (1): 153–58.

McCombs, Maxwell E., and Jack Nolan. 1992. "The Relative Constancy Approach to Consumer Spending for Media." *Journal of Media Economics* 5 (2): 43–52.

Michels, Robert. 1962. *Political Parties: A Sociological Study of Oligarchical Tendencies of Modern Democracy.* New York: Collier Books.

Napoli, Philip M., ed. 2006. *Media Diversity and Localism: Meaning and Metrics.* Mahwah, NJ: Erlbaum.

Negroponte, Nicholas. 1995. *Being Digital.* New York: Knopf.

Neuman, W. Russell, and Ithiel de Sola Pool. 1986. "The Flow of Communications into the Home." In *Media, Audience, and Social Structure,* ed. Sandra J. Ball-Rokeach and Muriel G. Cantor, 71–86. Beverly Hills: Sage.

Noam, Eli. 2009. *Media Ownership and Concentration in America.* New York: Oxford University Press.

Orlikowski, Wanda. 1992. "The Duality of Technology: Rethinking the Concept of Technology in Organizations." *Organisation Science* 3 (3): 398–427.

Pool, Ithiel de Sola. 1973. "Communication in Totalitarian Societies." In *Handbook of Communication,* ed. Ithiel de Sola Pool and Wilbur Schramm, 462–511. Chicago: Rand McNally.

Pool, Ithiel de Sola. 1983. "Tracking the Flow of Information." *Science* 211:609–13.

Saggs, H. W. F. 1989. *Civilization before Greece and Rome.* New Haven: Yale University Press.

Schiller, Herbert I. 1989. *Culture, Inc.: The Corporate Takeover of Public Expression.* New York: Oxford University Press.

Schmidt, Susanne K., and Raymund Werle. 1998. *Coordinating Technology: Studies in the International Standardization of Telecommunications.* Cambridge: MIT Press.

Schudson, Michael. 1978. *Discovering the News: A Social History of American Newspapers.* New York: Basic Books.

Shapiro, Carl, and Hal R. Varian. 1998. *Information Rules: A Strategic Guide to the Network Economy.* Boston: Harvard Business School Press.

SNL Kagan. 2008. *Media Trends.*

Starr, Paul. 2004. *The Creation of the Media: Political Origins of Modern Communications.* New York: Basic.

Stukeley, William, ed. 1936. *Memoirs of Sir Isaac Newton's Life*. London: Taylor and Francis.

Winston, Brian. 1986. *Misunderstanding Media*. Cambridge: Harvard University Press.

Winston, Brian. 1998. *Media Technology and Society: A History*. New York: Routledge.

Wirth, Michael O. 2006. "Issues in Media Convergence." In *Handbook of Media Management and Economics*, ed. Alan B. Albarran, Sylvia M. Chan-Olmsted, and Michael O. Wirth, 445–62. New York: Routledge.

Zittrain, Jonathan. 2008. *The Future of the Internet and How to Stop It*. New Haven: Yale University Press.

Newspaper Culture and Technical Innovation, 1980–2005

PABLO J. BOCZKOWSKI

On August 2, 2005, Bill Keller, executive editor of the *New York Times,* and Martin Nisenholtz, senior vice president of digital operations for the New York Times Company, distributed to *Times* employees a memo—later made publicly available on the Web—announcing the integration of the *Times* print and online newsrooms. After commenting on the rationale for having two separate newsrooms during the first decade of the *Times on the Web,* Keller and Nisenholtz wrote, "In those ten years, the world has changed" (Keller and Nisenholtz 2005). According to Keller and Nisenholtz, one of the directions of this change was their public's desire for a product that could be better delivered by integrating the newsrooms. "Our readers are moving, and so are we." One remarkable aspect of this rather unremarkable phrase is its resemblance to a statement made ten years earlier, when the world was supposedly very different, by another top executive of a leading U.S. daily, to explain another important change.

During its early 1990s forays into electronic publishing, the *Los Angeles Times* had decided to make its content available exclusively to subscribers of Prodigy, the online service provider. Shortly after it became evident that consumers were migrating massively from closed online services, such as Prodigy or CompuServe, to the more open space of the Web, the *Times*' publisher and chief executive officer, Richard Schlosberg III, announced that the newspaper was moving from Prodigy to the Web. "In the rapidly evolving world, it is important to go where the customers . . . are going" ("*L.A. Times* Exits Prodigy" 1995).

The similarity between the statements made by the leaders of the *New York Times* and *Los Angeles Times* about different events separated by ten years illustrates two issues that will be central in this chapter's treatment of how the newspaper industry has approached the first quarter century of electronic and online publishing. One issue is the *resilience of interpretive schemes*—in this case, a stated need to "follow the users." The second is a persistent intention to change. The usefulness of these schemes and the success of the resulting changes become obvious if they are contrasted with another pair of events that also took place roughly a decade apart.

On November 20, 2006, Yahoo and seven of the largest newspaper chains announced a new partnership to share advertisements, content, and technology.[1] The first phase of this agreement was to have the job ads of the newspapers displayed on Yahoo's *HotJobs* site, but the larger goal of this partnership was to "have the content of these newspapers tagged and optimized for searching and indexing by Yahoo" (Helft and Lohr 2006, C1). Industry analysts and leaders reacted quite enthusiastically to the news, as has often been the case with announcements of this kind during the past decade. For instance, longtime industry analyst John Morton argued that "newspapers now fully recognize that the Internet is a threat, and this is a way for newspapers to try to preserve their franchise, with a partner that has huge online distribution" (Helft and Lohr 2006, C1). To William Dean Singleton, vice chairman and chief executive officer of the MediaNews Group, one of the participating newspaper chains, "There has been a big question asked for a while as to how newspapers will navigate the online future. . . . I think this [partnership with Yahoo] is the answer to that question" (Helft and Lohr 2006, C1). Other industry sources echoed Singleton's excitement and cited "the announcement as the most ambitious collective effort by the industry to deal with the Internet since the New Century Network of a decade ago" (Helft and Lohr 2006, C1).

What was the now nearly forgotten New Century Network, and what can its connection to the current partnership between newspapers and Yahoo reveal about how newspapers have approached their digital future? The formation of the New Century Network, a consortium of eight newspaper chains, was announced in April 1995.[2] It was launched with great fanfare by the participant organizations. For instance, its first, and temporary, head, Cox executive Peter Winter, seemed to anticipate the question that MediaNews executive William Dean Singleton would pose a decade later apropos the partnership with Yahoo: "We have seen the Internet and we get it" (Garneau 1995a, 15). At a time when most newspapers were only beginning to explore the Web, the consortium, he said, aimed to become an "enabling company" and to "evangelize the online concept" (Garneau 1995b, 9). Thus, two months later, at a meeting prior to the start of the Newspaper Association of America's annual marketing conference, Winter said that New Century Network had a three-stage strategy: to have seventy-five papers connected to the network within two years, to interconnect the members and create a shared archive of information, and to fine-tune the content and sell ads on the network (Consoli 1995). Some industry observers received the initiative, like the one with Yahoo, with great enthusiasm. An *Editor and Publisher* editorial called it "probably the most exciting development in the newspaper business at this point in the ever-changing world of cyberspace" (NCN Alliance 1995).

New Century Network executives, however, did not anticipate that newspapers were going to establish web sites on their own at great speed throughout 1995. Therefore, a year after its formation, they decided that the consortium would shift gears and aim instead to integrate the already existing sites by putting the most relevant information from each paper on a single site, helping to create niche content and selling targeted ads in relation to the pages served (Consoli 1996). The rationale behind this idea was to give maximum visibility to local content—a distinctive asset of print newspapers—in the online space that was seen by many as favoring global, or at least translocal, information. All pages would feature banner advertisements, and the New Century Network would get a 10 percent facilitation fee, the seller would receive a 15 percent commission, and the rest of the proceeds would be split among the participating newspapers according to usage patterns (Consoli 1996).

In May 1997, under the new slogan "The Net with a hometown point-of-view," the consortium unveiled the aggregation site, called *NewsWorks* ("NCN Previews" 1997). However, despite the high expectations and strong promotional efforts, *NewsWorks* amounted to no more than a collection of interesting stories from more than one hundred papers. The numbers did not look good either: during the second half of 1997, the initiative employed seventy people and delivered 775,000 page views a day—an average of less than 8,000 page views per day for every participating newspaper. Its annual gross revenue was less than $1 million, and its operating losses were estimated to be as high as $8 million (Meyer 1998). Rumors of disagreement among the partners began to spread in the industry. Thus, unsurprisingly, in March 1998—almost three years after its formation had been announced and with total losses of $27 million—the New Century Network closed. It issued a statement that read in part as follows:

> We were unable to agree on a business plan that would receive the support of enough partners to enable us to move forward. The world of content and commerce on the Internet has been transformed since [New Century Network] was created in 1995. The challenge of finding a strategy for [New Century Network] in this fast changing marketplace has proved too daunting. (Outing 1998, 12)

The comparison between the New Century Network and the partnership with Yahoo reiterates the two common themes mentioned briefly in regard to the previous pair of stories: the resilience of key interpretive schemes—in this case, the value of developing interorganizational networks to protect local franchises in the online environment—and the persistent championship of initiatives for change. But this comparison also makes clear what a difference a decade can make. In the mid-1990s, newspapers were undertaking these initiatives with partners in their own industry and aiming to establish a leading position in the online environment. Ten years later, newspapers are partnering with a nonnewspaper company that scarcely existed a decade ago, but has grown to achieve a market capitalization unmatched by any of the publicly traded newspaper firms and that may hold the commanding position in their joint venture.

How can we make sense of the common themes that cut across these two pairs of stories and the differences between then and now? Since the early 1980s, the newspaper industry has made innovations in electronic and online alternatives to print publishing. By switching the reference frame and looking at this past quarter century, it is possible to assess in two ways how the industry has done. On the one hand, from the vantage point of the newspaper industry in 1980, print dailies have experienced significant editorial, technological, and organizational changes. They have also had a decent degree of market success with their current online ventures. Executives and journalists of the 1980s would no doubt have been content and surprised to hear about their online publications twenty-five years in the future. They would have been fascinated to learn that they would disseminate news on an ongoing basis; carry audio and video; let their users talk back to an unparalleled degree; have, in the case of the largest newspapers, unique users in the millions; and routinely find themselves in the top twenty of the most visited online news sites. On the other hand, looking at the situation from the vantage point of the larger "information industries"—a broader set of players that includes print and broadcast news media and also companies such as Microsoft, Google, Yahoo, and America Online that have evolved to become important competitors in online news space—yields a different picture. In 2005, we saw how even the most resourceful and creative newspaper companies were less innovative editorially, technologically, and organizationally than new competitors not associated with traditional media, and thus missed key opportunities and lost overall leadership positions. Knight-Ridder—at the time the second-largest newspaper chain and one of the most aggressive players in electronic and online publishing since 1980—was sold for a price that would have been unthinkable only five years earlier. Layoffs took place in newsrooms across the nation, and a sense of pessimism cut across newspapers. Thus from the standpoint of the larger information industries, it became impossible by 2005 to ignore that newspapers had done far worse in conquering the digital landscape than other competitors in the information industries.

Newspapers have not stood still in the twenty-five-year period between 1980 and 2005. Hence the significant change from the 1980 vantage point of the newspaper industry. However, they have moved in more conservative and less successful ways than new competitors—hence the lower level of innovation and market success from the 2005 vantage point of the information industries. How are we to make sense of the disparity between these two assessments and the many lost opportunities for newspapers during this period? Building on themes I first developed in *Digitizing the News: Innovation in Online Newspapers* (Boczkowski 2004), in this chapter I argue that these disparities arose partly from newspapers' culture of innovation, marked by three traits: it has been reactive, defensive, and pragmatic. First, even though they tinkered with several new electronic and online publishing options before some competitors even existed, newspapers have tended to react to events, following trends rather than proactively setting them. Second, when they did act, newspapers have often focused more on maintaining their position and values in the print world rather than on experimenting with radically new ways of doing things. Third, when they have pursued new initiatives, they have been more concerned about short-term results than long-term horizons that are riskier but can have much bigger payoffs. Some of the issues raised by the two contrasting pairs of stories that opened this chapter—

the resilience of certain interpretive schemes, the persistent attempts to change, and the growing realization of a loss of relevance—illustrate the major role played by this culture of innovation during the past quarter century. These issues also suggest how little this cultural configuration has changed in a historical period of remarkable transformations in the world of news and information, and the extent to which it has become more a liability than an asset for the press in the digital age.

A Quarter Century of Innovation

American newspapers have changed their production and distribution technologies considerably over the years, but their dissemination vehicle—ink on paper—has not been much modified until the early 1980s. Exceptions were brief forays into telephone and facsimile communication in the first half of the twentieth century (Hotaling 1948; Marvin 1988; Shefrin 1949). As a result of learning about electronic publishing initiatives that had begun taking place in other parts of the world, mostly in Europe, in the late 1970s, a handful of newspaper companies in the United States started in 1980 to tinker with videotex and teletext (Carlson 2003; Compaine 1980; Pool 1983; Stone 1987; Weaver and Wilhoit 1986).[3] Unlike the European initiatives, usually led by public sector organizations, the newspapers, together with firms in the financial services sector, were among the first private sector organizations in America to experiment with the new capabilities created by the marriage of computing and telecommunications (Aumente 1987; Baer and Greenberger 1987; Davenport 1987; Mantooth 1982; Noll 1980). For the most part, these companies pursued innovative initiatives to ascertain their potential challenges to the core print product. Thus, James Batten, chief executive officer of the newspaper chain Knight-Ridder, said his company decided to undertake Viewtron, a videotex project, because "we were concerned that some of these new systems might someday represent a competitive threat to the daily newspaper. And if that was to be the case, we wanted to discover that fact earlier rather than later" (Batten 1981, 18). A survey conducted in 1983 of newspapers involved in electronic publishing concluded that "one of the reasons cited by most of those newspapers for entering the field is franchise protection—holding on to their markets" ("Quality and Technology" 1983, 17).

Two of the most highly visible videotex projects of the first half of the 1980s were an initiative in electronic publishing that the Associated

Press coordinated with the participation of twelve newspapers, and the Viewtron endeavor by Knight-Ridder already mentioned (Brown and Atwater 1986; Fidler 1997; Hecht 1983; Laakaniemi 1981; Mantooth 1982). Although very different in many regards, the fate of both projects and how this fate was represented by members of the industry exhibit interesting similarities that are worth considering.

The Associated Press initiative consisted of making the content of twelve newspapers available to subscribers of the online system provider CompuServe for an additional fee. The Associated Press and the participating newspapers ran this project partly as an experiment to have a better sense of users' behavior and interests. The experiment lasted two years. Although it worked from a technical standpoint, it was discontinued because it did not seem commercially appealing to the participating newspapers. Although the complete results of this project have never been released, they include findings that led Lawrence Blasko, the director of information technology for the Associated Press, to conclude that "there is no clear and present danger to newspapers from electronic delivery of information to the home" ("Electronic Newspaper" 1982).

Knight-Ridder spent more than five years developing, prototyping, testing, and then deploying a stand-alone videotex system, first in South Florida and then in several cities across the nation. It was an ambitious endeavor that delivered news, advertisements, information, and transactional content to dedicated terminals via a telephone line. Viewtron anticipated some of the features of online services that became prevalent a decade later, but most users found it slow, expensive, and unresponsive to their broader set of communicative interests. For instance, users were more interested in communication among themselves than in reading the news, but Viewtron executives preferred to reproduce the typical newspaper one-way communication model rather than to enable two-way exchanges. According to Fidler, "Nearly everyone involved in the trial saw Viewtron as an advertiser-supported electronic newspaper. Its potential role as an interpersonal communication medium was considered secondary" (1997, 148). After accumulating losses of more than $50 million, Viewtron was discontinued in 1985. At that time, James Batten, then president of Knight Ridder Newspapers, justified the closing of Viewtron with a rationale that strongly resonates with Blasko's: "Videotex is not likely to be a threat to newspapers in the foreseeable future" ("Knight-Ridder 'Pulls Plug'"1986, 14). Paul Orme, president of Viewdata Corporation of America, Knight-Ridder's wholly owned subsidiary in charge of Viewtron, echoed Batten's short-term focus by stating, "In the long term, everyone is very bullish about the business. The question is, how do we get through the short term of the business?" (Fitzgerald 1985, 33).

Although most videotex initiatives had folded by the mid-1980s, some small-scale ones continued through the second half of the decade, a period when newspapers began to set up facsimile publications and audiotex services (Boczkowski 2004; Carlson 2003). These two options of delivering content became commercially viable in some cases, but on such a small scale that they were never considered strong alternatives to print. In the 1990s there was renewed interest in trying new ways of exploiting the power of computerized networks to communicate with the public (Carveth, Owers, and Alexander 1998; Dizard 1997; Molina 1997; Willis 1994). This was still a small and open domain of innovation, and some newspaper companies were again among the first players trying to make sense of it. For instance, in 1991 the Tribune Corporation acquired 10 percent of the nascent online service provider America Online, allegedly for less than $10 million. This was part of a partnership to develop local portals in the cities where the *Tribune* had a strong media presence, starting with the launch of *Chicago Online* in 1992.

During the first part of the 1990s the public interest in online communication continued to grow and with it the market penetration of online service providers. As we saw in the first pair of stories mentioned in the introductory section, when the popularization of the Web triggered a qualitative leap in the public's interest, newspapers began to move aggressively again into the domain of online publishing, following what they perceived to be a clear trend in user behavior (Boczkowski 2004; Beamish 1997; Garrison 1997; Martin and Hansen 1998). But, by then, companies such as America Online—which had been relatively small players only a few years before, as suggested by the dollar figure of the aforementioned transaction by the Tribune Corporation—had acquired a leading position in the digital world, and newspapers had lost the opportunities that often accompany first movers into new markets. According to industry analyst Steve Outing:

> Newspaper online services have been around since the early 1990s, yet the industry didn't get excited about online service until the end of 1994, when the Internet became a household word and subscribing to a service like America Online began to become mainstream.

But while Internet providers and the big commercial online services were making money, the newspaper industry, in general, was not. (1996, 81)

Once they settled on the Web as their online platform of choice, newspapers tried to develop products and services to protect their leading position in the parts of their business that were considered more at risk. One such area was classified advertisement, long regarded as very well suited to the technical properties of electronic and online systems. For instance, at the 1981 annual conference of the Association of Newspaper Classified Advertising Managers, there was discussion that "the most serious threat to newspapers classified advertising revenues is being posed by the emergence of new interactive video technology that makes possible the electronic transmission of classified advertising" (Gloede 1981, 11). At the 1993 annual convention of the Newspaper Association of America, Jay Harris, Knight-Ridder vice president of operations, "warned newspapers to 'keep an eye on classified,' because new technologies 'lend themselves to stealing that base' and pose a 'more near and present danger' than they do to other ad categories. 'It's going to happen,' [Harris] said. 'Somebody is going to take classified electronic'" (Garneau 1993, 15). Thus, it is not surprising that, starting in the mid-1990s, newspaper companies put substantial effort into online classified ventures, such as Careerpath.com. This was an employment site launched in October 1995 that pulled together the ads of many individual papers, such as the *New York Times*, the *Washington Post*, the *Los Angeles Times*, and the *Chicago Tribune*.

However, because of their failure to move in a significant manner at a time when there were no serious competitors—the 1980s and the early 1990s—the efforts of newspapers in online advertisement that were initiated in the mid-1990s have had mixed results. They have furthered the position of newspapers in the online world, but, at the same time, have been unable to contain the rise of new competitors that had no presence in the print world. Thus, for example, by 2005, although newspaper sites received about 44 percent of local online advertisement dollar—local advertisement comprises employment, real estate, and automotive ads—which amounted to about one-third of all online advertisement spending, online companies such as Google and Monster.com received 40 percent of these expenditures (Journalism.org 2006).

How did newspapers fare after this first quarter century of innovation in electronic and online publishing? Before examining some key indicators of audience and revenue for online newspapers as of 2005, it will be helpful to put these numbers into perspective by placing them within the context of the general evolution of print newspapers during this period.

During the twenty-five years preceding 2005, the story that print newspaper figures tell is one of steady and significant decline—a decline that arguably began earlier but has accelerated more recently. In 1980 there were 1,745 dailies in America that employed 403,000 people, or 0.45 percent of the country's total employment. These dailies had a combined weekly circulation of 62 million, at a time when the population of the United States was 227 million, and had a 28 percent share of the total advertising expenditures in all media (Newspaper Association of America 2001; Picard and Brody 1997). One-quarter of a century later, all of these indicators had moved downward. By 2005 the number of dailies had dropped to 1,452, and the level of employment to 376,000, or 0.29 percent of the total employment. The combined print newspaper weekly circulation decreased to 53 million, whereas the population of the United States had increased to nearly 300 million, and the newspapers' share of the advertisement pie was reduced to 17 percent (Newspaper Association of America 2006).

Key indicators paint a mixed picture of online newspapers in 2005. A significant growth in site traffic and advertisement revenue coexisted with the lack of a leadership position in the new media space. Furthermore, there were widespread doubts about the ability of online newspapers to regain for their parent companies the stance that print dailies had once held in the world of news.

On the positive side, during the last quarter of 2005, newspaper web sites combined had, on average, 53 million monthly unique users and reached about one-third of the Americans who were online (Newspaper Association of America 2006). Moreover, online newspapers had combined advertisement revenues of more than $2 billion for 2005, representing a 75 percent growth from just two years earlier (Journalism. org 2006). However, to put things into perspective, these revenues represented less than 5 percent of the total revenues of the parent companies of these sites and less than 1 percent of the total advertisement pie (Journalism.org 2006).

On the negative side, in terms of audiences for online news, the best-positioned newspaper company was Gannett, in fifth place. The company was behind two sites belonging to "pure play firms" such as Yahoo and AOL and two coming from the broadcast world such as CNN and MSNBC (Journalism.org 2006). Although advertisement revenues had experienced significant growth in recent years, online newspaper sites competed fiercely with online-only players in key categories where they had once held dominant positions in the traditional media world, such as in classified advertisements.

Furthermore, newspaper sites have not achieved a commanding position in any of the major areas of action online. Google and Yahoo lead in information organization, eBay and Amazon.com in electronic commerce; Wikipedia, OhMyNews, and blogs are first in user-authored content, MySpace in social networking, and YouTube in multimedia, to name but a few. This failure accounts, in part, for the belief that the relative audience and revenue success of online newspapers is not enough to imagine that their future will be as bright as their print counterparts' past has been. In turn, it helps to explain why the market capitalization values of the new competitors are quite high in light of their actual revenues, but the reverse is the case for newspaper companies. For instance, Google achieved a market capitalization of $80 billion and surpassed that of the largest traditional media company, Time Warner, in 2005. A year later Google's stock market valuation had continued to grow to the point that it was worth eleven times more than that of Gannett, the largest publicly traded newspaper chain.

Newspapers' Culture of Innovation

How are we to make sense of the trajectory pursued by newspapers during the past quarter century in their attempts to innovate beyond ink on paper? In this section I argue that a culture of innovation marked by defensive and reactive traits illuminates key dynamics that have shaped this trajectory. Although this cultural argument cannot fully account for all the relevant factors, it is my contention that it helps to understand the resilience of certain modes of interpretation and action in the industry as well as their resulting consequences.

The term *reactive* is used to underscore that "quite often newspapers acted only after it seemed evident to key decision makers that relevant technical and social developments had reasonable chance of taking hold, rather than more proactively trying to take advantage of them earlier in the game" (Boczkowski 2004, 48). The first pair of stories in the introduction to this chapter is a clear illustration of this trait. Separated by a decade, top executives at the *New York Times* and the *Los Angeles Times* framed significant changes in production processes and resulting products, respectively, in essentially the same way—as a stated need to follow users in order to succeed. That is, instead of developing products and services that were aimed proactively at leading the users in a direction that would generate maximum advantage to their respective newspapers, the strategies were conceived as reactions to what was then considered an established trend. For the *Los Angeles Times*, users wanted to get digital news on the Web instead of on Prodigy, and, for the *New York Times*, they demanded a more integrated print-online product. Moreover, we find evidence of this reactive attitude a decade earlier, too, with regard to videotex. American newspapers embarked on the videotex journey as a reaction to developments then well under way in Europe, especially the United Kingdom, that were considered potentially damaging to the newspaper industry. This, in turn, leads to the second cultural trait: defensiveness.

The notion of a defensive culture of innovation highlights that newspapers "were usually more interested in finding out what the new technologies meant for the print enterprise than in more offensively developing new technical, communication, and organizational capabilities" (Boczkowski 2004, 49).[1] In other words, a critical focus of the first quarter century of innovation in electronic and online publishing was to defend the editorial and advertising spaces occupied by print rather than to conquer new territories in the digital domain. Thus, Knight-Ridder spent $50 million and five years developing, testing, and deploying Viewtron to "protect print's franchise" rather than to explore new communication products and market horizons. When their own user data suggested that people preferred to communicate among themselves rather than to read the news, Knight-Ridder dismissed this interest because it meant no harm to print's franchise. Thus, Knight-Ridder failed to exploit what a decade later became the first "killer app" of the digital space: user-to-user communication in the form of electronic mail and chat. Moreover, Knight-Ridder was not alone in pursuing videotex endeavors for this reason. In fact, as was mentioned in the 1983 survey of electronic publishing, most newspaper companies did so also to defend print from a potential threat and ceased to move in this direction after concluding that videotex posed "no clear and present danger."

Two additional illustrations of the defensive character of newspapers' culture of innovation can be found in the second pair of stories and in the fate of classified advertisement. A key motivation for both the New Century Network of the mid-1990s and the partnership between a group of newspapers and Yahoo a decade later was to protect the local franchise in an environment perceived to be increasingly beneficial to translocal products and services. Most American newspapers have local editorial and advertisement foci, and the Web seems to favor arrangements that take advantage of localities while at the same time connecting them to larger units. Therefore, newspaper companies have undertaken that interorganizational initiatives as mechanisms to defend their eminently local enterprises from the potential threat of nonlocal competitors.

The same defensiveness characterizes classified advertisements. Because industry players recognized long ago that this key element of the newspaper business is highly amenable to improvements when distributed electronically or online, the focus of most decision makers was to defend the status quo instead of moving aggressively to develop alternatives before new competitors did. This meant that when the newspaper industry finally started to move forward in the second half of the 1990s, the new competitors that had not existed in the early 1980s, when the topic first entered industry conversations, had already acquired a strong position. They continued to grow to nearly match the newspapers' share of this vital source of revenue, at least for local online classified ads.

The third trait of newspapers' culture of innovation is pragmatism. Having a pragmatic culture suggests "that with their non-print innovations, American dailies were often more interested in the short-term health of their core print businesses than, more idealistically, in projects that seemed more promising with comparatively higher payoffs that could only pan out in the longer term" (Boczkowski 2004, 49). Examples of this pragmatic attitude abound during the twenty-five-year period I have focused on. Building on the two illustrations previously mentioned, videotex had been all but abandoned in the mid-1980s, not because it did not work from a technical standpoint or did not have long-term promise, but because it appeared to pose "no clear and present danger" to print in the short term. To paraphrase Knight-Ridder's Paul Orme, the issue would have been to withstand short-term uncertainty in the midst of a perceived bright long-term future. Why such a focus on short-term results for organizations that had enjoyed significantly high levels of profit margins for a mature industry? This focus was partly because the pragmatic culture of innovation has made these organizations risk- and uncertainty-averse. For instance, speaking at the 1997 Interactive Newspaper conference, Bob Cauthorn, director of new technology at the *Arizona Daily Star*, argued that "the dairy industry spends more on R&D

[research and development] . . . than the newspaper industry does . . . We want an ROI [return on investment] . . . on everything. . . . Companies are investing risk capital to do business with us and we are investing almost nothing in risk capital" (Consoli 1997, 10). This risk-aversion partially accounts for the lack of development in the area of classified advertisement between the early 1980s and the mid-1990s, a period in which the short-term results for this kind of initiative were absent, even though there was a widespread belief that this vital part of the revenue stream was at risk.

The combination of these three traits helps to explain the coexistence of the two assessments made in the introductory section to this essay about how newspapers have fared in their electronic and online initiatives during the 1980–2005 period. On the one hand, because they have tried to react, defend, and be pragmatic, they have not stood still at all. This is why contemporary online newspapers look significantly different than the print artifacts of the early 1980s and have achieved a relative degree of audience and advertisement success. On the other hand, because they have evolved in a reactive, defensive, and pragmatic way, they have moved more slowly and more conservatively than their competitors, especially those without ties to traditional media enterprises. Therefore, they have lost the commanding position that they once held in the world of news and information.

This culture of innovation has been remarkably resilient in a quarter century of marked technological and societal changes. This is illustrated by the contrasting pairs of stories used to open this chapter as well as by the endurance of certain types of responses to key issues addressed here, such as user-generated content and classified advertisement. The resilience of this cultural constellation and its role in preventing newspapers from dealing with innovation in a less conservative fashion suggest that perhaps the major challenge that the industry faces to ensure its viability as a large and leading component of the media landscape is not exogenous but endogenous. That is, the key challenge may not come from outside the industry—for example, from unforeseen technological developments, unanticipated consumer choices, or creative strategies of competitors. Rather that challenge comes from the industry's very core: the set of beliefs, values, and norms that guide its members to make sense of their world and act upon it. This culture, in the end, may prove more difficult to deal with than technological, social, and market forces.

NOTES

I thank Russ Neuman for inviting me to contribute to this volume and for the most helpful comments received from him. I also thank Limor Peer, Rich Gordon, and the other participants of the workshop that led to the volume, held at the University of Michigan in Ann Arbor in March 2006. This text was conceived in preparation for that workshop and the bulk of this writing was completed by early 2007.

1. The chains are Belo, Cox Enterprises, Hearst, the Journal Register Company, Lee Enterprises, MediaNews Group, and E. W. Scripps.

2. These chains were Advance Publications Incorporated, Cox Newspapers, the Gannett Corporation, the Hearst Corporation, Knight-Ridder Incorporated, the Times Mirror Corporation, the Tribune Corporation, and the Washington Post. Two of these chains—Cox and Hearst—also participate in the partnership with Yahoo. At that time, these chains owned 185 papers with a combined circulation of about one-third of all U.S. dailies.

3. Whereas videotex consisted basically of content transmitted over telephone lines to computerized terminals, teletext consisted of content sent over television signals to modified television sets that had interactive capabilities.

4. From the cultural standpoint, the combination of reactivity and defensiveness complements Gilbert's (2005) findings about the behavioral dynamics of threat-induced rigidity in newspaper companies' responses to the first years of online publishing on the Web.

REFERENCES

Aumente, Jerome. 1987. *New Electronic Pathways: Videotex, Teletext, and Online Databases.* Beverly Hills: Sage.

Baer, Walter S., and Martin Greenberger. 1987. "Consumer Electronic Publishing in the Competitive Environment." *Journal of Communication* 37:49–63.

Batten, James. 1981. "A History of K-R's Viewdata Project." *Editor and Publisher,* July 4, 18, 20.

Beamish, Richard. 1997. "The Local Newspaper in the Age of Multimedia." In *Making Local News: Local Journalism in Context,* ed. Bob Franklin and David Murphy, 140–53. London: Routledge.

Boczkowski, Pablo J. 2004. *Digitizing the News: Innovation in Online Newspapers.* Cambridge: MIT Press.

Brown, Natalie A., and Tony Atwater. 1986. "Videotex News: A Content Analysis of Three Videotex Services and Their Companion Newspapers." *Journalism Quarterly* 63:554–61.

Carlson, David. 2003. "The History of Online Journalism." In *Digital Journalism: Emerging Media and the Changing Horizons of Journalism,* ed. Kevin Kawamoto, 31–55. Lanham, MD: Rowman and Littlefield.

Carveth, Rod, James Owers, and Alison Alexander. 1998. "The Economics of Online Media." In *Media Economics: Theory and Practice,* ed. Alison Alexander, James Owers, and Rod Carveth, 2nd ed., 247–73. Mahwah, NJ: Lawrence Erlbaum Associates.

Compaine, Benjamin M. 1980. *The Newspaper Industry in the 1980s: An Assessment of Economics and Technology.* White Plains, NY: Knowledge Industry Publications.

Consoli, John. 1995. "Online Timetable." *Editor and Publisher,* July 1, 17.

Consoli, John. 1996. "NCN Makes Some Strides." *Editor and Publisher,* May 4, 9–10.

Consoli, John. 1997. "Where Are the Cowboys?" *Editor and Publisher,* March 1, 10–11.

Davenport, L. 1987. "A Coorientation Analysis of Newspaper Editors' and Readers' Attitudes towards Videotex, Online News and Databases: A Study of Perception and Options." Ph.D. diss., Ohio University.

Dizard, Wilson. 1997. *Old Media, New Media: Mass Communication in the Information Age.* New York: Longman.

"Electronic Newspaper Found Unprofitable." 1982. *Editor and Publisher,* August 28, 7–8.

Fidler, Roger. 1997. *Mediamorphosis: Understanding New Media.* Thousand Oaks, CA: Pine Forge Press.

Fitzgerald, Mark. 1985. "Bullish on Videotex." *Editor and Publisher,* June 1, 32–33.

Garneau, George. 1993. "The New Media Landscape." *Editor and Publisher,* May 8, 14–15.

Garneau, George. 1995a. "Big-Time, Online Alliance Formed." *Editor and Publisher,* April 22, 15–16.

Garneau, George. 1995b. "New Alliance Raises Industry Concerns." *Editor and Publisher,* April 29, 9–10, 54.

Garrison, Bruce. 1997. "Online Services, Internet in 1995 Newsrooms." *Newspaper Research Journal* 18 (3–4): 79–93.

Gilbert, Clark. 2005. "Unbundling the Structure of Inertia: Resource versus Routine Rigidity." *Academy of Management Journal* 48:741–63.

Gloede, Bill. 1981. "ANCAM Proposes System for Electronic Classified." *Editor and Publisher,* June 27, 11, 40.

Hecht, J. 1983. "Information Services Search for Identity." *High Technology* 3:58–65.

Helft, Miguel, and Steve Lohr. 2006. "176 Newspapers to Form a Partnership with Yahoo." *New York Times,* November 20, C1.

Hotaling, Burton. 1948. "Facsimile Broadcasting: Problems and Possibilities." *Journalism Quarterly* 25:139–44.

Journalism.org. 2006. *State of the News Media.* Project for Excellence in Journalism. Retrieved June 9, 2006, from http://www.stateofthemedia.org/2006/.

Keller, Bill, and Martin Nisenholtz. 2005. A Message from Bill Keller and Martin Nisenholtz. August 2. *Poynter Online.* Retrieved March 16, 2007, from http://www.poynter.org/forum/view_post.asp?id=10027.

"Knight-Ridder 'Pulls Plug' on Its Videotex Operation." 1986. *Editor and Publisher,* March 29, 14.

"*L.A. Times* Exits Prodigy, for Now." 1995. *Editor and Publisher,* December 2, 37.

Laakaniemi, Ray. 1981. "The Computer Connection: America's First Computer-Delivered Newspaper." *Newspaper Research Journal* 2 (4): 61–68.

Mantooth, S. S. 1982. "The Electronic Newspaper: Its Prospects and Directions for Future Study." Ph.D. diss., University of Tennessee, Knoxville.

Martin, Shannon E., and Kathleen A. Hansen. 1998. *Newspapers of Record in a Digital Age: From Hot Type to Hot Link.* Westport, CT: Praeger.

Marvin, Carolyn. 1988. *When Old Technologies Were New: Thinking about Electric Communication in the Late Nineteenth Century.* New York: Oxford University Press.

Meyer, E. 1998. "Why NewsWorks Didn't." *AJR NewsLink.* April. Retrieved April 21, 2000, from http://ajr.newslink.org/emcolncn2.html.

Molina, Alfonso. 1997. "Issues and Challenges in the Evolution of Multimedia: The Case of the Newspaper." *Futures* 29:193–212.

NCN Alliance. 1995. *Editor and Publisher*, May 6, 6.

"NCN Previews Web Gateway." 1997. *Editor and Publisher*, May 3, 16.

Newspaper Association of America. 2001. *Facts about Newspapers 2001*. Retrieved March 20, 2002, from http://www.naa.org/info/facts01/index.html.

Newspaper Association of America. 2006. *The Source: Newspapers by the Numbers*. Retrieved January 3, 2007, from http://www.naa.org/thesource/.

Noll, A. Michael. 1980. "Teletext and Videotex in North America: Service and System Implications." *Telecommunications Policy* 4:25–31.

Outing, Steve. 1996. "Where's the Money?" *Editor and Publisher*, February 17, 8I, 34I.

Outing, Steve. 1998. "NCN Goes Belly Up; Total Shutdown Announced." *Editor and Publisher*, March 14, 12, 14.

Picard, Robert G., and Jeffrey H. Brody. 1997. *The Newspaper Publishing Industry*. Boston: Allyn and Bacon.

Pool, Ithiel de Sola. 1983. *Technologies of Freedom*. Cambridge: Belknap Press of Harvard University Press.

"Quality and Technology Stressed at ANPA/RI Show." 1983. *Editor and Publisher*, June 18, 12–17, 38, 42–44.

Shefrin, D. 1949. "The Radio Newspaper and Facsimile Broadcasting." Master's thesis, University of Missouri.

Stone, Gerald. 1987. *Examining Newspapers: What Research Reveals about America's Newspapers*. Newbury Park, CA: Sage.

Weaver, David H., and G. Cleveland Wilhoit. 1986. *The American Journalist: A Portrait of U.S. News People and Their Work*. Bloomington: Indiana University Press.

Willis, Jim. 1994. *The Age of Multimedia and Turbonews*. Westport, CT: Praeger.

From the Telegraph and Telephone to the Negroponte Switch

RICH LING

In this chapter I will explore a series of historical case studies examining technical evolution and the interaction of this technical development with the *visionary rhetoric* used to help organize the institutional development of the technologies.

Sometimes visionaries produce inspiring and empowering words on new technologies that will result in social-structural changes. But not always. We have Gordon Moore's 1965 law describing developments in computing and David Sarnoff's 1920s description of radio as a type of music box. At the same time we also have Herb Grosch's law (also in 1965) describing the need for large computers and William Orton's 1876 suggestion that the telephone was only an interesting toy. Sometimes these descriptions are the rallying cries that move an industry in one direction or another as they crystallize complex issues into a comprehensible insight. At other times they do not even receive their Warholian fifteen minutes of fame.

Such examples of visionary rhetoric have careers that wax and wane and can constrain opportunities for invention as well as stimulate them. When ideas become slogans embedded in political, policy, and commercial interest, as they often do, we might want to rethink our taken-for-granted notion of their heroic inventors.

Harmeet Sawhney has suggested that access to *excess capacity* in a technical system results in creativity (see Sawhney's chapter in this volume). While that may be true, I will posit a corollary that the sudden access to new technical possibilities, be this via technical development or regulatory fiat, unleashes creativity, a round of catchphrases and slogans, and in some cases, the majority of the seven cardinal sins. Indeed Winston posits the "'law' of the *suppression of radical potential*," which states that between the initial invention of a technology and its mass acceptance there is a period of slower development when the preexisting structures need to rearrange themselves in relation to the new arrival (1998, 11). Winston, however, discounts the visionary rhetoric associated with the development of technology as rodomontade or pretentious self-importance. Thus, he points to the same situation as Sawhney but puts another spin on it.

This chapter will examine three episodes in the history of technology where either technical advancement and/or regulatory contortions resulted in new possibilities for mediation: the first instance is the development of broadcast radio; the second is the rise of the integrated circuit; and the third, as indicated in the title of this chapter, is the potential of digital TV and the cotemporal development of mobile telephony. In each case, there was some type of technical advancement either on the doorstep or in the recent past. In each case there was also a crystallizing description of the situation that helped to organize the institutional reaction to the development. There was Sarnoff's description of the radio music box, Moore's law, and finally the Negroponte switch. The first two were, indeed, associated with developments that eventually led to the situation described by the latter. There was new capacity and a rush to innovation—as suggested by the Sawhney principle—and there was the channeling and constraining of the innovation as it interacted with various institutions.

With hindsight, it is possible to say that a phrase was, or was not, visionary. At one level, that is beside the point. It is also possible to assert that phrases or slogans such as the Negroponte switch are a necessary part of the glue that links techno-political developments with the people who are implementing them. In the heat of the institutional scramble to deal with a changing field, these phrases light the way. It is through the establishment and elaboration of these catchphrases that institutions set their course. In some cases they help to organize and direct efforts. The problem is that in other cases they point in a direction that leads off the edge of the nearest cliff. Finally, some of them never really catch on and end up being historical curiosities.

The basic mechanism here is technological or regulatory development. It is not enough, however, that the elements of new mediation forms are in place; there is also the need to organize institutional capacity for these developments. It is here that catchphrases such as the

Negroponte switch or Sarnoff's comment on the radio come into play. These slogans encapsulate a complex technical and policy issue, they come from a legitimate source, and they need to be so pithy that they are ingrained in the institutional culture where the developments are taking place. That is, they need to be a rallying cry for the troops who are busy with the development of the technology.

The History of Wired and Wireless Mediation

In this chapter, I will look specifically at the historical context that led up to and coincided with the so-called Negroponte switch. In addition, with almost two decades of hindsight, I will look into the fate of the phrase and set it into the broader context of the politics of technology development.[1]

To set the Negroponte switch into a broader historical context, it is useful to trace the development of electrical and electromagnetic technology as applied to interpersonal communication and the broadcast of entertainment, news, and commercial content. It is these two threads of development that laid the foundation for the mediation of voice, images, entertainment, and interpersonal communication. That is, they are the technical core of the Negroponte switch.

The general line of development is that wired point-to-point—and generally interpersonal—communication developed in the mid-nineteenth century in the form of the telegraph and later the telephone. About the turn of the century radio communication developed and by 1920 was also transmitting audio content, not just Morse code. During the early 1920s in the United States there was a brief point of convergence—at least at the institutional level—for these two forms of mediation, but basically until the late 1980s, after the development of the transistor, wired and wireless communication lived their separate and largely parallel lives.[2] With the rise of digital TV and cellular telephony the potential again suggested itself that the given practice was not necessarily set in stone. It is at this point that Gilder and Negroponte suggested the idea of the switch.

Ultimately, the prophecies suggested by the switch have, to some degree, been achieved, but the picture here is quite muddled. The phrase, however, provides us with good insight into the politics of technology development, particularly when innovators face the need to mobilize institutions either for certain types of development or to protect themselves from the assault of new techno-regulatory regimes.

Electricity Applied to Communication

Joseph Henry was the first person to use electricity for the purpose of communication. Henry used the principles developed by Michael Faraday, and indeed it is Faraday who laid the groundwork for both wire-based and wireless communication.[3] Henry applied the principles of electricity to various applications in the early 1830s. He developed a system for using magnetism to remotely ring a bell that was the forerunner of telegraphy. In 1837, of course, Samuel Morse received his patent for telegraphy after learning of Faraday's work and that of Henry.

Moving now to the institutional realm and Sawhney's period of creativity, we note that wire-based telegraphy found two niches that immediately assisted in its growth. The first was as a signaling channel for the control of the railroad, and the second was the transmission of time-sensitive financial information (Standage 1998). While there was a period of competition in the industry, the structure of the telegraph industry moved toward monopolization, and by the end of the 1800s, Western Union in the United States, the British Post Office in the United Kingdom, and Telegrafverket in Norway were the monopolists. Internationally, the International Telegraph Union was formed in the 1860s to develop standards for international interaction.

The roughly parallel but time-shifted development of telephony for interpersonal communication followed somewhat the same development as telegraphy. In the United States, based on the developments of Alexander Graham Bell, the Bell telephone eventually formed into American Telephone and Telegraph (AT&T). Western Union was offered the possibility of purchasing the patents for the telephone. From this episode we have one of the oft-repeated quotes—as well as an illustration of the suppression of radical potential highlighted by Winston—made by William Orton, the head of Western Union, who believed that the telephone was an interesting toy but would not have practical implications (Winston 1998, 54). As with the later Negroponte switch, the fact that this quip is remembered—and even savored by telephone people—points to the social dynamics of institutional adoption of technology. It is an example of just how wrong we can be. Orton was so thoroughly entrenched in the hegemony of Western Union he failed to grasp the fundamental shift presented by the telephone.[4]

Through a series of consolidations and the idea of "universal service"—another catchphrase that has organized the efforts of many policymakers—the reach of the telephone expanded. By the start of the

1920s wire-based interpersonal and voice-based communication was a well-established institution in major cities and in many rural areas (Fischer 1992). The telephone and the telegraph coexisted for many years, with the telephone gradually taking more and more of the traffic.[5]

The role of the telephone was, however, not simply interpersonal communication. While the telephone was not designed to send or receive audio with any fidelity (Pool 1983), it was nonetheless used for the transmission of entertainment. Here again is the Sawhney principle at work. In the 1870s music was transmitted over the telephone. It seems that "telephone concerts" were the rage in the late 1870s. One affair was in Warren County, Pennsylvania, where on January 29, 1878, musicians performing in Jamestown, New York, were heard in the hall through the use of the telephone. Also heard was a speech by Thomas Edison, who introduced his new "phonograph" (Warren County Historical Society 2005). From New Orleans in 1879 we hear of a "telephone concert" given by the telephone company in 1879 with Miss Minnie Wolf singing "Pizzicato Polka" and other pieces (New Orleans Public Library 2005). And in lonely Lake City, Colorado—a town without telephony at the time—in March 1878 we learn of William Penn Harbottle, the temporary editor of the local *Silver World* who, among his other talents that were presumably played out in other locations, claimed to be a telephone-concert tenor horn soloist (Thompson 1974). Marvin reports on telephone concerts sent from New York to Rochester and Buffalo in the 1890s (1988). Similar services were offered in Paris, London, and Budapest. Indeed the last telephone concert sent from Paris seems to have been in 1932 (Crook 1999). Thus, there was the embryonic idea of broadcasting that, while mediated by the telephone, included the one-to-many structure of the later industry.[6]

Turning to radio-based communication, we note that Marconi was at work during the latter part of the nineteenth century to develop a practical method for the transmission of telegraph signals. During this period he continued to push the boundary for the transmission of telegraph signals until transoceanic communication became possible. By 1900 he had sent a message across Newfoundland and the United Kingdom.

At the dawn of the twentieth century, radio was basically unregulated, limited to Morse code, and largely the realm of hobbyists.[7] However, its unfulfilled role in the *Titanic* disaster and the use of radio in World War I led to the regulation and the eventual commercialization of the airwaves. This along with the technical development of voice modulation led to a genuine radio craze in the 1920s.

The amateur handling of news regarding the *Titanic* along with a deep and lurid interest in the fate of so many people changed public opinion regarding the lassez-faire regulation of the radio spectrum (S. Douglas 1987; Hargittai 2000). In 1912 the International Radio-Tele-graphic Convention was convened in London, where it was decided to require oceangoing passenger vessels have a wireless communication system that was staffed twenty-four hours a day. In addition, the U.S. Federal Radio Act of 1912 was passed, the first U.S. government involvement in radio. It required the licensing of operators and set aside frequencies for emergency communication.

The movement from radio-based Morse code to the modulation of voice continued into the twentieth century. The work of Lee de Forest resulted in the vacuum tube. This was essential since it amplified signals and allowed for the wireless transmission of voice. This period also saw some of the first use of radio for the distribution of entertainment. The idea of broadcasting was staring to coalesce. Mapping onto the idea that phrases help to organize the development and adoption of technologies, one metaphor that captured the idea of using the technology for the distribution of entertainment was Sarnoff's idea of the "radio music box."

> The "Radio Music Box" can be supplied with amplifying tubes and a loudspeaking telephone, all of which can be neatly mounted in one box. The box can be placed on a table in the parlor or living room, the switch set accordingly and the transmitted music received. There should be no difficulty in receiving music perfectly when transmitted within a radius of 25 to 50 miles. Within such a radius there reside hundreds of thousands of families; and as all can simultaneously receive from a single transmitter, there would be no question of obtaining sufficiently loud signals to make the performance enjoyable. (Sarnoff 1920)

In January 1917 Lee de Forest used his vacuum tube radio system to broadcast music in a "Concert by Wireless" and a month later broadcast a "Wireless Dance" (*QST* 1917).[8] Writing in the April 1917 edition of the magazine *QST*, de Forest reported:

> A novel request was one from two gentlemen in Newark, N. J., who asked that on a certain evening we play dance music. This, in order that their guests of that evening, to the number of one hundred,

might dance to our Graphonola Orchestra furnished us nightly by the Columbia Graphophone Company. We heard afterwards that this dance was a great success, as was the previous one in Morristown, N. J., for which we also provided the music at Highbridge, N. Y., thirty odd miles away. (de Forest 1917)

The entry of the United States into World War I temporarily halted this development. Amateur radio was suspended during the war for fear of spying and the U.S. Navy took over all radio signaling. Further, the fear of losing control of the radio spectrum prompted the government to regulate it in the years after the war. This included the organization of Radio Corporation of America (RCA), which resulted from the nationalized Marconi America. The company, which was controlled by AT&T and General Electric, was given the license to produce radio equipment in the United States. Further, the government started the regulation of the radio spectrum and required licensing for those who wished to operate a radio station (for a discussion see Hazlett 2001). This meant that RCA controlled the patents for vacuum tubes, which gave it a de facto monopoly. After a short and troubled marriage to AT&T, it controlled radio for some time.

Thus, by the end of World War I wired and wireless mediation were channeled into their separate directions. On the one hand, point-to-point communication was carried out via wired systems, the somewhat competing systems of telegraph and telephone. On the wireless side, the elements for the development of broadcast radio were on the table, and they were starting to be used for what we recognize as broadcast entertainment.

Embedding of the Channels

Several issues resulted in the canalization of telephony in the wired world and broadcast in the wireless world. Not to be a technological determinist, but there are good technical reasons for the paths chosen in the early years of telephony and radio. Following Farley:

As the vacuum tube and the transistor made possible the early telephone network, the wireless revolution began only after low cost microprocessors, miniature circuit boards, and digital switching became available. (Farley 2005)

Thus, as of the 1920s, technical means were unavailable for any form of switched interpersonal radio communication such as we now have with mobile telephony. The development of cellular telephony awaited the rise of enhanced processing power. This is not to say that there was not overlap. Indeed, early radio operators sent personal messages to one another, and, as we have seen, the telephone was used for the distribution of entertainment and news.[9]

Looking at radio, we see other considerations. In the early 1920s there was little understanding of whether broadcast technology would attract an audience. Up to that point, what we consider as broadcast radio had been dominated by amateurs who were interested in both sending and receiving transmissions. This metaphor was, to a certain degree, explored by AT&T in a period when they investigated the development of radio broadcasting. According to John Brooks, there was a notion that AT&T-owned radio stations, starting with WEAF in New York, would allow a telephone subscriber to call into the station and give a radio talk. Thus, radio would be supported by rental of the transmitter. The open time was to be filled with music (Brooks et al. 1976).

Radio broadcasts for the purpose of entertainment or news started with the Westinghouse-owned station KDKA and its reporting of the presidential election in 1920. Soon major events such as the Dempsey-Carpentier boxing match and baseball games were becoming a regular feature of radio broadcasts (Ackerman 1945).

The first use of the medium for advertising came in August 1922 when a real estate developer bought fifteen minutes to promote a housing development called Hawthorne Court. There were soon others, and eventually radio developed a mixture of entertainment and news (music, sports, comedy, theatrical performances, etc.) and commercial pitches. The owners of the station managed the boundary between entertainment and commercials. The pattern of multiple types of content was nonetheless set. In addition, many types of organizations applied for and received licenses for broadcasting during this period. In addition to major corporations and newspapers, there were department stores, YMCA clubs, universities, and churches. Some of the connections were logical, while others reflected the breadth of interest in radio during this period.

In those euphoric months of early 1922 radio stations were licensed to some very eccentric and inexplicable owners. There was the Yahrling-Rayner Piano Company of Youngstown, Ohio (WAAY); the Palmer School of Chiropractic, of Davenport, Iowa (WOC); the C. F.

Aldrich Marble and Granite Co., of Colorado Springs, Colo. (KHD); the Omaha Grain Exchange (WAAW); and even the Nushawg Poultry Farm of New Lebanon, Ohio (WPI). (Douglas 1997)

While there was a clear commercial drift in the United States, the situation was different elsewhere. The BBC was being organized in the United Kingdom. After a short period of commercial radio, broadcasting in Britain was nationalized and developed programming to be broadcast to its wide-flung colonial empire. The model, still widely copied, relied on licensing fees in lieu of commercials. Thus, the listener paid for radio use with an annual licensing fee, as opposed to supporting the station by buying toothpaste or shampoo advertised on the radio (as in the commercial U.S. system). In addition to catering to the desires of listeners, the BBC model also had the explicit mission of educational and public service programming. Its motivation, in the words of its first director general, John Reith, was (in typically gendered terms) "making the nation as one man." Thus, we come again to the interaction between ideological perspective and the development of a techno-institutional organization (see Schwartz in this volume).

When we think of the fast-coming canalization of wireless broadcast and wire-based telephony, this seems to be a particularly plastic moment in history. On the one hand, the soon to be premier radio broadcasting company, RCA, and the premier telephone company, AT&T, were indeed in a loose partnership. By 1923 AT&T was able to open a second radio station in Washington that used its telephone network to carry the signal between New York and Washington. Later that year, AT&T even used its telephone system in conjunction with local radio broadcasters to air the first nationwide address by President Harding.

The cooperation between RCA and AT&T was not easy to maintain. AT&T tried to enforce various monopolies and set what RCA believed to be inappropriate prices for use of the telephone transport between radio markets. There were lawsuits and bickering between the two. By the middle of 1926 AT&T had sold its radio stations and had agreed to supply RCA with the telephone network so that RCA could distribute its radio programs. Thus, anticipating the discussion of the Negroponte shift, while there was a wire-based network for the transport of what we have come to call *content* between local radio stations, the final distribution in a city was via ether.

By the mid-1920s the pattern had been established. While both telephony and radio communication had been used for several decades at this point, it was only when AT&T backed out of the broadcast industry that the pattern upon which Negroponte and Gilder commented became the norm. In the first two decades of the twentieth century there was the well-entrenched wire-based transmission of interpersonal communication (the telephone system) and the nascent broadcasting of entertainment, news, and, not incidentally, commercials via local radio.

The Convergence of Wired and Wireless

From the early 1920s until the late 1970s the model of wired interpersonal communication and wireless broadcasting went almost unquestioned. However, the development of the transistor by Shockley, Barden, and Brattain in 1947, and the resulting development of the integrated circuit in 1959 by Jack Kilby and independently by Robert Noyce, changed the situation. Their development radically reduced the energy and size needed for electronic devices and thus enabled much of the technology development in the latter part of the twentieth century (Winston 1998, 220). These developments paved the way for the changes brought by cable TV, the promise of HDTV, and the growing development of wireless communication.

Looking first at wireless telephony, in the period after World War II there were several small trials with the intention of introducing a wireless local loop into the "switched" telephone service. These were the first steps associated with the eventual development of mobile telephony. As reported elsewhere (Ling 2004), one of the first such trials was carried out in eastern Colorado near the town of Cheyenne Wells. It was expensive to set up the telephone lines to the widespread farmers in the area. As an indication of the distances, some of the "local" farmers used airplanes to commute into town. From the perspective of the telephone company, it was potentially more efficient to connect the farmers into the system via radio. In town a telephone operator could patch the calls into the traditional wire-based system. In this case, the cells were many tens of miles in diameter. The installations at the farmers' homes were stationary. Thus there was no need for systems to deal with "handoff" between cells, and indeed the cells were quite spacious when compared with today's. Radio had, however, entered into the realm of switched telephony.[10]

The next advancement in cellular telephony came in the late 1960s with trials on the New York–Washington Metroliner. In this trial a system was developed by AT&T that allowed the calls from the train traveling between the two cities to be handed off between cells. In order to deal with this system the engineers had to plan frequency use so that adjacent cells were not operating on the same frequency and thus interfering with each other. The development of the transistor as a supercharged version of the vacuum tube also allowed the development of first "luggable" and later quite portable handsets. Thus, in the latter part of the twentieth century the development in telephony has seen the rise of smaller and smaller mobile handsets that move away from the geographically fixed landline telephone.

Looking back to the realm of broadcast, TV arose as a popular medium in the 1950s and 1960s (Schwartz 2002; and see Schwartz in this volume). Advances in television included the rise of cable TV, the attempted development of HDTV, and digital TV, which also arose from the development of the integrated circuit (Winston 1998, 140). Cable TV started to become a force in television distribution in the late 1970s with the rise of channels such as HBO and CNN. Since that time it has been a major conduit of information into the home. The greatest impact has been in terms of broadcast TV, but also Internet and telephony have been delivered via the "TV" cable.

Interestingly, as these words are being written we see a new technical twist. Broadcast TV as well as "on demand" services such as YouTube clips are being offered via mobile telephone handsets. Almost as if to make a mockery of the Negroponte shift, if the broadcast material is being remotely gathered by a news team, the transmission involves a radio link into the wire-based system, where it is carried to the production center of a content provider and perhaps mixed with other programming (for example, the anchorperson talking to the remote reporter). From there it is sent back out through a cable system to a mobile phone tower, where it is sent via a radio link to the final viewer.

Technical Paradigms in Historical Perspective

Faraday did not come close to envisioning the two paths of development traced here. His ideas on electromagnetic induction were, however, basic for the development of both wired and wireless communication. Electricity was used as a medium for communication via wired channels first in the guise of the telegraph, followed by the telephone and later by broadcast communication that also can include telephony. Electromagnetism developed first into radio-based Morse telegraphy and later into voice and visual broadcast. With the development of the transistor it also was pressed into service as a form of mediated interpersonal interaction in the form of the mobile phone—which is now also becoming a TV terminal.

These developments have spun off various phrases to describe the different technologies. Sarnoff's "music box," Moore's prolific transistors, and Gilder's formulation are three central examples. Each of them was a prognosis, and each of them also functioned to direct the institutional mobilization required for the development of the respective systems.

The Context of the Negroponte Switch

The Negroponte switch was posited in 1989 by George Gilder. Based on interaction with Nicholas Negroponte he asserted, "What goes over the air (broadcast TV and radio) will go via wire and what goes via wire (telephony) will go over the air." Expanding on this dictum, Negroponte wrote:

> George Gilder and I have shared the podium frequently, and I have learned a lot from him. One of our first encounters occurred about 10 years ago at an executive retreat organized by Northern Telecom (now called Nortel). At this meeting, I showed a slide that depicted wired and wireless information trading places. This idea had been prompted, in part, by some early HDTV discussions, during which I and others questioned whether broadcast TV should get any spectrum at all, since stationary TV sets could be better served by wires (read: fiber).
>
> In contrast, the theory continued, anything that moves needs to be wireless. Phones, largely wired at the time, would go wireless, and TV, largely wireless, would get wired. Gilder called this "the Negroponte Switch." (Negroponte 1997)

The Negroponte switch was posited in the era when "fiber to the home" was a popular notion. It was also the era when high-definition TV was under development, mobile telephony was becoming more common, and we were at the dawn of the popularized Internet. The technologies on the horizon at that point indicated that perhaps the public would be better served if the signals that had traditionally traveled wirelessly (TV and radio) were transported by landline techniques, while those that had traditionally been wire-bound (telephony) were transported through the ether. The need for capacity to transmit huge amounts of video material and the fact that telephony required much less bandwidth indicated that the switch would be logical.

Today, there are large numbers of mobile phone users as well as a large reliance on cable TV. Thus, we might assume that the prophecy is true. Seen in this light, the idea of the Negroponte switch is prophetic. However, while there are some general lines of agreement, there are also devils in the details. In another sense, the phrase also provides insight into the need to develop institutional ideologies in the sense of Berger and Luckmann (1967). That is, there is the need to mobilize institutions in the implementation of a technical or a regulatory vision. Slogans such as the Negroponte switch serve this goal.

Problems with Heroic Prophecy

With almost two decades of hindsight we now have a chance to see the value of the prophecy. As noted in the introduction, the widespread adoption of mobile telephony and cable TV seems to indicate that yes, this switch has indeed happened. In addition, the growing use of mobile communication points in the same direction. Point-to-point interpersonal communication had a long life in the wired world and has started to move into the wireless sphere. Movement of wireless to wired has also occurred. Thus, we can perhaps assume that Gilder and Negroponte's prophecy has come true.

However, the details are not quite so clear. If we are thinking only of "plain old telephony," as seems to be the case with Gilder and Negroponte, the slogan holds up. However, if we take a few steps back, other issues arise. From the perspective of mobile communication, there is undeniably a wireless element. However, a lot of interpersonal communication happens over wired systems. A lot of e-mail, chatting, and IM'ing is still wired. Further significant portions of the population, particularly the elderly, still use wire-based voice telephony.

Consider local radio connections. If we are using a traditional mobile telephone (GSM, CDMA, etc.) or if we use an advanced phone with a WiFi connection and, for example, a Skype client, or if we use a so-called wireless local loop system such as Little Smart (which is widespread in China), the interaction makes the first part of its journey through the ether (Castells et al. 2007; Sandvig, Young, and Menrath 2004). After that, however, it is back into the wired world. The series of base stations, routers, backbone, and so on are all wire based.

If we look at the local situation, Gilder was right; if we look at the broader system, he was not. While in some countries and for some groups, wireless is the dominant form of voice mediation, the pattern does not hold up in all cases.

To argue from a slightly different perspective: a lot of entertainment has become cable based. This said, there is still a relatively large public for satellite-based TV, and increasingly radio (see Carey's chapter in this volume). In addition, the traditional terrestrial TV broadcast system is still in place and occupying radio frequency. Thus, the shift that Gilder suggested has taken place, but it is partial and has not resulted in tidying up resource allocation issues.

There is also a definitional question here. Increasingly, people are using local WiFi (read wireless) connections within their homes to afford them mobility and to avoid some of the "wire spaghetti" that seems to be a part of the PC world. Through these local wireless connections people are working (and engaging in interpersonal communication). They are also surfing the net as a form of entertainment. More to the point, they are downloading music and viewing videos that are decidedly entertainment and formerly the turf of the broadcast industry. While the bits that constitute the entertainment flow through different pipes (cable, copper-based DSL, etc.) the last critical "local loop" is wireless. To the degree that this is going on, the accuracy of Gilder's prophecy becomes an issue of framing. In this case, the outcome is the opposite of that in interpersonal communication.

Thus, if we look at the broader system, Gilder was right on. If we look at the immediate user configuration, the answer is not so clear. Negroponte himself has raised the same point:

> *Was the Negroponte Switch Correct After All?* . . .
> A decade later, it seems that this whole switching of places has been contradicted left and right. Satellite TV is doing fine. HDTV just got new spectrum. And the cable business is starting to include telephony. So how should one look at RF [radio frequency] today? (1997)

George Gilder, the person who originally posited the switch, was also in doubt. He wrote, "By 1994 the vision of scarce spectrum behind the Negroponte switch was in a rout" (1993). In a subsequent article he sketched some of the scenario I have already outlined:

> In an era of bandwidth abundance, the Negroponte switch—with voice pushed to the air and video onto wires—may well give way to this

division between fibersphere and atmosphere. With the fibersphere offering virtually unlimited bandwidth for fixed communications over long distances, the local loop will be the bottleneck, thronged with millions of wireless devices. Under these conditions, a move to high-frequency cellular systems is imperative to carry the increasing floods of digital video overflowing from the fibersphere (1993). Others have suggested that economic mechanisms can address some of the spectrum constraints and ease the issues associated with the transition of TV from its analogue era into the coming digital era. (Hazlett 2001)

There are clear prophetic elements in the idea of the Negroponte switch, and indeed some of the technological changes suggested by it have been realized. However, it would overstate the case to say that reality has followed the plan. The unforeseen rise of WiFi and other technological changes have skewed the picture. In spite of this, for a brief period, the Negroponte switch was seen as a clear vision of technical development. It crystallized the direction of technical developments at the time and pointed to the problems being faced by those developments. However, the introduction of other technologies into this mix changed the situation.

The Negroponte Switch as Visionary Rhetoric

Were the Negroponte switch simply a technical prophecy, it would soon have been forgotten. It was, however, much else. The phrase is so well entrenched because it summarized a complex technical situation, stated a probable outcome, came from a legitimate source (in the form of Gilder and Negroponte), and also helped to marshal activity in important sectors of the society. In later life it serves as a benchmark with regards to the political, technical, and social vectors of the time and it is indeed still being debated. Further, the statement came at a time when extra capacity was problematic. Policy issues and technical futures were at play. For these reasons, it registered in the minds of persons who were engaged in the daily work of developing or marketing technologies where the turf of the "other" group was for some reason desirable.

The Negroponte switch was a successful slogan. It was used in the mobilization of social forces pushing for, or alternatively resisting, the establishment of a new technological regime. It was a call to arms for those wishing these chances to be made, and it was also a warning to those wishing for the status quo.

As we have seen, the broad sweep of the phrase has been achieved—or perhaps not, depending on the framing of the data. What is interesting from a sociological perspective, however, is that the phrase crystallized the tensions between significant institutional actors. Coined at a meeting of landline telephone executives, it may have scandalized the meeting, or at least those executives whose jobs it was to maintain the copper-based telephone system. It probably also energized the troops associated with the development of HDTV and mobile telephony.

To be sure, it was pithy and quick, it seemed to easily encapsulate broad trends in society, and it came from highly credible sources who also had access to publication systems where it could be spread to the far corners of the earth. Thus it is not difficult to imagine that it soon appeared in hundreds, if not thousands, of corporate presentations associated with planning and development.

The cable industry saw it as a summary of how the development of technology would eventually trump the terrestrial broadcasting industry. In a similar way, radio-based communication industries, such as mobile telephony, saw it as fitting into their campaigns to gain access to additional radio spectrum. For policymakers it outlined issues of who needed spectrum and who might not need it in the future.

In this respect, it is far from unique. Many phrases and slogans are pressed into service in this way. William Orton's description of the telephone as a toy, Sarnoff's "radio music box," and Moore's law have also served a similar function.[11] Consider for a moment Moore's law. An interesting contrast is seen in the form of Grosch's law from 1956, which noted that "computer performance increases as the square of the cost. If you want to do it twice as cheaply, you have to do it four times slower" (see Edwards's chapter in this volume). This formulation competed with Moore's law, which observed that the computational power of computers would double every eighteen months. The former statement suggested that the direction of development for computers would be for larger and larger machines. Here the politicking was between those advocating a few big computers and those advocating many small ones. In the early phase of computer development, the period when Sawhney suggests we look for creativity, we see two ideas that help to frame development efforts.

Time has shown that Grosch's side lost. Interestingly, however, there is a metatext associated with each of these two alternatives. First, the notion of Moore's law helps developers, investors, and users to think about possible future developments. Its seeming validation lets them orient themselves. Second, Moore's law is perhaps associated with the inevitability of the PC revolution. To the degree that it is remembered, Grosch's law is used to show just how bad we—or perhaps poor Grosch—can be when trying to make prognoses. These other "laws" and slogans have played a role similar to that of the Negroponte switch.

The Social Framing of Technology Development

The development of technical regimes is a complex process. The development phase of a technology sees the introduction of new potential and what Sawhney describes as a creative phase. Soon enough the potentials become institutionalized and interact with other preexisting systems that deal with the same realm. In this phase we see Winston's suppression of radical potential. In this process there are technical developments, regulatory issues, and the need to mobilize large institutions either in support of or in opposition to the change in technology. In an era of convergence we meet these issues increasingly.

It is in these circumstances that phrases such as the Negroponte switch find their role. These phrases, coined by central people in the development milieu, often summarize a complex system, help others to understand the issues at play, and organize their efforts.

We can see the results of these processes by looking at a perhaps flawed, but interesting meter of popularity. Specifically, as of this writing, there are 136,000 mentions of the Negroponte switch on the Web when queried via Google. There is, however, certain confusion as to its application. In most cases it refers to the cable/mobile phone exchange I have outlined. In other cases it is a reference to a physical switch that would reroute these two streams of information, and in some cases it refers to Negroponte's idea regarding the replacement of atoms with bits. By this measure Moore's law is more thoroughly ensconced, since it is mentioned on approximately 10.1 million pages, while poor Grosch has his law mentioned only about 800 times. Sarnoff's comment on the radio as a "music box" is cited 19,600 times, and the quip made by Western Union about the telephone being nothing more than a toy has 43,000 referrals.

These statistics show that these catchphrases have careers. They can become received truth regarding the inevitability of a certain type of development (Moore's law), a cliché that may even become a parody (Western Union's preliminary evaluation of the telephone), a phrase with perhaps limited shelf life (the Negroponte switch), or a largely forgotten erroneous formula (Grosch's law). These outcomes are determined by the degree to which they are oversold, and by the degree to which they are overtaken by events.

NOTES

1. While the Negroponte switch points to the comments of Nicholas Negroponte, it is not necessarily the case that Negroponte or George Gilder, who actually coined the phrase, was motivated to establish a catchphrase. They may have simply meant it as an off-the-cuff statement. Nonetheless it captured the imagination of others.

2. The technology for mobile cell-based telecommunication was not mature in the 1920s.

3. To trace fully the development of mediated interpersonal and broadcast communication, it is convenient to go back to the time of Michael Faraday. It is perhaps one of the quirks of history that the fundamental scientific basis for both the generation of electricity and the understanding of the electromagnetic spectrum came from the same person. From relatively simple origins Faraday rose to be Humphrey Davy's assistant and eventually a member of the Royal Institute in London.

Looking first at electricity, basic to landline telephony, Faraday discovered the method for generating this type of power. Previous to Faraday electricity was basically equivalent to Leyden jars and lightning. It was Faraday, along with Ampère, Ohm, Volta, and Galvani, who worked out the basis for modern electrical technology. Thomas Edison, of course, was a telegraph operator early in his career and went on to make improvements in telegraphy and also to engage in a pitched battle with George Westinghouse over the relative benefits of AC and DC power. Foreshadowing the later discussion of Negroponte, Edison and Westinghouse saw the unmet niche of electrification of the home, and each pressed his case using forms of what we would call spin. Thus, Faraday's work led to the development of reliable production of electricity. Along the way electricity was used for a variety of odd, morbid, and even bizarre functions including therapy, execution, and entertainment (Elsenaar and Remko 2002). This obviously found its application in terms of electrification, and more interesting for our purposes, telegraphy and telephony.

The same work on electrical generators led to the development of electromagnetic communication, in other words, radio. Inspired by the work of the Dane Øersted, Faraday carried out experiments that resulted in the discovery of electromagnetic rotation. Faraday's work on electromagnetism inspired the work of Maxwell in Scotland, Hertz in Germany, and finally, at the turn of the twentieth century, Marconi, in the development of radio broadcasting (Winston 1998).

4. Interestingly, this phrase is also recorded for other persons in different countries. According to various sources, when the Norwegian first was shown the telephone, he also called it an interesting toy (Bastiansen 2006). This indicates that the phrase is an urban legend, or that the banker somehow knew of the comments by the Western Union executives.

5. Western Union had a niche in the area of financial services and the "wiring" of monies that is still essential in many Third World countries. This niche is, however, being threatened by mobile phone companies that are developing other methods of transferring monies.

6. Interestingly, the idea of broadcasting concerts is still alive. Concertgoers use mobile phones to transmit the concert to friends elsewhere. One version is the so-called cellcerts associated with the singer Clay Aiken (Watkins 2005). In this case, the remote friend sometimes uses a PC to post a quasi-real-time blog to other fans describing which song is being played, the style of costume, etc.

7. Perhaps this might be described as the "Sawhney" period.

8. De Forest's vacuum tube was a variation of the tube developed by Ambrose Fleming. The similarity between the two led to endless patent disagreements. Until Fleming's patent expired in 1922 these disagreements caused the delay of broadcast radio (Winston 1998).

9. There are still vestiges of the interpersonal form of radio contact as seen in ham and also CB radio.

10. Similar radio-based "local loops" have been used in telephony in developing countries. See, for example, Castells et al. 2007 on Little Smart in China.

11. In a more contemporary example, this time coming from Norway, there is a slogan regarding the increasing reach of Internet Protocol that states, "Alt over IP og IP over alt" (Everything via IP and IP everywhere). As with Moore's law, this is a statement used in the mobilization of resources.

REFERENCES

Ackerman, W. C. 1945. "The Dimensions of American Broadcasting." *Public Opinion Quarterly* 9(1): 1–18.

Bastiansen, H. G. 2006. *Det piper og synger overalt: Mobiltelefonen i Norge fra ide til allemannseie.* Oslo: Norsk Telemuseum.

Brooks, J. 1976. *Telephone: The First Hundred Years.* New York: Harper and Row.

Castells, M., M. Fernandez-Ardevol, J. L. Qiu, and A. Sey. 2007. *Mobile Communication and Society: A Global Perspective.* Cambridge: MIT Press.

Crook, Tim. 1999. *Radio Drama: Theory and Practice.* London: Routledge.

de Forest, Lee. 1917. *Wireless Dance* (Electronic Version). Retrieved 8 May 2009 from http://earlyradiohistory.us/1917df.htm.

Douglas, G. M. 1997. *The Early Days of Radio Broadcasting.* Jefferson, NC: McFarland and Co.

Douglas, S. 1987. *Inventing American Broadcasting 1899–1922.* Baltimore: John Hopkins University Press.

Farley, T. 2005. *Privateline.com: Telephone History.* Retrieved 9 May 2009, from http://www.privateline.com/TelephoneHistory3A/numbers.html.

Fischer, C. 1992. *America Calling: A Social History of the Telephone to 1940.* Berkeley, CA: University of California Press.

Gilder, G. 1993. "The New Rule of the Wireless." *Forbes ASAP* March 29.

Hargittai, E. 2000. "Radio's Lessons for the Internet." *Communications of the ACM* 43.

Hazlett, T. W. 2001. "The U.S. Digital TV Transition: Time to Toss the Negroponte Switch." The Brookings Institute, Washington, D.C.

Ling, R. 2004. *The Mobile Connection: The Cell Phone's Impact on Society.* San Francisco: Morgan Kaufmann.

Marvin, Carolyn. 1988. *When Old Technologies Were New: Thinking about Electric Communication in the Late Nineteenth Century.* New York: Oxford University Press.

Negroponte, N. 1997. "Wireless Revisted." *Wired* August.

New Orleans Public Library. 2005. *Index to Riders' Digest.* Retrieved 9 May 2009, from http://nutrias.org/~nopl/info/louinfo/ridersdiges/indext/html.

Pool, Ithiel de Sola 1983. *Technologies of Freedom.* Cambridge: Belknap Press of Harvard University Press.

Sandvig, C., D. Young, and S. Menrath. 2004. "Hidden Interfaces to 'Ownerless' Networks." In *The 32nd Conference on Communication, Information, and Internet Policy.* Washington, D.C.

Sarnoff, D. 1920. "Radio music box" memo. Retrieved 9 May 2009, from http://earlyradiohistory.us/1916rmb.htm.

Schwartz, E. I. 2002. "Televisionary." *Wired* 10 (4 April): 5.

Standage, T. 1998. *The Victorian Internet.* London: Weidenfeld and Nicolson.

Thompson, T. G. 1974. *Lake City, Colorado: An Early Social and Cultural History.* Oklahoma City, OK: Metro Press.

Warren County Historical Society. 2005. Retrieved 9 May 2009, from http://209.85/209.85.229.132/search?q=cache:_oy8KJHE95gJ:www.warrenhistory.org/PHMCapp5.htm+"Warren+county+historical+society"+"thomas+edison"+music&hl=en&gl=no&strip=1.

Watkins, E. E. 2005. "Instant Fame: Message Boards, Mobile Phones, and Clay Aiken." in *Association of Internet Researchers Conference 6.0.* Chicago.

Winston, Brian. 1998. *Media Technology and Society: A History.* New York: Routledge.

Hollywood 2.0:
How Internet Distribution Will
Affect the Film Industry

ELI NOAM

When it comes to film, everybody is an expert. Film is art, entertainment, role model, trendsetter. It is also an industry. The United States is currently the largest exporter of commercial films in the world. But now Hollywood's global engine of content is facing a new distribution method—Internet TV—and the question is how its dominance will be affected. The conventional wisdom is that entry barriers will decline rapidly for both production and distribution, and that the audience will fragment in the *long tail* (Anderson 2006) of options. Will today's Hollywood studios become tomorrow's past attraction? Our surprising conclusion is probably not. In fact, the *industrial efficiency* of the Hollywood dream factory may lead to an even more dramatic economic dominance in the digital age.

It is an important question for analysis, because it foretells the nature of the world's central medium of the not-so-distant future. Yet to conduct such analysis in a clear-eyed fashion is hampered by two self-imposed set of blinders: the gloomy conventional wisdom on what leads to the strength of Hollywood in content, and the rose-colored stereotypes about the problems that the Internet will solve. Both sets of clichés lack a historical or economical perspective, and in combination they prevent an understanding of the future of content production and distribution.

To answer the question one needs to analyze why one particular content production center (Hollywood) has been so successful, for so long, in so many countries, and across so many distribution media. It is successful even though it is by far the high-cost producer, and even though it never had much of a strategic vision. At first it totally missed the opportunities of broadcast TV, instead fighting it tooth and nail. It then exhibited the same myopia with pay cable, with home video, and it may be now doing so with the Internet.

But none of this seems to have made much of a difference. For almost a century Hollywood has been predominant around the world, and despite many efforts, subsidies, and restrictive rules by other countries, going back even before World War I, not much has changed. There is always some hopeful news from the film industries of other countries. All of them get much ink and hope, since so many dislike the strength of Hollywood—but somehow none of this has diminished its dominance. In 1920, Hollywood had over 70 percent of world film revenues. In 2005, that share was still above 70 percent. The industry consists pretty much of the same six firms for ninety years, minus MGM and RKO, plus Disney, all in close proximity in one metropolitan area. I know of no other set of firms with such long-term global dominance, even including the oil industry.

In 1998, of the forty most successful movies worldwide in terms of box-office revenues, Hollywood films occupied the top thirty-nine. Britain's *The Full Monty* was number 40. In 2003, of the world's top twenty films, twenty were American, or American co-productions (which usually means that some of the financing comes from other countries). The British movies' market share in the domestic market was 13 percent in 2003, and German films took less than 10 percent.

At the same time, the global audience for European films was declining. In the 1960s and 1970s, there were decent-sized audiences for quality European films. Truffaut, Goddard, Fellini, Antonioni, Bergman, Fassbinder, Pasolini, Werthmüller, Richardson, Tanner were icons. But this audience has been steadily graying. In 2002, French films' total box office in the United States was an anemic $36 million. That's about five million tickets a year, for the films of a country that makes about 200 films a year.

This is bad news to Europeans, because after all, for several centuries culture flowed largely in one direction: out of Europe to the rest of the world. Then, before World War I, the flow reversed direction for the young and populist medium of film. Around the world, audiences flocked to American movies. European cultural elites promoted government protectionism. In the 1920s, Germany's near-monopoly producer Ufa was already advocating the protection of "European films," and established a European cartel together with the French film trade association. Restrictive contractual arrangements were agreed upon with other countries, supplemented by import quotas.

Today, various forms of film protectionism abound. In Canada, the government subsidizes film production directly, and 60 percent of TV schedule must be Canadian in content, as a production. In Australia, government money makes up around 37 percent of overall investment, plus the lost tax revenues from a 100 percent tax deduction for film investments. In Europe, the European Union provided in 2002 subsidies of $850 million for films that generated box-office revenues of around $400 million. On top of that, some European countries provide subsidies for over 50 percent of a film budget. There is also substantial support for production through public service TV whose budgets derive from a quasi tax. And on top of that, there are tax shelters for rich investors in films.

But even with these generous subsidies, non-Hollywood films are rarely an international success. They are watched domestically, somewhat. But audiences are reluctant to see the films of neighboring countries. European films, outside their national market, draw in other European countries only 6.3 percent of audiences, and worldwide less than 5 percent.

The predominance of a handful of Hollywood firms for almost a century raises the question—how come?

The first and perhaps most popular explanation is *cultural imperialism*. This term is conveniently vague enough to match a lot of inkblots. But the fact is that Hollywood was dominant already before World War I, before America's ascendancy to a superpower that could make its themes those of the world. So there must be more to the story.

The second basic explanation is that of economic conspiracy.

Hollywood favors itself, discriminates against others, gains from the combination of production with distribution. The practices of Hollywood firms were also the target of U.S. antitrust actions for decades. But the basic economic case for the importance of vertical integration is questionable.

These synergies are stressed by empire-building CEOs and investment bankers in search of deals. Yet firms that have enlarged themselves by merger and acquisition are now splitting or tottering: Viacom, Vivendi, Time Warner, and Disney all with well-publicized dysfunctionalities, barely able to contain their centrifugalism and to provide enough management attention.

For vertical firms, discrimination in favor of one's own product is sensible only as long as that product is not inferior. It rarely makes sense for a distribution organization to push its own unpopular films into theaters and reject other producers' potential blockbusters. Ultimately, the market power of Hollywood distributors depends on their access to attractive films, not vice versa. In the 1980s, when the Hollywood studios were readmitted into theatrical exhibition, the general expectation was that this vertical integration would lead to their renewed dominance in movie theaters. Instead, almost all of the efforts at entry were unsuccessful.

The third explanation is that of market size. The U.S. (and the English-language) markets are just too large for anyone else to keep up, with the possible exception of India. But actually the U.S. domestic audience, while large, is more fragmented than those of most countries because many more movies are being produced. The domestic population per feature film produced in the United States is half a million, whereas in the United Kingdom and Germany there are twice as many people per film produced.

It is similarly argued that because Hollywood programs can recover their production costs domestically, they can export them at a low price. But such two-stage thinking—that a film must first make money domestically, with exports only an added windfall—is a flawed economic analysis. With that kind of thinking nobody would produce watches in Switzerland, grow Kiwi fruits in New Zealand, or make cell phones in Korea. The film and TV companies of even small countries can be successful if they produce films for the world market rather than primarily for their domestic audiences. The successful Dutch TV production company Endemol is perhaps the leading example.

The fourth alleged factor for Hollywood's success is its content style: down-market, down-culture, down-creativity. A simplistic dichotomy is alleged: in the one corner, there is Hollywood where moviemaking is show business: no business, no show. And in the other corner, the "auteur" approach, centered on director and his artistic sensibilities. That perspective is epitomized by celebrated French director Jean-Luc Godard who wrote: "Who is the enemy? The audience!"

To some people, it is comforting to believe that it is the uncompromising integrity of European filmmakers that limits their popularity, in contrast to Hollywood's pandering. But actually, most European (or Japanese, Korean, Indian, and Chinese) films are not artsy at all. Those outside of public TV are mostly commercially oriented. There are big and established media firms in many a country, often centered around commercial TV operations. In Italy, Berlusconi. In Britain, Murdoch and Granada. In Germany, Bertelsmann. In France, Vivendi and Garmont. In Brazil, Globo. In Mexico, Televisa. In India, Murktar and others. In Japan, Shoshiko, Tokyo, and Tohn. All try to be popular in their home markets. Most of their commercial films never reach America, and usually deservedly so.

At the same time, the American independent film production is alive and vibrant. For the 2005 Sundance Film Festival there were 2,600 feature-length submissions, 29 percent more than the year before. While it is much smaller in terms of audience attendance than Hollywood, Sundance is its talent pool.

Thus, the image of culture versus commerce is not really an explanation.

If so, then what is? The main success factor for content production is *the efficiency of Hollywood.* This seems counterintuitive. Hollywood movies are vastly more expensive than European or Indian ones. It is the place of the $600 haircut. A Hollywood film cost over $70 million to produce, ten times as much as in Europe, fifty times as much as in India. The budget for two minutes of Hollywood produces an entire feature film in India.

But this is not the whole story. Hollywood's big budgets are spread over a large audience size, and are actually smaller per ticket sold than for a European film. In Europe, it takes $12.5 of a film budget to generate a ticket, while for Hollywood films, it's only $1.65, almost one-eighth. India's "Bollywood" is still lower by a factor of four: $.43. But movie tickets in India are dirt cheap. If one looks at revenues generated per budget dollar. Hollywood and Bollywood are about equal, and Europe is in the red.

Efficiency is also gained by superior risk reduction through portfolio diversification. Film projects are enormously risky. Eighty percent of films, even allowing for the elusiveness of the concept of profits in the industry, lose money. Hollywood has managed to create a portfolio of investments, each with a certain riskiness, that achieve a lower risk than any individual part of the portfolio. The studio pools many risky projects, making their aggregate cash flow reasonably safe for the lenders. And this in turn generates investments in film projects of Hollywood.

In contrast, missing in Europe and other production centers are strong financing structures to invest significant capital in movies. In

India, a good part of film financing for a long time was through organized crime cartels that liked its glamour and cash basis. In Europe much
of the financing comes from the state, directly and indirectly.

But the most important success factor of Hollywood's efficiency is
that it has developed a new business model. And that business model
is important to *all* industries and *all* companies, not just in the media
sector. Hollywood has developed this model not because of its superior
access to management gurus but because it has been engaged in a Darwinian process. Each year, about 200 major films are being produced.
Each of the major films cost about $70 million to $100 million to make,
and $40 million or more to promote. As mentioned, many of these films
disappear within days. Thus under the pressures to sink or swim, companies and business practices evolve and reengineer themselves continu-
ously.

Most people still talk about the "studios" and believe that a few highly
concentrated conglomerates are producing all these movies. Not so. The
Big Six are mostly in the business of distributing films made by small
independent or semi-independent firms. The studios also finance some
of them fully or partly. They may rent out production facilities. But
their share in actual production of the major films they distribute keeps
declining, and is probably less than 20 percent now. (There are many
gray shades between outright studio production and truly independent
production.)

Thus, Hollywood today is hundreds of small independent production companies, which in turn use hundreds of specialized films with
special skills. All use mostly freelancers, that is, independent contract
labor rather than regular staff. Even management staff is project-based.
The studio companies are the integrators of this system, but relative to
their activity level, they are characterized by *low bureaucracy, low overhead,
low risk, low employee benefits, and low operations cost.*

This has restructured the industry from one of vertically integrated
firms with in-house skills—which is the traditional image of the Hollywood firms—to one of horizontal specialists for hire.

Specialization and decentralization of skill provide a central role
for coordinators, who are, in particular, independent producers, talent
agencies, and the distributors (the studio).

This is important far beyond the film industry. The model of the proj-
ect-oriented, almost "virtual" production firm is perhaps the forerunner
for many business firms and industries in general. It is an organizational
model that integrates creativity with business in a way that's better than

anyone else's model. It is decentralized, networked, virtual, freelance, global, disaggregated (not integrated), and able to draw on diverse creativity. It combines the creativity of small organizations with the economies of scale of large ones.

We can see similar developments reacting to consumer electronics, IT, and automotive industries. Specialist firms do the design. Others produce the components. Still others assemble. Still others the marketing. The major firms are mainly coordinators, integrators of the specialist firms, and the branders of the final products. This might be, for many industries, the business model of the future.

It would not be the first time that media has led the way for a general business transformation. The printing press led the way for the industrial mass production system, and to machinery with interchangeable parts. And now, the film industry model, created in the Darwinian process described, is a forerunner for the next stage, the postindustrial production system and economy.

And what of the future? A new medium is knocking—television over the Internet—and the question is what will enter when the door is opened. Will it be a multicultural richness of many national sources, or will it be more of Hollywood?

The knee-jerk response to this question is to invoke Internet platitudes. Anybody can enter, you can't tell who's a dog on the Internet, the long tail. For many in the Internet community, staunchly internationalist and multicultural by outlook and background, the very idea that their medium will further the ascendancy of American mass culture is unthinkable.

So let us look at the elements that come together for a successful film production, along the lines we analyzed and identified earlier.

STYLE. It is true that Internet-distributed video content lowers entry barriers through lower production and distribution costs and reduced regulatory barriers. Thus, there will be many more small providers, including the users themselves, and a new and specialized content will proliferate. However, the lower costs apply to everybody and as a result much more content is being produced and supplied. As the supply of content rises relative to the fairly steady stock of attention, the general expectations on production quality standards rise, and with them the cost of production. Even so, supply will clearly be much larger than before and with a richer diversity of sources and content. This is the long tail end of the content spectrum. However, at the same time there will even greater pressure for "blockbuster" content that stands out from the crowd, and for content that makes the most of the multimedia and interactive features of broadband and ultrabroadband communications. Internet TV is for applications that go beyond regular linear TV: interactive, asynchronous, linked, multimedia.

To produce such content is expensive. It requires creativity, programmers, performance testing, and continually new versions. Such content exhibits strong economies of scale on the content production side, and strong network effects on the demand side. Both favor content providers that can come up with big budgets, can diversify risk, distribute over multiple platforms, create product tie-ins, and establish global user communities.

INDUSTRY ORGANIZATION. In creating such new types of content, new ideas on content, format, and interactivity will come from new directions and new firms. New types of specialists will emerge, on the technology side often in Silicon Valley, another cluster. For games, there might be subclusters in Japan and Korea.

But the networked structure of the established Hollywood media companies will absorb these innovators seamlessly. It is precisely this structure that can cope with change and innovation brought about by others. In fact, this network structure is strengthened by more powerful communications pipes, since the clustering can spread beyond those of geography. Thus, "Hollywood" will become less of a description of geography, and more of an industry structure.

RISK REDUCTION AND FINANCE. It is likely that such integrators will also emerge in other production centers, such as India, Europe, or Japan. Some such firms will certainly emerge there, based on those regions' cultural, technological, and financial resources. But none is likely to have quite the advantages of U.S. firms: a large domestic market and Internet community; significant hardware and software entrepreneurial energy; a financial system that provides risk capital; big content-producing companies that can diversify risk and access the capital markets; access to worldwide distribution and experience in reaching popular audiences; talent in content creativity and technology from all over the world; efficient geographic clusters in production and technology; the cultural prowess of the world's superpower; language; a culture of diversity; and a university system that generates technology and entrepreneurship. These factors are also available elsewhere, but probably nowhere quite in such combination or magnitude. (On the other hand, the United States lacks the supportive mechanism of public TV that exists in Europe and Japan.)

DISTRIBUTION. At the same time, the broadband Internet means that programs can be distributed globally at relatively low cost. It's been termed the death of distance. People in Peru, Panama, and Portugal can select, click, and download. The protection of distance is thus giving way. And, similarly, the protections of regulation and licensing. The content itself exhibits strong economies of scale. Once produced, it can be reproduced at almost no cost. And it can be distributed, with the Internet, quite cheaply, and without much sensitivity to distance. This means that the content of Hollywood, adapted for interactivity, can be all over the world.

True, there will be opportunities for other producers to create and distribute specialized programs for niche and general audiences. And those could be met by providers from other countries. But the main audience will still be attached to big-budget, technically sophisticated productions that combine Hollywood glitz with Silicon Valley tech. And that means that Hollywood will be even stronger, because it now has a more direct link to global audiences. It does not need to go through the intermediaries of TV networks, and pass through the regulation of governments. It has the ability to fine-tune prices. And it can deploy in its network of specialists also the talent and creativity from everywhere—animators from Japan; special effects software in India; postproduction in Shanghai; venture finance in London; advertising companies in New York. Thus, Hollywood will become, even more than before, the entertainment content integrator to the world.

I reach this conclusion without much pleasure. But a century of history should teach us some lessons. Artistic creativity is not enough. The transition to packetized and Internetworked communications will not reverse an industry structure built on underlying economics. The only way for other countries' film industries to become a bigger factor for the attention of global audiences is for them to resort to managerial responses rather than to find comfort in cultural criticism and political protectionism.

REFERENCES

Adorno, Theodor W. 1954. "Television and the Patterns of Mass Culture." *Quarterly of Film, Radio, and Television* 8:213–35.
Anderson, Chris. 2006. *The Long Tail: Why the Future of Business Is Selling Less of More.* New York: Hyperion.

Caves, Richard E. 2000. *Creative Industries: Contracts between Art and Commerce.* Cambridge: Harvard University Press.

Curwen, Peter. 1999. "Television without Frontiers—Can Culture Be Harmonized?" *European Business Review* 99 (6): 368–75.

DeVany, Arthur. 2005. "Laws of Production and Cost." *The Movies,* April 29, 46–65.

Eliashberg, Jehoshua, and Mark A. A. M. Leenders. 2006. "Antecedents and Consequences of Third-Party Products Evaluation Systems: Lessons from the International Motion Picture Industry." *Knowledge@Wharton,* October 10. Retrieved January 22, 2007, from http://knowledge.wharton.upenn.edu.

Epstein, Edward Jay. 2005. *The Big Picture: The New Logic of Money and Power in Hollywood.* New York: E. J. E. Publications.

European Audiovisual Observatory. 1999. *Developments in Digital Television in the European Union.* Ed. André Lange. Version 2, December 4. Retrieved April 5, 2009, from http://www.obs.coe.int/online_publication/expert/00002497.pdf.fr.

European Audiovisual Observatory. 2004. *Focus 2004: World Film Market Trends.* Retrieved April 5, 2009, from http://www.obs.coe.int/online_publication/reports/focus2004.pdf.

Film and Television Action Committee. 1999. *U.S. Runaway Film and Television Production Study Report.* Retrieved January 22, 2007, from http://www.dga.org/news/pr_runaway.pdf.

Kotkin, Joel, and David Friedman. 1999. "Why Every Business Will Be like Show Business." *Inc. Magazine* 17 (3): 64–75.

Lampel, Josh, Theresa Lant, and Jamal Shamsie. 2000. "Cultural Industries: Learning from Evolving Organizational Practices." *Organizational Science* 11 (3): 263–69.

Murray, Janet H. 2005. "Digital TV and the Emerging Formats of Cyberdrama." In *Creative Industries,* ed. John Hartley, 188–96. Malden, MA: Blackwell.

Nikoltchev, Susanne. 2001. "National Film Production Aid: Legislative Characteristics and Trends." *IRIS Plus Legal Observations* (European Audiovisual Observatory) 4:5.

Ortega y Gasset, José. 1957. "The Coming of the Masses." In *Mass Culture: The Popular Arts in America,* ed. Bernard Rosenberg and David Manning White, 41–45. Glencoe, IL: Free Press.

Sojcher, Frederic. 2002. "The Economics of Cinema: History, Strategic Choices and Cultural Policy." *Contemporary European History* 2:306–16.

United States Department of Commerce. 2001. *Media Migration Report.* Retrieved April 5, 2009, from http://www.media-services.com/common/pdf/states/migration11901.pdf.

Vogel, Harold. 2007. *Entertainment Industry Economics.* 7th ed. New York: Cambridge University Press.

Waterman, David. 2005. *Hollywood's Road to Riches.* Cambridge: Harvard University Press.

The Evolution of Radio

JOHN CAREY

Do monopolies lead to greater, not less competition? This counterintuitive hypothesis, generally attributed to Peter Steiner (1952)—the Steiner Paradox—suggests that under some conditions, a monopoly, for example, satellite radio, may provide consumers with more diverse content than a competitive environment. An examination of current trends and future prospects for radio can illuminate this and other key theories about media generally. A second general question is whether we are experiencing the end of mass media and the emergence of a new era of special-interest niche media or if mass media will continue to prosper (Neuman 1991). A third general media observation that can be illuminated by radio trends is offered by Leo Bogart (1995), among others: that over time people are paying for more of the media they consume and advertisers are paying a smaller share of the bill. Who would have thought that people would pay for radio?

There is much controversy surrounding the *theory of long tails* (Anderson 2004). The concept of long tails suggests that many new media can aggregate audiences from diverse geographic areas and sets of interests, which will support niche content that would not be economically feasible in the old media world. Lowering the cost of production is also said to enhance the possibilities for long tails. So, for example, jazz can find an audience on the Web and satellite radio, which cover large geographic areas, whereas it cannot in most local radio markets. Further, small jazz groups can create high-quality recordings for a fraction of what it cost a decade ago, putting jazz recordings in the marketplace that might not otherwise be available if production costs were high. Others argue that the theory of long tails is greatly exaggerated and that a small share of content still attracts the greatest share of audiences even in the new media environment (Gomes 2006).

This chapter takes a brief look at the history of radio, identifying patterns that can inform what is happening in radio today and in the future. It reviews the recent history of commercial AM and FM radio, which set the stage for the changes that are currently under way by homogenizing radio content and monetizing the radio listener (*monetizing* is a business term that, in this case, means extracting every last nickel and dime from the medium through excessive commercials). It then assesses current trends in radio and positions these against sixty years of research about the core functions of radio in people's lives. This provides a basis for discussing the future of radio.

This chapter will also examine whether the new radio environment has created a renaissance of innovation that will be with us for a long time or if we are experiencing a brief window of opportunity that will shut once traditional economic and marketplace forces begin to work on the new radio media. Radio has experienced bursts of innovation before, but for how long did the window of opportunity remain open?

The Past as Prologue

The future of radio is rooted in its past. As rapid technological advances change the face of radio, very little in the new environment is without parallel in the medium's history. Understanding this history can inform the development of scenarios suggesting where radio may be heading in the future and provide clues for both entrepreneurs and policymakers about business opportunities and citizens' needs. Some of the current issues that run in parallel with the past include uncertainty about the level of interest in new radio services; the high cost of early receivers for new radio technologies and the need to find a group of early adopters who are willing to pay those high prices; the influence of amateurs on commercial radio; struggles to find a workable business model for new radio services; the role of well-known personalities in attracting audiences; the appeal of listening to radio in mobile settings; how changes in technology affect radio listening; whether traditional radio can reinvent itself in the face of stiff competition; and the roles of serendipity and risk in shaping radio.

In coming to grips with the future, there is a surprising and basic definitional issue—what do we mean by "radio"? A few years ago, it was relatively easy to answer. Radio included commercial and noncommercial AM and FM stations (all that most people understood) plus a few complementary services such as shortwave international broadcasts, amateur radio (ham and CB), and services that piggybacked on radio broadcasts such as talking books for the blind carried over SCA (subsidiary communications authority). The new environment includes those services plus satellite radio, HD radio (digital terrestrial radio), web radio, cable and satellite TV radio, podcasts, radio downloads to MP3 players, radio for cell phones, and WiFi radio sets. The academic thing to do would be to sort all of these technologies and services into neat categories, excluding some as not truly radio and embracing others as core to radio, but it may be too early to derive a neat taxonomy and, in any event, the marketplace is likely go in its own direction without regard to academic classifications. For the foreseeable future, the radio landscape is likely to remain open and messy.

An assessment of radio organizations, technologies, markets, and content cannot escape the much-hyped, but in this case appropriate, term: *convergence.* Several technologies are converging in the distribution of radio programming, for example, over-the-air broadcast, the Web, digital satellite, digital terrestrial broadcast, and cellular networks. The organizations that provide radio are also converging, as web portals such as AOL and Yahoo offer radio, newspapers offer radio podcasts, music downloading service such as Real Networks provide radio to MP3 players, and traditional AM/FM conglomerates such as Clear Channel invest in satellite radio. Markets are also converging. AM and FM stations reach a finite geographic area, typically in a circular dispersal pattern, reaching twenty to seventy miles' distance from the transmitter in a typical local market. Satellite radio has a continental footprint, reaching the contiguous forty-eight states plus parts of Mexico and Canada. Web radio has an international footprint, reaching anywhere that listeners have access to the Web. Content has been converging in traditional AM/FM markets, but it is becoming more diverse in satellite and web radio.

Key Patterns in the History of Radio

Several patterns in the history of radio are especially relevant to the modern era of satellite radio, web radio, podcasts, and HD radio.

Uncertainty and the Search for Early Adopters

The uncertainty surrounding recent radio technologies and services mirrors the early days of radio. Radio began in the late 1890s with wireless telegraphy, using the electromagnetic spectrum and Morse code to send messages across distances. It was a substitute for the telegraph in locations where you could not easily build a wired network, such as ships at sea. Notably, radio was two-way and it was run primarily by young males. Some were hobbyists; others worked for the Marconi Company, founded by Guglielmo Marconi, who many consider the father of radio. They were called, appropriately, "Marconi Men." By 1920, it was possible to send voice over radio, but no one knew quite what to do with it or if ordinary people would want to listen to radio. So, groups tried many different things. WEAF in New York, which was owned by AT&T, thought that people might lease time on their station to give speeches. They even developed a rate card: forty dollars for a fifteen-minute speech. There were few takers. Many radio stations were owned by department stores that wanted to sell radio sets. It was not uncommon for the station to stay off the air until a prospective buyer came in to the radio section of the store. The salesperson would then go in the back, turn on the transmitter and hook up a phonograph, so the customer out front could hear something on the radio (Barnouw 1966). Over the course of a few years, with much experimentation, radio pioneers discovered what worked: live events such as a musical performance from a hotel ballroom; comedy; coverage of events at a great distance such as a baseball game from another city or a political convention; and telling people the time (Lewis 1991). Drama, vaudeville acts, and news coverage also became popular. Could this have been predicted in 1920? Not likely. It required experimentation and *an innovation champion* unafraid of potential risks—an important lesson for the modern era of new radio technologies and services.

When radio sets were first offered to the public, they were very expensive. To save on costs, many early radio listeners purchased kits and built radios themselves. The first wave of radio listeners was mostly males who liked to tinker with technology. Typically, they listened alone on a headset and were thrilled just to tune in and receive signals from stations (Douglas 1997). As more radio sets were manufactured and the price came down, millions of households purchased radios for the entire family, who listened to radio for entertainment. It should be noted that many people first experienced radio in a public setting such as a department store, a hotel ballroom, or from loudspeakers that were posted outside newspaper offices. Finding early adopters and exposing the larger public to new forms of radio are just as important for the current wave of radio services.

Business Models, Stars, and the Role of Amateurs

If radio was to survive in the 1920s and beyond, it would either have to follow the path of the British, who put a tax on radio sets to subsidize the creation of content, or find a way for radio stations to make money. There was no shortage of ideas about how to make money. Department stores that sold radios and manufacturers that built them provided some support for radio programming but it wasn't a long-term solution. Many newspapers owned radio stations, and they supported broadcasts to help sell newspapers, but this too was not a good solution. Remember WEAF and its idea of selling time on radio for people to give speeches? They actually stumbled on a workable business model. One of the first people to come forward and buy time was not a budding politician who wanted to sell his ideas but a real estate developer who wanted to sell homes. This inspired others with different commercial applications. WEAF soon realized that people would not likely listen to an evening of sales pitches, so they interspersed entertainment between the commercials, using employees at first and later professional entertainers. It was the start of a working business model. By 1927, the business model of entertainment mixed with commercials was widely in place (Hilmes 1990). A key lesson for the modern era is that early business models are often wrong. They have to be tested and abandoned if they don't work or modified, as in the case of WEAF, until they do work.

As business models evolved, the star system came to radio. At first, the stars who attracted very large audiences were entertainers, many of whom came from vaudeville. They included Jack Benny, Fred Allen, and Bing Crosby, among many others. There were also a few star reporters, sports announcers, and commentators in the 1930s and 1940s such as Edward R. Murrow, Graham McNamee, and H. V. Kaltenborn. The era of star entertainers diminished in the 1950s, as television attracted many radio stars, but star commentators and sports announcers continued and a new era of star DJs (disc jockeys) emerged. This system of radio stars continued through the end of the twentieth century. In many cases, radio stars are syndicated, which means that they distribute their programs to many stations, collecting fees from each of them. The most popular ones can earn several million dollars per year. The challenge for the new era of radio services is whether to embrace the star system or compete by bringing in new talent. If new radio services go with star power, how do you determine what a star personality is worth?

Amateurs have been an important part of radio from the beginning, but they are often ignored by both academics and those in the radio industry, and their creative contributions overlooked. Amateurs played a major role in the early period of wireless telegraphy, bringing a passion and a dedication to radio that became legendary and was even celebrated in books of the time (Douglas 1997). They also developed a worldwide league of two-way "ham radio" hobbyists and emergency responders that is a few million strong. Amateurs have been a strong force in low-power radio stations, college stations, and citizens band (CB) radio. With fewer restrictions than their commercial counterparts, amateurs have been able to experiment with new formats and have been at the forefront of two-way radio applications. In the modern era, amateurs play a significant role in web radio and podcasts, and a contributing role in satellite radio through channels that carry unsigned artists and experimental programming.

Advances in Technology and the Growth of Radio in Mobile Settings

Advances in radio technology have come in spurts. Radio technology itself was considered a marvel in the late 1890s and the early twentieth century. The idea that Morse code signals and later sound could travel through buildings and over long distances was mesmerizing. There were many technological advances in the first quarter of the twentieth century that the public knew little about. The average person simply knew that by the early 1920s, radio worked. Advances that followed were a mixture of failures, a few overnight successes, and technologies that took a long time to be widely accepted. A radio fax newspaper was tried in the 1930s but it failed. FM radio began in the late 1930s but it took more than three decades before FM was widely accepted by the public. FM stereo began in the early 1960s and it was an important factor in helping FM to overcome the dominance of AM. When AM stereo was authorized by the FCC in the early 1980s, it was bogged down by multiple standards and an industry with little vision. It went nowhere. Subscription radio on cable was tried in the 1990s but it failed. Against this mixed history, a broad set of advances in radio technology and services entered the marketplace beginning in the late 1990s. The history of technological advances in radio suggests that not all of the new radio services will succeed.

Mobility saved radio. From the 1920s through the early 1950s, radio was primarily a service for homes. The first portable radio was built by Edwin Armstrong, inventor of FM radio, for his wife in the 1920s. However, it was very heavy and bulky. Radios were built into some cars in the 1930s but the number of cars with a radio was very small. In the 1950s, just as radio was coming under heavy competition from television, the portable transistor radio, small and lightweight, was introduced and became an overnight sensation. Teenagers, in particular, adopted it in large numbers and made portable radio a symbol of their generation (Douglas 1999). At about the same time, car manufacturers were preinstalling radios in millions of cars. By 1955, 60 percent of all cars on the road had a radio (Sterling and Haight 1979). The trend continued into the 1960s and 1970s as combined AM/FM radios were introduced into cars. In the 1980s, the boom box became another cultural icon for a new generation of young people. By the end of the twentieth century, 70 percent of all radio listening was in cars. Mobility was the baseline for most uses of radios just as a new generation of technologies and services was being introduced.

Risk, Serendipity, and the Reinvention of Radio

Risk was a constant companion of radio entrepreneurs at the turn of the twentieth century, when it was not clear if wireless telegraphy would work or if there was any way to make money with it. The period 1920 to 1927 was also filled with technological and marketplace risks for radio. Competition from television in the 1950s threatened the radio business, but from approximately 1960 to 2000, radio was a relatively low-risk venture. In 2000 and beyond, radio once again became a high-risk business for the many entrepreneurial startups that challenged traditional AM/FM stations. An environment of risk seems to attract certain personalities— people who are risk-takers. Marconi certainly fit this profile, as did David Sarnoff in the 1920s. Who will be the risk-takers in the future?

Serendipity involves unplanned, often accidental events that affect other events, people, and organizations. Early radio was filled with serendipity. It included the developer who came forward to buy time on WEAF and helped radio find its business model. It also included "batterymen." In 1925, only half of U.S. households had electricity. How could a household buy a radio and use it without electricity? It turns out that local entrepreneurs spontaneously created a business of providing homes with large batteries to run their radios, batteries they replaced every week or so. They operated much like icemen who delivered ice regularly for household ice boxes. This helped radio to grow, while electricity was spreading to additional homes. This happened not just in the United States, but in Europe as well (Morley 1986).

In the late 1930s, a confluence of serendipitous events helped to make news a vital part of radio. These included the development of equipment for on-the-scene reporting, shortwave broadcasting from overseas, and the beginning of World War II in Europe. As battles flared, radio reporters were able to broadcast live from the scene to radio listeners in America. The listening public was transfixed. By its very nature, serendipity can't be planned. The lesson from early radio for new radio ventures is to be open to serendipity, recognize it when it comes along, and take advantage of it.

In many ways, the modern era of radio services is an attempt to reinvent radio. This has happened a few times before. In the 1950s, under the threat of competition from television, radio reinvented itself as a service for mobile environments (cars and portable radios) and changed from many forms of content on each station to single-format programming. In the 1940s, most stations broadcast a combination of comedy, drama, musical performance, and news—each in specific time slots. Television adopted this style of mixed-format programming. Radio countered it with single formats such as all rock, all country or all news. From listeners' perspective, the schedule became irrelevant and they had to do less work in finding what they wanted: at any time of day or night, they could tune to a specific station and know what content they would hear. Radio reinvented itself again the 1970s with the "FM revolution." Up until this time, AM dominated radio listening. Through a combination of strong DJ personalities, a counterculture attitude, and a willingness to play new artists, FM reinvented radio and came to dominate AM for audience share. Reinventing a medium requires a willingness to change the established ways of doing things. It can be motivated by threats from a competitor or an entrepreneurial spirit.

Commercial Radio, 1980–2000: The Formula Becomes Stale

Many of the new radio services launched after 2000 were able to establish a beachhead with the public because their main rival had fallen asleep. After the FM revolution of the 1970s, commercial radio began a slow descent into stale and formulaic programming formats. This was driven in part by simplistic research that characterized audiences narrowly into demographic groups, losing the nuances of farming communities, college towns, fast-paced urban centers, and other social qualities of audiences (Lynch and Gillispie 1998). Radio consultants traveled from town to town imposing cookie-cutter formats that often increased ratings for a given station in the short term but had the longer-term impact of making radio sound the same all over the country. There were more than 10,000 commercials AM and FM stations but relatively little variety. Radio became homogenized.

At the same time, conglomerates began to purchase many stations and program them in the same way. Clear Channel and Infinity Broadcasting emerged as industry titans. The number of commercials increased, in some cases to more than twenty minutes per hour. The strategy was successful in increasing revenue. Between 1990 and 2000 revenue doubled (Manly 2005). Later, in response to listeners' anger and competition from satellite radio, many stations cut back on the number of commercials but asked advertisers to make up the difference by paying more for less air time (McBride 2005). While revenue increased during this period, programming suffered. The number of formats available in markets shrank. Niche content such as jazz, classical, and folk music all but disappeared. The most popular formats such as country and talk increased, pushing aside formats with niche audiences. Many stations played fewer than thirty songs; some stations played only ten songs (MacFarland 1997). If there were five country stations in a market, chances were pretty good that all five had nearly identical playlists. At the same time, local news coverage decreased or was dropped completely. The Project for Excellence in Journalism reported that the number of full-time employees in radio newsrooms dropped 44 percent between 1994 and 2000.

In small and medium-size markets, many stations were programmed from another city. This sometimes led to DJs mispronouncing the name of a local street or landmark; in more cases, DJs stopped talking about the local community at all and used air time simply to promote the station. In one case, police in Minot, North Dakota, called the local radio station to get help in broadcasting a warning to the public about a toxic gas accident. No one answered. The station was automated to carry a feed from another city (Lee 2003).

Innovation also suffered. DJs and station programmers had less freedom to try new songs and new styles of programming. There was little enthusiasm for technological innovation. AM stereo was available in the 1990s but stations did little to promote it. Digital broadcasting was technically feasible in the 1990s, but the industry could not agree on a standard or timetable to implement it. Some sources of innovation outside mainstream commercial radio were blocked. For example, the National Association of Broadcasters fought the expansion of low-power radio stations, arguing that they would cause interference. This effectively blocked many local colleges, community groups, and other amateurs who wanted to start low-power stations and could have provided an important source of experimentation. This is not to argue that innovation came to a standstill. Many public radio and full-power college stations along with some commercial stations tried new forms of programming, but commercial radio in general was tired and predictable.

By the early 2000s, commercial AM and FM radio was a mass medium with a very large but tenuous audience. Fewer people were waking up to radio. Instead, many turned on morning TV shows. The mainstream radio audience was aging, many young people relied on CDs and later MP3 players for music, and the Web was beginning to compete with radio for people's time. The Web was not yet a viable way to distribute radio programming because relatively few households had the broadband connections necessary for a good audio experience. The local DJ was not as important as in earlier periods, but national radio personalities such as Howard Stern and Rush Limbaugh had very large audiences. It is not clear whether the popularity of shock jocks and conservative commentators may have turned off other groups of listeners. Overall, however, the enthusiasm for radio that was present in earlier decades was diminished. This was reflected in many ways, including the scarcity of magazines or newspaper columns about radio. The radio establishment was asleep just as a new set of rivals was about to enter the scene.

Radio Visionaries Arrive Anew

In the early 2000s, satellite radio was launched; web radio existed but was waiting for more households to get high-speed access to the Internet that would make it an enjoyable experience; MP3 players were owned by millions and poised to accept radio content; and HD radio was in a prelaunch phase. The radio landscape was about to change.

Satellite Radio

In 1997, the FCC held an auction for satellite radio services in the S-band section of the radio spectrum. Two licenses were awarded, one to American Mobile Radio, later to become XM Satellite Radio, and another to CD Radio, later to become Sirius Satellite Radio. XM was first to launch, in November 2001; Sirius followed in July 2002.

The concept of satellite radio was greeted with much skepticism in the press and the radio industry. Some skeptics asked why would anyone pay for radio when free radio was so widely available. Others argued that radio is a local medium, so a national satellite service couldn't compete, or pointed out that satellite radio technology was untested and might not work in large cities with tall buildings or rural areas with dense clusters of trees.

Satellite radio faced a number of challenges and risks, including competition from more than 12,000 existing radio stations, a need to raise $2 billion for the launch of the satellites and a five-year startup phase, the possibility of launch failures for the satellites, obtaining agreements with car manufacturers to install a new generation of radios in vehicles, and the existing habits of millions of listeners who already had AM/FM radios in their cars and homes.

When satellite radio was launched, there was a window of opportunity for innovation. Because it was a new service, users had not yet formed expectations about what content would be provided or the style of programming. Further, satellite radio had the advantage of controlling all of its channels. Whereas most radio organizations in a local market controlled only their own station and competed with up to 125 others, satellite radio could program across its 100-plus channels, finding niche groups of listeners for each, and even using one channel to promote other channels. There was competition with AM/FM and the other satellite service provider, but within each satellite service provider's lineup, there was in effect no competition.

As first to launch a satellite radio service and with a six-month lead over its rival, XM was able to establish a baseline of programming content and style. The program directors at XM consciously referred to the FM revolution in the 1970s and said that they wanted to reinvent radio once again. In the context of the early twenty-first century, reinventing radio involved a breadth and depth of content, and taking advantage of satellite radio's freedom from content regulation. It also involved customized text content such as the name of the song and artist playing and, later, personalized content such as stock quotes and sports scores, for stocks and teams selected by the subscriber.

With more than one hundred channels, satellite radio could offer a wide diversity of content. Formats such as folk or classical music that could not attract a sufficient audience for a commercial station in one market could aggregate listeners across satellite radio's continental footprint. Even if listenership was low at a national level, niche music formats could be justified if enough people listened occasionally and felt that the channel added benefit to their subscription. Depth of content involved much longer playlists within a music format. Further, since all content was stored in a huge database, the DJ or channel programmer could easily access any song. They did not need physical media such as CDs or tapes. If there were five country channels on the satellite radio service, instead of each one playing the same 20 songs to compete for the largest share of country listeners, the five could divide the field into classic country, southern country, modern country, and so on, and provide greater depth in playlists for each niche format.

Satellite radio is free from the content regulations that govern over-the-air stations. This is because satellite radio providers paid for the spectrum they use and the service is private—only those who pay a subscription and own a satellite radio can receive it. The program lineups of XM and Sirius contain comedy channels with off-color jokes and radio personalities such as Howard Stern (on Sirius) and Opie and Anthony (on XM) who use off-color language and discuss topics that would not be permitted under FCC content rules. This freedom appeals to many but has the potential to offend others. To deal with this concern, the satellite radio companies let subscribers block channels.

At first, the channel lineups for XM and Sirius were different. Over time, they began to look very similar, except for the exclusive deals each has with sports groups such as the National Football League or Major League Baseball and major personalities such as Oprah Winfrey or Martha Stewart. Each has core content in the areas of music (more than sixty channels each), comedy, news, and talk. In addition, each has a few niche content areas such as radio drama, talking books, and unsigned bands. Nearly all of the music channels are commercial free; some of the other channels have a few commercials but far fewer per hour compared to local commercial stations. Commercial-free content has been a core part of satellite radio's appeal to listeners.

Some of the channels on satellite radio borrow types of content that were popular on commercial radio decades ago. For example, comedy was very popular on radio during the 1920s through the 1940s; it found a resurgence of interest on satellite radio. Drama was also very popular on radio in the second quarter of the twentieth century, but it was pushed aside by television drama in the 1950s. With satellite radio, it has found a new home, including some shows from the 1930s and 1940s that are replayed and some new dramas, but it is a much smaller niche than the one for comedy.

Many of the channels on satellite radio have content that is targeted to specific groups such as women, truckers, Hispanics, gays, evangelical Christians, baseball fans, liberals, and conservatives. Well-known brands from broadcasting and cable are also represented. Channels are programmed by Disney, CNN, MSNBC, Fox News, ESPN, and the Weather Channel, among others. Some of these channels have original content created for satellite radio, and some carry the audio feed from a television channel, for example, from CNBC's cable channel.

The winter of 2003 was a major turning point for satellite radio. The change began with an announcement by Sirius of a $220 million deal, over seven years, with the National Football League to carry all of the NFL games. Up until then, both companies had relatively low programming budgets, relying on new styles of programming and greater variety, rather than major stars, to compete with commercial radio and each other. Sirius's announcement signaled that it was going for star power and strongly associating its brand with sports in order to appeal to sports fans. Subsequently, Sirius announced deals to carry games of the National Basketball Association and the National Hockey League. It was an appeal to Wall Street as much as potential subscribers, and the financial community responded favorably, driving the price of Sirius's stock up. XM in turn announced an eleven-year $650 million dollar deal ($60 million per year) with Major League Baseball and followed up with deals for Big Ten football and basketball. The quest for star power did not end with sports. Sirius signed Howard Stern and Martha Stewart. XM signed Oprah Winfrey and Opie and Anthony.

There are a number of issues associated with star power, including the impact on the programming budget, the ability of stars to draw new subscribers, the potential loss of subscribers who may be offended by some stars, and the relationship between mass media and stars. During the period 2003 to 2005, the programming budgets for both Sirius and XM more than tripled. This was before the full impact of major deals such as Sirius's acquisition of Howard Stern. This affected not only the cost of new high-profile personalities but existing content providers who sought more money as their contracts came up for renewal. The satellite radio companies bet that well-known personalities and brands would attract their fan base to satellite radio. But might some potential subscribers to Sirius or XM go with a rival because they felt that their subscription dollars would go to a personality they did not like or a service they wouldn't use? This also raises the question—are stars with very high salaries inevitable in the mass media? Seven years after launch, satellite radio had more than 18 million subscribers and could claim the status of a mass medium. Could it have continued to grow without bringing in major stars?

By the middle of the decade, satellite radio had established its place in the radio marketplace, but neither XM nor Sirius was profitable and both faced many challenges. Competition between the two rivals was fierce, and both struggled to find successful business models. In January 2007, they proposed a merger of the two companies as a way to reduce costs. They argued that even though the merged companies would be a monopoly in satellite radio (as opposed to a duopoly under existing regulations) there was far more competition—in the form of iPods, web radio, HD radio, and so on—than existed when the services were launched. The merger was completed in 2008. The two services continued to transmit independently but they shared many channels. Meanwhile, AM and FM had started to fight back, and new competitors such as web radio and podcasts were on the scene.

Web Radio, Podcasts, and MP3 Radio

There are many competitors to traditional over-the-air and satellite radio providers, including web radio, podcasts, and MP3 radio. Web radio began in the 1990s, but it was not an enjoyable experience until many people adopted broadband web service. By the middle of the next decade, most commercial and public radio stations had a web presence. This was supplemented by international radio stations and web-only radio stations, many of which are created by amateurs. International radio stations appeal to immigrants and people with a special interest such as European football (soccer). The BBC is very active in international web radio, offering more than a dozen stations with a variety of formats. Web-only radio includes services provided by large web portals such as AOL, Yahoo, and MSN. In fact, portals have the largest web radio audiences in the United States. AOL and Yahoo create some radio content and carry content from other sources. For example, AOL carries some channels from satellite radio; Yahoo has many international radio stations.

In the middle of the first decade of the new century, nearly 30 million U.S. web users were listening weekly to 14,000 U.S. web radio stations

(McBride 2007). Web radio has attracted some serious amateurs, people who aspire to create radio programming that is commercially successful on the Web or becomes syndicated programming for commercial radio stations. One example is Grape Radio, which consists of talk programs about wine. It has advertising on its site and places ads on other web sites to attract listeners. Grape Radio is a good example of a station that would have difficulty attracting a sufficiently large audience in a local market to be financially feasible, but which on a national or international platform like the Web can aggregate enough listeners to be viable. There is also much amateur radio and musical performances on social networking sites such as MySpace.

All but a few web radio services are ad supported or free. Many commercial stations simply rebroadcast their over-the-air signal and include the commercials that are on their regular station. Many sell text or graphical advertising on their web sites that is not available on a broadcast station. Relatively few services have been successful in selling web radio as a subscription service. Real Networks, which has a subscription music service, includes radio content as part of the subscription. Radio services on MSN and Yahoo are free with advertising, but a listener can pay a subscription fee to get the services without advertising. Web radio is not restricted to audio. Some web radio services carry music videos.

Podcasts are audio files on the Web that can be listened to live, stored on a PC and accessed later, or downloaded to an MP3 player. They emerged out of the world of blogs, their text cousins on the Web. Podcasts include individuals offering their opinions on a wide range of subjects, audio files created by other media organizations such as newspapers, and syndicated radio programs distributed over the Web. For example, Rush Limbaugh distributes his radio show as a podcast. Among other mainstream media, the wine critic of the *New York Times* has a podcast, as does the editor of *Business Week*. Many education organizations offer podcasts as well, for example, audio recordings of a lecture for students who missed a class or more general educational services such as teaching a foreign language.

In the world of amateur podcasts, there are programs about religion, politics, computers, sex, stocks, and sports, among many other topics. One of the more popular subjects is cooking. Many podcasts have a homespun quality to them, the type of down-to-earth conversation that might be heard at a local diner. The large number of podcasts has encouraged the creation of directories such as PodcastAlley that help people search by topic or source.

Most podcasts are free with no advertising. They are created by amateurs who want to publish their opinions to the world or who aspire to be discovered by mainstream media. Podcasts from media organizations often have advertising, but their main purpose appears to be creating a deeper relationship with a reader, listener, or viewer of the primary media source or promoting their newspaper, radio station, or TV program to potential new audiences. There has been talk but little evidence that podcasts might "cannibalize" audiences away from other media sources; for example, a person listening to a podcast of a magazine columnist might not feel a need to read the magazine. Podcasts have also become a vehicle for long-form advertising—infomercials. General Mills and Sub-Zero, among other companies, have created podcast infomercials about their products.

A number of web radio stations and podcasts can be downloaded to MP3 players such as the iPod, for listening inside or outside the home in locations such as a car or the gym. In this form, a user can fast forward, rewind, and replay the content. There are other new radio services for car and mobile environments. These include WiFi networks that can be picked up in cars and cellular networks that transmit radio programming to cell phones anywhere in their coverage areas.

Web radio and podcasts are feasible in homes and offices because people spend so much time at the computer. The PC has become ubiquitous on office desks and is installed in multiple rooms of many households. Further, most PCs are now equipped with good speakers, which was not the case some years earlier. Web radio and podcasts also lend themselves to multitasking, just as broadcast radio has been used as background sound to other tasks in the home or office. At the computer, a listener can minimize the radio station home page and still listen to the audio while surfing the Web, checking e-mail, or doing homework.

HD Radio

HD radio (many think the HD stands for "high definition," but iBiquity, the company that licenses HD radio to stations, says that the letters do not stand for anything) represents a major initiative by AM and FM broadcasters to renew their services for the public and compete with satellite radio. It is a form of digital broadcasting similar to satellite radio, but broadcast locally. A prototype of digital radio (at the time, it was called Digital Audio Broadcasting, or DAB) was tested in the early 1990s but not implemented for more than a decade because of debates about standards and the perception by many in the industry that it was not needed (Trautman, Rathe, and Carey 1993). HD radio allows both AM and FM stations to broadcast one or more additional signals in digital format. HD AM can broadcast with the quality of existing analog FM stations; HD FM can broadcast a signal with near-CD quality. However, this assumes that each broadcasts only one digital signal, in addition to their regular analog broadcast. HD radio can be used for multicasting or the transmission of two or more extra signals, and many stations split their signal in this way. As a second or third extra channel is added, the quality of all the digital signals from the station is degraded. HD radio also supports datacasting—the transmission of text information such as the weather, traffic information, or stock quotes. Two limitations of HD radio are that the digital signals do not generally travel as far as the regular analog signal and there is a lag in acquiring a signal, sometimes as long as several seconds.

After nearly fifteen years of debate, the FCC finally chose a standard for HD radio in 2003; a limited number of services were launched in 2004. By 2008, nearly 2,000 of the 13,000 radio stations in the United States were broadcasting in HD radio along with their regular transmission, reaching all of the top one hundred markets. There are no plans to convert all radio broadcasting to digital transmission since so many people have multiple analog radio sets. So HD radio and traditional AM/FM broadcasts will likely exist side by side for a long time. It cost stations between $75,000 and $100,000 to add HD radio transmission, a modest investment for large stations but a significant cost for many smaller stations. Like satellite radio, HD radio requires listeners to purchase a new radio. The initial sale of HD radios was slow, due in part to high prices. Consumer understanding of the new service also appears to have been weak.

A number of radio organizations formed the HD Radio Alliance to encourage the development of HD radio and provide stations with support in adopting it. A major radio conglomerate, Clear Channel, also created the Format Lab and developed more than seventy new radio formats that are licensed to local stations for transmission in HD radio. Many of the formats are similar to satellite radio channels—niche content that is not generally supported on regular AM or FM. National Public Radio (NPR) has been very active in developing content for HD radio and provides multiple feeds to its member stations. The HD Radio Alliance encouraged stations to avoid commercials for a few years, to make the service more appealing to listeners. HD radio is free, but individual stations or a consortium of stations have the ability to charge a subscription if they wish, since each radio set can be addressed in the transmission and authorized or prohibited from receiving the signals.

HD radio faces many of the same hurdles as satellite radio when it was introduced. It needs to find early adopters who will buy expensive radios to pick up services that are relatively unknown. Even though HD radio service is free and, in its introductory phase, generally without commercials, it must convince radio listeners that it provides a valuable experience. The strategy of the radio industry places more emphasis on multicasting extra channels than on one extra channels with the highest quality. Another hurdle is how HD radio service providers can coordinate data services and ensure that radio manufacturers build these capabilities into all HD radios. The HD Radio Alliance may serve this function. It is also serving the important function of experimenting with new formats and not assuming that the public wants the same content in this new digital medium.

The Core Functions of Radio and the Challenge of Functional Equivalence

It is important to ground a discussion of the future of radio in terms of major forces of influence. Some industry analysts would choose technology itself as the determinant of the future of radio and assess how changes in technology are likely to lead to changes in behavior and, in turn, reshape the industry. The perspective presented here on the future of radio is grounded in six decades of research about the core functions of radio in people's lives. To understand the survival of radio in the media mix requires we put the notion of *functional equivalence* to work. Functional analysis of radio began with Lazarsfeld (1948), Cantril (1935), and their colleagues. They asked not only what people listened to on radio but why. What functions does radio serve in everyday lives? In reviewing this research, it is necessary to ask whether these functions evolved over time or have been replaced by other core functions.

One of the core functions of radio is to entertain. This was important as early as the 1920s. By the 1930s, radio was also becoming a daily habit and part of the rhythm of everyday life (Spigel 1992). During the 1930s and 1940s, radio, particularly in the form of comedy and drama, provided relief and escape from the stress of the Great Depression and World War II. In addition, radio fed the imagination. People listened and filled in details, especially visual details, that were not present in the audio. For example, they used their imagination to fill in the visuals of a baseball game. By the 1950s, radio served the multitaskers of the day. People used radio to accompany reading, eating, homework, cleaning the house, and, more and more frequently, driving a car. Radio also served to keep people company, connect them to the world, and support or change a mood (Mendelsohn 1966). Douglas (1999) demonstrated that two core functions of radio are to mark periods of the day—for example, to wake up, go to sleep, or take a break from another activity—and to create a community for the listener.

Some of these functions have evolved; a few are less important in the modern era of HD, satellite, and web radio. People still use radio to mark periods of their day but fewer people use it to wake up (many young people wake up to a ring tone from their cell phone) and more use it to mark the beginning and end of a commute. Radio still serves an entertainment function, especially in the car, but it is more likely to be background accompaniment to other activities in the home. Keeping people company, changing or supporting moods, and creating communities remain vital functions of radio.

One example of how these core functions play out in the modern era of radio is illustrated in the mantra of the commercial radio industry: "Radio is local." If so, it would be very difficult for satellite radio with its national footprint to compete with local radio stations. But if Douglas is right and radio is about community, then a radio station that appeals to people in its coverage area by covering local events, traffic, and weather is creating one type of community. Radio can also create a community for baseball fans, people who love jazz, long-distance truck drivers, or people who were teenagers in the 1960s.

Another way in which these core functions may play out in the future is the role of DJs, people who talk to the listener between songs and host radio programs. Technology and economics are squeezing the DJ out of many radio services. In some cases, the radio service is simply a playlist of songs with no program announcer at all; in other cases, the playlist is interspersed with prerecorded promotional announcements and commercials. This is an inexpensive way to create radio programming. It can be automated, recycled, and run for months or years with no human intervention. The rationale for this style of programming is that it is like a playlist on an MP3 player. However, is that what people want from radio? Does it keep them company, can it create a community? MP3 players are about control—a listener determines what he or she hears and in what order. Radio is more about spontaneity and the relationship between a listener and the personality on the station.

Content that serves these functions is likely to be a significant part of radio's future. This is not a signal that highbrow and socially responsible radio will dominate: Howard Stern serves all of these functions very well.

Evidence from Radio about Media Theories

It's time to return to the set of theoretical issues that opened the essay. Peter Steiner's theory (1952), sometimes called "the munificent monopolist," suggests that under some conditions, a monopoly may provide consumers with more diverse content than a competitive environment. It is most relevant to satellite radio, which has only two service providers (from one merged company), though the theory could apply to HD radio if a group such as the HD Radio Alliance develops a service that coordinates content across multiple stations in a market. With control of more than one hundred channels, satellite radio provides considerably more diverse content than one hundred separate radio stations in large markets. Competition among the one hundred stations has led them to provide the same content across a few formats, as each station tries to attract the same large blocks of listeners. Satellite radio can serve many different audiences with diverse content and accumulate them as a large block of subscribers. The economics and marketplace dynamics of a monopoly, satellite radio, leads to more choice for consumers than the competitive environment of local broadcast radio.

The second question raised earlier is whether we are experiencing the end of mass media and the emergence of a new era of special-interest niche media. In terms of radio, there is little evidence that mass media are disappearing. Traditional AM and FM radio have felt the sting of competition, but they continue to attract large audiences and billions of dollars a year in advertising revenue. The two satellite radio services have become mass media. Web radio is dominated by a few large organizations that attract millions of listeners. The most popular podcasts are created by mass media organizations. There is more niche content, but the audience for very specialized radio services is small. As Neuman forecast (1991), the movement toward fragmentation and specialization has been modest. In the future, economic and marketplace forces could lead to less niche content. For those who hoped to smash the mass media model and replace it with small, local entrepreneurs who create content that is local and contextual, this may be disappointing. For those who feared a form of communication anarchy if society did not retain some common perspectives on the world around us that mass media provide, it is likely to be encouraging.

Changes in radio can also inform the debate about long tails (Anderson 2004). Can new media such as satellite and web radio aggregate audiences from diverse geographic areas and sets of interests, supporting content that would not be economically feasible in the old media world? The new radio environment provides support for the concept of long tails, but it does not contradict the generally accepted principle that a relatively small share of content attracts the largest share of the audience. What is most interesting is the aggregation of content from many sources, including competitors. Satellite radio carries cable TV content and some commercial radio station content. Web content aggregators such as MSN and Yahoo carry international stations and commercial radio stations, each of which have their own web sites.

Does the new radio environment support the thesis presented by Bogart (1995) and others that over time people are paying for more of the media they consume and advertisers are paying a smaller share of the bill? Clearly, yes. In the 1990s, no one was paying for radio and an attempt to sell subscriptions to a pay radio service on cable failed. A decade later, more than 18 million people were subscribing to satellite radio; several million were paying for a web music service that included radio; and, a more modest number were paying subscription fees for commercial-free web radio services on MSN and Yahoo. Satellite radio demonstrated that people would pay for more choice and fewer commercials.

The new radio environment has led to a renaissance of innovation. However, will it be with us for a long time, or have we experienced a brief window of opportunity that will shut? In the case of satellite radio, traditional economic and marketplace forces have begun to put pressure on the merged company. Satellite radio has become a mass medium and embraced the star system. There is a temptation to view the signing of a new star as innovation, and for some users it will build a stronger relationship because they like the star personality, but there is a high price to be paid that may preclude other innovations. In the end, satellite radio's battle with the commercial radio industry will rest on the user's experience and the ability of satellite radio to continue to innovate while controlling costs.

In the case of web radio, the low cost of creating and distributing content will continue to provide opportunities for innovation. However, as large groups control more of the audience, they may have less incentive to experiment. For many garage radio entrepreneurs, the goal is become large and profitable; for others it is to become recognized and bought by one of the large web radio groups. This process may be tougher over time as those who control the largest share of the web radio audience settle on a working model and feel less need to change.

What about commercial AM and FM radio? They have placed a bet on HD radio, but there has been surprisingly little innovation within their traditional world. In response to complaints from listeners about excessive commercials, and to competition from satellite radio, some stations have trimmed advertising time. They have created a new format, "Jack" and several imitators, that has a more eclectic mix of music. In small markets, some stations have experimented with auctions and trading among listeners (Barry 2007). For the most part, however, commercial radio has continued along the same path. This stability has benefited satellite radio and also noncommercial broadcasters such as NPR and many college radio stations that have been more innovative. Following a formula that has worked does not necessarily signal a decline of commercial radio; many have predicted the demise of radio in the past and were always wrong (Matelski 1993). Commercial AM and FM radio may be able to milk their cash cow for some time.

REFERENCES

Anderson, Chris. 2004. "The Long Tail." *Wired Magazine,* October.
Barnouw, Erik. 1966. *A Tower in Babel: A History of Broadcasting in the United States to 1933.* New York: Oxford University Press.
Barry, Dan. 2007. "A Community Swap Meet, on Your AM Radio Station." *New York Times,* July 15.
Bogart, Leo. 1995. *Commercial Culture: The Media System and the Public Interest.* New York: Oxford University Press.
Cantril, Hadley. 1935. *The Psychology of Radio.* New York: Harper and Brothers.
Douglas, Susan. 1997. *American Broadcasting, 1899–1922.* Baltimore: John Hopkins University Press.
Douglas, Susan. 1999. *Listening In: Radio and the American Imagination.* New York: Random House.
Gomes, Lee. 2006. "Many Companies Still Cling to Big Hits to Drive Earnings." *Wall Street Journal,* August 2.
Hilmes, Michele. 1990. *Hollywood and Broadcasting: From Radio to Cable.* Urbana: University of Illinois Press.
Lazarsfeld, Paul. 1948. *Radio Listening in America: The People Look at Radio—Again.* New York: Prentice Hall.

Lee, Jennifer. 2003. "On Minot, N.D., Radio, a Single Corporate Voice." *New York Times,* March 31.

Lewis, Tom. 1991. *Empire of the Air: The Men Who Made Radio.* New York: HarperCollins.

Lynch, Joanna R., and Greg Gillispie. 1998. *Process and Practice of Radio Programming.* Lanham, MD: University Press of America.

MacFarland, David. 1997. *Future Radio Programming Strategies: Cultivating Listenership in the Digital Age.* Mahwah, NJ: Erlbaum.

Manly, Lorne. 2005. "Satellite Radio Takes Off, Altering the Airwaves." *New York Times,* April 5.

Matelski, Marilyn. 1993. "Resilient Radio." *Media Studies Journal* 7 (3): 1–13.

McBride, Sarah. 2005. "Clear Channel Scales Back Ad Time." *Wall Street Journal,* July 19.

McBride, Sarah. 2007. "Internet Radio Races to Break Free of the PC." *Wall Street Journal,* June 18.

Mendelsohn, Harold. 1966. *Mass Entertainment.* New Haven: College and University Press.

Morley, David. 1986. *Family Television: Cultural Power and Domestic Leisure.* London: Comedia.

Neuman, W. Russell. 1991. *The Future of the Mass Audience.* New York: Cambridge University Press.

Spigel, Lynn. 1992. *Make Room for TV: Television and the Family Ideal in Postwar America.* Chicago: University of Chicago Press.

Steiner, Peter. 1952. "Program Patterns and Preferences and the Workability of Competition in Radio Broadcasting." *Quarterly Journal of Economics* 66:194–223.

Sterling, Christopher, and Timothy Haight. 1979. *The Mass Media: Aspen Institute Guide to Communication Industry Trends.* New York: Praeger.

Tedeschi, Bob. 2005. "As Clear Channel Enters the Fray, Online Radio Looks to Be Coming of Age." *New York Times,* July 18.

Trautman, James, Steve Rathe, and John Carey. 1993. *Digital Audio Broadcasting.* Washington, DC: Corporation for Public Broadcasting.

Inventing Television:
Citizen Sarnoff and
One Philo T. Farnsworth

EVAN I. SCHWARTZ

Some believe we are undergoing a fundamental transformation of mass communication as the Internet replaces TV as the primary means of public communication and entertainment. This could have important consequences for the distribution of political and cultural power in society. Recently Nielsen//NetRatings reported that the average American online household is actively online over an hour a day and that Internet advertising is growing faster than any other medium. One way to better understand the political, technical, and economic character of these possible transitions is to look back at the issues that arose in the early days of radio and television broadcasting. One story comes immediately to mind.

It is the story of the invention and commercialization of television. Independent inventor Philo Farnsworth will play the role of our protagonist in our little teleplay. The antagonist is General David Sarnoff, the chairman of RCA and founder of NBC. He was a shrewd and ruthless businessman but also a visionary who laid the groundwork for our modern media system.

Whereas Farnsworth viewed Sarnoff as a gigantic but surmountable obstacle, Sarnoff viewed Farnsworth as just one more inventor to be held under his thumb. Buy him out cheap and reap the rewards. He did not realize that Farnsworth was different from all the other scientists and engineers he controlled, that this inventor was a throwback to an earlier era. Out of the confrontation between these two mismatched men, the modern television tube would emerge, ingesting images of reality deep inside itself, then spitting out reordered flickers of phosphorescence into living rooms everywhere. By the time the inventor and mogul would die, in the very same year, the number of homes with televisions would surpass the number of homes with indoor plumbing. Philo T. Farnsworth and David Sarnoff were fighting over something more than just a box of lights and wires.

Fields of Vision

Philo T. Farnsworth grew up in a time not unlike our own. A war was being waged overseas (World War I) and people's lives were being transformed by new technology (the automobile, radio). Philo was a farm boy in Idaho and a young genius who read about electricity and Einstein, who won the Nobel Prize in 1919 for his theory on the photoelectric effect. *Science & Invention* magazine offered a twenty-five-dollar prize each month for the best invention to improve the automobile. The month before the winner had been Edna Purdy, who devised the first car alarm by attaching a horn to the bottom of the rear fender. If a stranger stepped onto the running board a circuit would be completed that would set off the horn. Philo had an idea that would top Purdy's. Instead of an alarm, why not have a lock on the steering column? At the time, all Model Ts were started with the same flat metal key. Philo had been reading about atoms, and realized that by magnetizing the starting mechanism and key, one could create a unique trigger that would enable the car to start. Philo won first prize and used the money to buy himself a suit from the Sears catalog.

Philo rose before dawn every morning to give himself time to read and think. Among his favorite science journals was *Radio News,* which was mailed to his farmhouse every month for a two-dollar annual subscription. He became particular interested in the German inventor Paul Nipkow, who had devised a theoretical system for scanning images called the Nipkow disk. Bright light reflected off a person or object would pass through a spinning black disk that was punctured with small holes. As the wheel spun around, it would mechanically scan the image, turning the patterns of light picked up by the holes into electrical impulses. The impulses would then travel by wire to another disk spinning at the same speed as the first. The receiving side would transform the impulses back into the original image, projecting it onto an adjacent screen.

The more Philo thought about it, the more he became convinced that this mechanical setup would never work. How could the disk ever spin fast enough to pick up an image in enough detail? If it transmitted only shadows and flickers, people wouldn't watch it. There had to be a better way, a method of sending images so quickly that it could fool the eye into perceiving pulses of light as sharp, fluid pictures. He had read about vacuum tubes, thus named because all the air was sucked from them before the glass was sealed. Inside was an environment perfectly suited for transmitting electrons without any interference from air molecules. He was especially intrigued by an article about a special oversized vacuum tube. In 1897, a German scientist named Karl Braun found a way to shoot an electron beam through a tube to a screen on the other end. The inside of the screen could be coated with a fluorescent substance that would light up when struck by the electrons. It was called a cathode ray tube . . . Philo was amazed.

One early morning in the summer of 1921, when Philo was about to turn fifteen, he once again rose to read and then head out to the fields, again to cultivate potatoes. The birds were chirping, the sun was coming up, and a clear blue sky slowly emerged. He climbed into the seat of a single-disk harrow that was pulled by two horses. Philo lapsed into his typical trance, meditating on the problem at hand, brainstorming for an idea. He already knew that electron beams could be controlled, manipulated, and redirected by magnets. Why wasn't anybody capturing an image electronically, then using an electromagnet to guide the light through the tube and to project the signals onto the surface of the screen?

As Philo turned the horses to cultivate another row parallel to the previous one, he gazed back at what he had already done. He saw row after row of furrows. An inspiration struck him like a jolt of electricity to the heart. It hit him with so much force that he froze and nearly fell off his seat. He saw television in that field. Just as a field needed to be plowed line by line, light had to be captured line by line. Philo knew that light energy could be converted into electrical current. What if patterns of electrons could represent patterns of light? After an image was scanned, the process could be reversed. The electron beams could be shot through a tube and converted back into an image that could be re-created on a screen in evenly painted lines. Electrons moved so fast that an entire image could manifest itself this way in a wink. So you can say that the potato field led to the couch potato.

Philo wanted desperately to tell someone about his idea. He realized that he had sold his magnetic key idea much too cheaply. His father, lacking the scientific knowledge to evaluate his son's invention but recognizing its brilliance, urged Philo to keep this one a secret. The only other person Philo told was his high school science teacher, Mr. Tolman. Recognizing Philo's scientific brilliance after overhearing the young man articulate Albert Einstein's photoelectric theory of light to his rapt classmates, Mr. Tolman convinced the principal to let Philo stay after school for special advanced chemistry lessons. After swearing his mentor to secrecy, Philo explained to his invention to Mr. Tolman. Mr. Tolman listened with interest as Philo explained how this system would work and just how it would bring images from a distance into people's homes, just as radio was now transmitting sound. He explained his concept for scanning images and said that pictures needed to be encoded just as the plow traverses a field or the human eye reads a page of print—row by row. He tore out a page from his notebook with a sketch of the image-scanning device. The sketch was of a cylinder with a lens on one end that would focus the incoming optical image onto a photoelectric cell. Philo explained how varying current could travel by wire to a nearby transmitter that would project electromagnetic waves from an antenna, just as with radio sound. Mr. Tolman's conclusion was exactly what Philo wanted to hear. "This just might work," he said. Many years later this conversation would prove very important.

When I interviewed Philo's widow Pem, she told me that in the beginning, Philo was idealistic about what television would become. He was driven to find a way to bring the world together around great events. He thought television would be the world's greatest education tool, that it would wipe out ignorance and illiteracy, and that it would stop war—war being a by-product of misunderstanding. With the enlightened images of television coming into living rooms, we would no longer have misunderstanding.

To him, that was the purpose of television. That was the public need. Education. Enlightenment. Idealistic stuff.

Making a Great Man

Now the other side of the story, the commercialization of the invention. If Philo Farnsworth was the quintessential independent American inventor, David Sarnoff was the quintessential American capitalist of his time. Sarnoff was born to a poor family in Uzlian, Russia. He immigrated to America at the age of nine, and at the age of fourteen, when his father was dying of tuberculosis, he hit the streets of New York to find a job to support his family. After working several jobs as a newspaper delivery boy and messenger, Sarnoff showed up, with telegraph key in hand, at the Wall Street offices of the American Marconi Company, which was engaged in the radically new business of overseas wireless communications

Not long after Sarnoff joined the firm, Guglielmo Marconi himself paid a visit to the office. What happened next was later corroborated by the famous Italian inventor. Sarnoff went out of his way to shake the hand of Marconi and managed to strike up a lengthy conversation with him. In place of his real father, a weak man with a hacking cough, a man he hardly knew and didn't especially admire, Sarnoff had idolized Marconi and would come to regard him as a surrogate father. The young Sarnoff was struck by the elegant way the trim Marconi dressed, held his cigarette, and moved around with a gold-plated walking stick, graciously greeting all the employees. He identified with the fact that Marconi had only a grade-school education. On the spot, Sarnoff offered to act as Marconi's personal messenger. As luck would have it, his hero happened to need one at the time. On subsequent visits to New York, Marconi began treating Sarnoff not just as a messenger but as a protégé of sorts, answering Sarnoff's many technical questions and offering the teenager access to company files and papers. Sarnoff thus became the sorcerer's apprentice.

Sarnoff began to infuse his own life with a sense of destiny, as if every move he made was a step toward his final goal, and that goal was greatness. He began to see the birth of broadcasting not just as a once-in-a-lifetime event but a transformation that would only come along once in human history. He became determined to be the great leader of the most important company in the world's most dynamic industry. Not just a businessman, but a Great World Figure and a prophet of the electronic age.

Sarnoff's first big step on his march to greatness supposedly came after he was promoted at American Marconi, to the position of wireless telegraph operator. Ever the self-promoter, it was here that the first tale of Sarnoff's greatness emerged. According to the tale, at 10:25 p.m. on Sunday night, April 14, 1912, Sarnoff was at his post when he heard the message: *S.S. Titanic ran into iceberg. Sinking fast.* In Sarnoff's version, which was later adopted by the Radio Corporation of America as its official account, he was the sole link between the sinking ship and the rest of the world. The *Titanic* disaster not only cast a spotlight on the importance of radio, it also catapulted Sarnoff's career. Sarnoff was promoted to the high-profile position of patent policeman, and shortly after, commercial manager at the newly formed RCA. The corporation was born in 1919 not as an entrepreneurial venture but as a government proclamation. With its success during the war, wireless was deemed too important to be left to a foreign power, even a friendly one. The Marconi Wireless and Telegraph Company pioneered the proliferation of wireless, but the company was headquartered in Great Britain. The U.S. Navy, and later Congress, decided that all the patents of its American subsidiary must be controlled by Americans.

Because of its leadership building the most powerful radio transmitters, General Electric was granted that opportunity. By congressional mandate, GE engulfed the assets, including the entire staff, of American Marconi and pooled the Marconi patents with its own. RCA was thus born as a monopoly, but Sarnoff thought that it wasn't the right kind of monopoly. It was Sarnoff who convinced RCA leaders that the biggest opportunity for radio would be not as an overseas communications tool but as a domestic entertainment medium. In order to position RCA as the leader in entertainment radio, the company needed to obtain several patents held by other companies. In exchange for company stock, RCA struck deals for several components of the household radio receiver and broadcasting infrastructure, thereby consolidating the company's position as the lead coordinating body and sales agent for radio receivers, transmitters, and other gear.

Having secured the patent rights to all stages of the broadcast radio, RCA now had to promote radio as an entertainment medium. As legend has it, Sarnoff single-handedly orchestrated the move of radio from an obscure communication tool to a commercial craze. Sarnoff would later tell the press the dramatic story of his master plan to manufacture the first big electronic media event. A boxing match to be held at an outdoor arena in Jersey City seemed to be the ideal event to usher in the new radio era. Cast as the role of the villain was legendary heavyweight champion Jack Dempsey. The public loved to hate this man. Known as the Manassa Mauler, he was a scar-faced bruiser, alleged wife-beater, and, worst of all, a draft dodger. The valiant challenger was French champ Georges Carpentier, a handsome, graceful ladies' man and decorated combat pilot. Sarnoff convinced the promoter to allow a microphone to be placed ringside. He arranged for a RCA radio transmitter en route to the Navy Department in Washington, DC, to be diverted to a secret shed near the arena. To broadcast the signal he recruited some of his engineers to construct a makeshift transmission antenna nearby. He enlisted the help of Anne Morgan, daughter of financial baron J. P. Morgan, for PR. She arranged for charity listening events around the Northeast to be held at town halls, theaters, school auditoriums, Elks' clubs and other locations. In exchange for a donation to her charity, attendees could gather to listen to the world's first radio event. More than 300,000 people across the region gathered to listen as Jack Dempsey knocked out Carpentier in just eleven minutes (and it was a good thing the match ended so quickly as an electrical overload blew out the equipment moments after the referee's final call). Indeed, the event was a massive success. Of course, this telling, much like the *Titanic* story, was just one of several episodes that David Sarnoff selectively edited, embellished, positioned, sharpened, backlighted, and recast with himself in the spotlight. That a man named Julius Hopp actually masterminded the event, and that Sarnoff had only the limited role of equipment supervisor, mattered little. Suddenly, everyone in the United States seemed to want two things: a radio and an opportunity to be on the radio. The Roaring Twenties were now good to go.

Of course, radio's newfound popularity had its downside. Practically overnight more than 200 set makers at 5,000 parts manufacturers sprung up. Suddenly there were hundreds of applicants for radio broadcast licenses and hundreds more broadcasting without a license. A cover of *Radio News* magazine captured the situation with a cartoon cover of a monkey wearing headphones, operating a radio transmitter. Sarnoff thought the situation was a mess, and that people would soon lose interest in buying radio if the content didn't become more sophisticated. So he proposed in an internal memo to create a national broadcasting company, or a public broadcasting service. Sarnoff's idea for the service was, like Farnsworth's vision, very high-minded—education, objective news reporting, lectures by Marconi and Einstein, classical symphonies, and perhaps some sports and entertainment. Someone had to bring order to the industry. Someone had to subdue the mob that was running away with the radio business. Someone had to enforce the patents. Sarnoff, already the head of RCA's patent committee, was the logical choice to assume the role, and he jumped at the chance. In the spirit of the most wildly unpopular law of the day, Sarnoff would institute a prohibition on the radio industry. Sarnoff led a patent crackdown, suing smaller companies for patent infringement and refusing to sell radio components to dealers who did not exclusively carry RCA's entire line of radios. Small independent radio producers united to attack the monopolistic practices of RCA in general and Sarnoff in particular. Sarnoff's reputation as the lead bully of the repressive broadcasting industry was emerging. If you got on the wrong side of Sarnoff, he could steamroll right over you and see to it that no one looked back on your remains.

Community Chest

While David Sarnoff was a man obsessed turning radio into an entertainment device, Philo T. Farnsworth was obsessed with making his idea of television a reality. College seemed the obvious next step in Farnsworth's efforts to actualize his dream. In order to pay tuition, he briefly joined the navy, but quit when he realized that any progress he made on his device while enlisted would automatically become government property. Unable to make ends meet working odd jobs, Philo dropped out of college. Luck placed him with a job at the Community Chest, a national charitable organization where he would meet three of the most important people in his life—his future wife, Pem Gardner, and two well-connected young fund-raisers named George Everson and Leslie Gorrell.

One day during a casual conversation Philo explained his invention to Everson and Gorrell. While neither man much understood the science of the contraption, this was an era of wild speculation on Wall Street, and Everson revealed that he had dreams of making a killing. "I have about six thousand dollars in a special account in San Francisco, he said. This is about as wild a gamble as I can imagine. I'll put the money up. If I win, great. But if I lose it all, I won't squawk." Philo's dreams finally had a chance at becoming a reality. Philo Farnsworth, George Everson, and Leslie Gorrell formed a partnership right on the spot. Farnsworth would own 50 percent of the venture, with Gorrell agreeing to reimburse Everson half his start-up capital if the venture was to go bust.

Philo's personal life was looking up too. A romance was budding between him and his sister's high school friend Pem Gardner. Pem listened with interest to Philo's talk of sending pictures to the airwaves. Soon Philo asked the eighteen-year-old to become his wife and travel with him to Los Angeles, where he would be setting up shop to work on television full time. Indeed, young Philo was a man obsessed. Even on their wedding night it was his invention that was on Philo's mind. Phil carried Pem over the threshold, but as soon as he put her down, he explained that he had to return to Everson's office to work out final details before their morning departure to California. Phil went over his invention and business plans with his nervous investors through the night, all while Pem was waiting on her wedding bed in her gown. By the time Phil arrived back at the room, all disheveled and windblown, Pem was visibly racked with worry and dismay at the thought of having her wedding night ruined. To top it off, Phil opened his explanation of where he was with an attempted joke. "Pemmie," he said, embracing her and staring deeply into her eyes, "I have to tell you something." Pause. "There is another woman in my life. And her name is Television!" Indeed, television would be ever-present in their marriage, with Pem working side by side with her husband as he worked toward bringing his invention to the world.

Patently Brilliant

As prices for radios fell, this new entertainment medium became easily accessible to the middle-class masses. In the mad scramble to reach this new audience, everyone was starting stations. The *Chicago Tribune* launched WGN (for World's Greatest Newspaper), Sears started WLS (for World's Largest Store), and a preacher in Richmond began broadcasting over WLSV (Will the Lord Save Virginia?). Hospitals and colleges took to the airwaves, as did cities, towns, and states (KFKB stood for Kansas Folk Know Best). Clothing retailers and pharmacies, banks and insurance firms, poultry farms and ice cream parlors, electronics stores and radio dealers—all had their own stations. Companies saw radio as an efficient new way to communicate with their customers, and so they began hiring announcers and technicians by the thousands.

Of course, RCA still owned the patents to all the technology that radio broadcasting required. Yet Sarnoff knew that the company could not sue everyone. Additionally, claims that RCA was a monopoly that could stifle competition were gaining traction at the Federal Trade Commission, which filed to formally charge RCA and the entire radio combine, including GE, AT&T, Westinghouse, and United Fruit. This placed RCA in a peculiar situation. On one hand, RCA was being lambasted for its far-reaching powers. On the other hand, its stifling bureaucracy rendered it unable to compete. Start-ups were able to get newer, better designed, and cheaper radios to market before committees of the radio combine were able to circulate the minutes of their meetings. RCA was charged with holding a monopoly over radio at the same time that 75 percent of the radio market was being captured by other companies.

One late night at the office, David Sarnoff was struck with an idea. Instead of trying to put the other radio makers out of business through expensive litigation that would only inflict tremendous damage on RCA's already fragile image, why not just license RCA's patents? For 7.5 percent of sales RCA would provide its entire pool of patents to anyone who wanted them. The plan worked brilliantly, and soon 90 percent of radios sold were licensed by RCA. Radio was suddenly no longer just a craze but a burgeoning industry, and Sarnoff's patent-licensing scheme made RCA fabulously profitable, much more so than it could ever have been selling radios alone.

Now that RCA was in the business of patent licensing, it faced tremendous pressure to produce more patents. While Philo T. Farnsworth was toiling independently in California to produce his television, David Sarnoff was busy establishing RCA's first research and development department. Instead of purchasing patents from independent inventors, Sarnoff hired engineers from the best universities. He paid them competitive salaries, provided them with ample research budgets, and offered them a chance to join his crusade to change the world, working in the most dynamic industry the world had ever seen. Engineers would be paid their salary, and when their work led to a patent, the corporation would seize it. Producing patents was the engineer's job. To make sure this agreement was understood and enforced, the corporation would issue a check for each patent filing in the amount of one dollar, payable to the engineer.

One RCA engineer by the name of Bill Eddy thought that the one-dollar checks were an absurdity. To him, the honor of receiving the check was worth far more than the dollar itself. Each time he was issued a check, he would paste it on the wall of his working space. Like many RCA engineers, he was quite prolific in filing patent applications. Pretty soon, he proudly covered an entire wall with these checks. Meanwhile, the comptroller in the accounting department was wondering why he could not balance the books. After asking around, Sarnoff's finance chief found out about Eddy's wall. A team of accountants descended on Eddy's cubicle, but they couldn't pry the checks off the wall without ripping them. Finally, they called some maintenance workers to hack down the whole section of plasterboard. They carried the wall away from the premises, dissolved the plaster in a special solution, removed the checks, waited for them to dry, took Eddy to the bank, got him to endorse the checks, gave him his small pile of bills, and balanced the books of RCA.

Under the direction of Sarnoff, RCA brought such policies to a whole new level, systematizing the process of invention as never before.

Going Hollywood

As Sarnoff and the engineers at RCA were busy rationalizing the invention process, Farnsworth and his wife were going it alone. Philo set up a lab in the living room of their Hollywood apartment. It was a particularly exciting time to be in Hollywood, not because of the start-ups, but because the movie industry was on the cusp of a technological transformation, incorporating sound with images. Philo brought home lamps, crystals, prisms, lenses, different types of wires, a barrel of shellac, various epoxies and glues, a hand-cranked coil winder, an electric generator, and all sorts of tools. Before long, equipment was coming out of closets and overflowing into the backyard. Everson and Gorrell, Philo's financiers, were thrilled when they arrived. They offered to help in any way they could. Pem, Everson, and Gorrell helped Philo secure the equipment needed to make custom vacuum tubes and busied themselves constructing coils. The coils would guide and focus the electron beams through the vacuum tube. When juiced with electricity, the coils would develop a charge that would help deflect beams of electrons through the inner space to an anode, a positively charged metallic finger. In essence, Philo was trying to use an electromagnet to focus electron rays within the vacuum tubes. This would become the basis of Philo's first great invention—the image dissector.

One particularly exciting evening the doorbell rang. Pem answered it, only to be startled by two burly officers from the Los Angeles Police Department flashing their badges in her face and launching an accusation. "We've had a report that someone is operating a *still* around here," one of the officers shouted. As Philo invited him in to take a look around, Everson spied the cop and decided he wanted no part of this trouble. His hands were dripping with stinky, sticky, orange-colored goo, so he put them up in the air and fled, attempting to escape out the back door, where he was nabbed on the spot by two more policemen. One of them chided, "Oh, no you don't, buddy!" That cop escorted Everson back inside and joined with his partner to search through all the equipment. Basically, the officers ransacked the place. Farnsworth started explaining to one of the officers that he wasn't making booze but doing something completely different. He was trying to build an electronic television. The cop looked at him as if he were nuts. Finally, when these examples of

L.A.'s finest became convinced that there wasn't any alcohol, they shook their heads. "They're doing some kooky thing called electric vision, or something," mumbled one of them. "They ain't got no still in here."

As summer drew to a close Everson and Gorrell left L.A. to tend to business in other cities. Philo and Pem enjoyed their new life in California and continued to toil over the image dissector, but the initial money was running out. That fall Philo was prepared for the first test of his compete electronic television system. This system included a camera, transmitter, and small reception tube to accept the signal. He invited Everson and Gorrell to witness the event. When everyone was assembled, and everything was connected, Farnsworth switched on the electrical generator. First, everyone heard a loud bang. That was followed by a few pops, then a slow hissing and a sizzle. Pungent smoke rose from the assortment of devices. By the time Farnsworth could shut the power off, it was too late. He had blown up the entire contraption, including his prized image dissector.

Farnsworth was humiliated, but Everson and Gorrell were still optimistic. Even if they could not produce a working device, they could still use Philo's sketches to apply for a patent. The patent attorneys at Lyon & Lyon were intrigued by Farnsworth's idea and requested a meeting with him to discuss the issue. The meeting lasted the entire afternoon, and Farnsworth rose to the occasion. He put on a passionate performance, explaining his idea with a brilliant clarity and answering every question with confidence and precision. The attorneys and several engineering experts agreed that the idea had merit, and that Farnsworth and his crew should pursue a patent.

What Philo needed now was money. After months of searching he and his partners landed at the Crocker First National Bank in San Francisco in the office of J. J. Fagan, an executive vice president of the bank with a reputation as a shrewd businessman. After hearing their story Fagan proclaimed, "Well, that's a *damn fool* idea. Somebody ought to put some money into it!" The bank agreed to put up $25,000, with Farnsworth promising television transmission within a year. Additionally, the bankers would make available in San Francisco a laboratory space. There was a minor glitch, discovered when it came time to sign the papers. Still only twenty, Farnsworth was not yet old enough to enter into a contract on California. Everson had to assume the responsibility as the boy's legal guardian. It made for an embarrassing moment. Off Philo and Pem went to their new headquarters at 202 Green Street, on the base of Telegraph Hill.

Networking

In addition to his management duties, Sarnoff continued to brain-storm about the future. One of his favorite subjects—the future of radio programming—began as a series of internal memos starting in 1922. The novelty of radio was wearing off, Sarnoff wrote, and programming needed to improve greatly because "the broadcasting station will ulti-mately be required to entertain a nation." Not only would this endeavor be expensive, but it would call for specialists in talent and public taste. Let us organize a separate and distinct company, he wrote, to be known as the Public Service Broadcasting Company, or some similar name. As Sarnoff envisioned it, the business model of the company had to be one of a nonprofit organization. He didn't favor taxing the public to support programming, an idea that was being put into practice for the government-owned stations in England and other European countries, but Sarnoff clearly viewed broadcasting as a public service of the highest order. He favored putting aside 2 percent of RCA radio profits toward a programming fund.

At the same time, around 1925, a company called AT&T began what it called toll broadcasting. The model was simple. Come down to the sta-tion, say whatever you want into the microphone, and pay by the minute. Lots of companies took the company up on the offer. To fill in the small gaps of time between the ads, people would sing, play piano, and give lectures, but nothing too fancy. By sending the programming and com-mercials over phone lines to affiliate stations, AT&T was able to move radio from a local to a national communication tool.

Sarnoff was outraged. Radio was to be a public service, not a forum for crass commercialism. At a high-profile radio conference in Wash-ington, DC, organized by commerce secretary Herbert Hoover, Sarnoff denounced AT&T's actions and urged everyone to join him in his indig-nation. As it turned out, Hoover himself was Sarnoff's staunchest ally. "If a speech by the President is to be used as the meat between the sandwich of two advertisements," Hoover proclaimed at the conference, "there will be no radio left!" There was one problem with his protest. The Com-merce Department had no authority over radio. No one did, until the Federal Radio Commission, forerunner of the FCC, was established a few years later, thanks in part to a Supreme Court decision.

Sarnoff was convinced that AT&T was violating federal antitrust laws—using its telephone monopoly to gain a monopoly over radio. Sar-noff realized that he had two options: either enter into a lengthy and expensive court case, or settle the dispute using arbitration. Luckily, the patent-sharing agreements between RCA and AT&T contained a provision for secret and binding arbitration of any disputes. Both parties agreed to arbitrate the antitrust issue privately, lest they bring the messy battle into the public spotlight.

The settlement was a resounding win for RCA. AT&T was forced to divest its radio network. It was sold to RCA for $1 million. The new RCA network, transmitted over AT&T's phone lines for a modest fee, became known as the National Broadcasting Company (NBC).

As his reward for almost single-handedly founding NBC, Sarnoff was promoted to executive vice president and given a raise, to $60,000 per year. But here's the twist. When Sarnoff and RCA launched NBC in 1926, they forgot all about its high-minded, anticommercial ideals. NBC would be funded by advertisers right from the start. After all its effort and investment of time and money, RCA wouldn't have it any other way. It didn't want any government regulation. AT&T proved that there was big money to be made in broadcasting commercials. Herbert Hoover by now was running for president, and he forgot his original indignation over the airwaves being filled with advertised chatter.

Sarnoff's ego having been gratified by the glory of building RCA into the first electronic media conglomerate, the next order of business was something now getting considerable press attention, a technological leap that had been looming on his horizon for years. He now turned to focus on it almost exclusively. Sarnoff needed a plan for controlling the new art of television, which he envisioned supplanting radio and becoming, as one of his early memos put it, the ultimate and greatest step in mass communications.

Life on Green Street

Backing for his project secured, Philo headed to his new lab in San Francisco. The dream of television was on the horizon. Of course, much like Sarnoff's, Farnsworth's dream was a romantic one. Television would become the world's greatest teaching tool. Illiteracy would be wiped out. The immediacy of television was key. As news happened, viewers would watch it unfold live; no longer would they have to rely on people interpreting and distorting the news for us. They would be watching sporting events and symphony orchestras. Instead of people going to the movies, the movies would come to them. Television would also bring about world peace. If people were able to see those in other countries and learn about their differences, why would there be any misunderstandings? War would be a thing of the past.

Philo set up shop in the sparse Green Street lab, and was able to hire a few helpers, including Pem and her brother Cliff. Farnsworth had no experience running a laboratory. In fact, he had never seen the inside of a research lab or manufacturing plant. He had little idea how difficult it was to accomplish what he wanted. Instead, he would rely on instinct and old-fashioned trial and error. He attacked the assignment with no engineering experience, but to compensate he had courage and genius, Everson later wrote, "The courage was not the foolhardy type born of ignorance. His was the courage of the pioneer who knows the goal but has little knowledge of the intervening terrain." Lab journals show Farnsworth moving at a furious pace. The small staff was working twelve hours a day, six days a week, trying out one technique after another, and doing their best to learn from their failures. "I'm a professional mistake maker," Philo told Pem.

By August 1927 Farnsworth had conducted eleven failed experiments of his complete system, but he was sure that he was coming close. September 7, 1927, was the day that they were to conduct experiment number 12, a test of the entire apparatus. They had partitioned the room into two parts. Cliff placed a slide with the image of a triangle in front of the image dissector in one section of the lab, while everyone else gathered around the receiving tube behind the partition. The two tubes were connected by an amplifier and wires. Within a couple of seconds, a line appeared across the small bluish square of light on the end of the tube, wrote Pem. It was pretty fuzzy, but Philo adjusted the focusing coil, and the line became well-defined. "Turn the slide, Cliff," shouted Philo. When he did so, the received line also turned ninety degrees. They didn't see the full triangle, but even so, this line represented a historic first. "That's it folks," Farnsworth exclaimed. "We've done it! There you have electronic television." In a telegraph to his backers Philo announced his good news in one short line: "THE DAMN THING WORKS!"

While the staff at the Green Street lab was celebrating the achievement of electronic television, excitement was brewing in engineering circles over television of another kind. Achievements in mechanical television were receiving a great deal of press coverage. John Logie Baird of Great Brittan was proclaimed the winner of the race for television when he successfully broadcast a shadowy image of a Maltese cross using the spinning disk method. The well-funded staff at AT&T's Bell Laboratories used a similar method to transmit a blurred approximation of

Herbert Hoover's face while separate phone lines connected to remote speakers carried his statement: "Human genius has now destroyed the impediment of distance." Even though mechanical television was to electronic television what smoke signals were to radio, David Sarnoff kept a watchful eye on the activities and pushed his engineering department to develop a marketable mechanical set.

The press's attention to mechanical television posed a significant threat to Philo Farnsworth. Of particular national interest was the public showcase of Charles Francis Jenkins's Radiovisor, as detailed in Hugo Gernsback's radio and invention magazines. Jenkins's company became a Wall Street darling virtually overnight, securing $10 million in investment capital. The financial euphoria surrounding the Radiovisor put Farnsworth in a knotty bind. After all, the bankers who were backing his venture were not interested in television per se but in the highest return on their money. Farnsworth needed to get his electronic television system to a commercial stage as quickly as possible, but he didn't want to excite his investors so much that they would want to sell the company out from under him.

In January 1928 Farnsworth made his next great breakthrough when he wound electromagnetic coils around the camera tube so that it would sweep the image across the anode of the dissector one line at a time, a focusing technique used in commercial television systems for the rest of the century. By May, he brainstormed a theory for narrowing the transmission wave band, so that picture signals wouldn't crowd out sounds assigned to adjacent frequencies. By August, all the small improvements added up to something big. His scan was now up to 150 lines of resolution.

It was time to demonstrate the device to his investors at the bank. As the assemblage stared into the receiving tube, Farnsworth said, "Here's something a banker will understand." And at the center of the blue screen appeared the image of a dollar sign. The group broke out into laughter, as the men began slapping their knees in approval. Cliff, in the other room, then began smoking a cigarette in front of the camera tube, and the men saw the vague outline of smoke wafting on the screen. The bankers in their day had witnessed plenty of people blowing smoke at them, but nothing like this.

The demonstration was a huge hit with the bankers. As Farnsworth had feared, they recommended that he quickly try to sell the company. While their techniques were greatly different, Farnsworth, just like Sarnoff, envisioned himself as the father of television. He would not sell out. He did agree, however, to recommendations for a press demonstration. The bankers saw this as an opportunity to find a buyer. Philo, on the other hand, saw this as an opportunity to prove to the world the workability of electronic television. Indeed, papers across the country reported how a young inventor in San Francisco had revolutionized the television.

Confrontation

Given the limited success of Sarnoff's engineers in developing a commercially viable television, one can only imagine his shock when he read that some kid from California, working independently, had gotten so complex an invention near to a commercial stage. Sarnoff refused to be beaten, and he knew just the engineer that would help RCA compete. Vladimir Kosma Zworykin was a Russian-trained engineer who had himself been researching the potential use of cathode ray tubes to transmit images using electricity. He had been running some preliminary tests of his ideas at RCA's sister company, Westinghouse, in Pittsburgh. Zworykin promised Sarnoff that with a $100,000 research budget he could develop a working electronic television system.

By now, Farnsworth's elaborate demonstrations were attracting high-profile visitors. Among them were Guglielmo Marconi, David Sarnoff's longtime mentor; Herbert Hoover Jr., son of the president; as well as Hollywood leading man Douglas Fairbanks Sr. and his Oscar-winning wife, Mary Pickford. While the attention made Farnsworth feel like a celebrity, the bankers at J. J. Fagan wanted a visitor who was capable of swallowing the entire outfit, someone from one of the big electrical concerns, someone serious about pioneering the future, someone with real money in tow. The next guest fit the bill—the head of television research at the Westinghouse Electric Corporation—Vladimir Zworykin.

Zworykin arrived at Green Street in the middle of April 1930. For three days, all of the activity at the laboratory was centered on impressing this esteemed visitor. Farnsworth simply wanted to license his patents to Westinghouse, while the bankers wanted to sell the company outright. In any case, they showed Zworykin every courtesy as they revealed to him everything in the lab. No one was especially concerned that Zworykin would try to swipe intellectual property. Engineers at Zworykin's level were all members of international professional societies that promoted clear odes of ethics. Besides, virtually all the demonstrations at the lab were already described in patent applications and technical journals.

Little did they know that David Sarnoff was behind this visit. West-inghouse had no intention of licensing patents or buying the company. Sarnoff had planned to have Zworykin visit Farnsworth and then move the entire Westinghouse television operation to the RCA labs in Camden, New Jersey. After visiting Farnsworth, Zworykin took the train back to Westinghouse labs, where he and his assistants re-created, as best they could, a replica of Farnsworth's Image dissector while it was still fresh in his mind. Then Zworykin packed it up, collected the rest of his things, and boarded another train to New York, where he reported to Sarnoff. Any pretense that Zworykin had come to see Farnsworth as a colleague, on a cooperative scientific mission, was now shattered. This bit of corporate espionage was a clear act of aggression. The war over television was hereby declared.

The reorganization moving all research to the RCA labs placed Sarnoff in nearly complete control of the new field of television. But in light of the stock market's plummet, this strategy backfired. Having lost jobs and life savings, the public was eager to punish large corporations for their personal woes, and the Congress was happy to oblige. Years-old antitrust suits against the RCA radio behemoth reemerged. Suddenly, Sarnoff recognized the real risk—that the government would dissolve the radio monopoly. Leading the new television industry might be RCA's only hope for survival.

When Sarnoff peered into the future, he saw himself as the Moses of a great new industry, the television industry, developed around an invention that would lead humankind toward its destiny. Anything that would interfere with that goal had to be shoved aside. Nothing would ever stand between RCA and television, especially not a young inventor who had designs on controlling the patent structure of the new art. As a result, Sarnoff established a clandestine task force. Composed of both engineers and patent attorneys, this new team became known, informally, as the Get-Around-Farnsworth Department.

End Run

By 1931 it was clear that Zworykin was nowhere near finishing a marketable version of electronic television. David Sarnoff decided that he would pay a personal visit to Farnsworth headquarters at the Green Street lab in San Francisco. Throughout his visit he expressed interest in the equipment and seemed impressed with the demonstrations. Afterward, however, his entire demeanor changed. He asserted that Zworykin's work on his own television receiver made it possible to avoid Farnsworth's patents. As for a television camera, he said that RCA was working on something that could equal Farnsworth's image dissector. "There's nothing here we'll need," Sarnoff concluded. Shortly after Sarnoff's visit, RCA offered to purchase the entire company for the insulting price of $100,000. The offer was rejected outright.

Sarnoff had made up his mind about Farnsworth even before visiting Green Street. His lowball offer wasn't a matter of money, but of pride. To Sarnoff, the resulting publicity around Farnsworth would be far worse than the dollar cost. A large payment to Farnsworth could be interpreted by the press as a validation of this kid's status as the father of television. Sarnoff believed that television was destined to be invented at RCA under his own command, even if it had already been invented somewhere else. Sarnoff, it seemed, visited Green Street only so that he could to claim that he had satisfied his basic curiosity.

Not long after Sarnoff's visit, Farnsworth received an offer that he could live with. Philco radio company in Philadelphia was struggling to survive. Between patent-licensing payments to RCA and plummeting radio sales, profit margins were slim. The company wanted to spread into a new market. To Farnsworth's delight, the owners did not want to buy his company but rather form an alliance. Philco would fund all of the television laboratory's expenses and provide research space in exchange for broad, nonexclusive licenses on all Farnsworth's patents. Philo T. Farnsworth, along with his wife and several key employees, quickly moved to Philadelphia.

Back at RCA, Vladimir Zworykin and his team were making steady progress on his own electronic television. The most important of these achievements occurred by accident. In an attempt to create an original television camera not based on a Farnsworth design, an RCA engineer was experimenting with surfaces that could temporarily store electronic representations of images. He coated with silver a sheet of mica crystals attached to a wire mesh, then put it in the oven to bake. He forgot all about it and left it in way too long. By the time he pulled his sheet out of the oven, he felt like a failed pastry chef, figuring his creation was ruined and that he'd have to start all over. When he looked at the result, however, he saw that his concoction had crystallized into a beautiful uniform mosaic of insulated silver. When Zworykin tested it, he found that this new photoelectric surface worked wonderfully. He called it the "final link" in his plan to create the first electronic television camera using the principle of temporary storage, which made the camera far more sensitive and reduced the need for bright lights. Zworykin called the newfangled instrument the Iconoscope.

In Philadelphia, Farnsworth knew that progress was being made at RCA because his equipment would occasionally pick up broadcasts from RCA's experimental television studio across the river in Camden. Farnsworth was also making progress. His team was also running successful tests of an experimental television station. Of course, the RCA team would occasionally pick up these signals as well. One afternoon, the team at Philco received a phone call from the RCA labs. One of the Philco cameras was stationed at the University of Pennsylvania pool. "You know your camera at the swimming pool?" the RCA engineer queried. "do you know that some of the students are swimming without bathing suits?"

In 1932, the Great Depression took a toll on RCA. The company posted a million-dollar loss, and continued antitrust litigation distracted Sarnoff from his television project. Meanwhile, Philco was forced by RCA to sever its ties with Farnsworth. The end run to commercialize television without RCA had failed. Farnsworth later learned that when Sarnoff found out about the Philo-Philco plan, he threatened to rescind the Philadelphia company's license to produce radios under RCA's patents, which would effectively put Philco out of business. Farnsworth moved the laboratory to rented space near his home. To fund the enterprise, George Everson went to New York to sell stock in Farnsworth Television.

Who Owns What?

No matter how hard Philo T. Farnsworth worked at his suburban Philadelphia laboratory, he wasn't making progress in advancing television to a commercial stage. According to the party line laid down by David Sarnoff, it was RCA that was developing true commercial television, and when it was ready, RCA's own pending patents based on the work of Zworykin's team would be available to manufacturers for license. RCA notified all the potential licensees of Farnsworth's patents that the Patent Office must have made a serious mistake. This calculated and clandestine campaign of misinformation and threats cut off Farnsworth's ability to license his patents, which he had counted as his main source of potential revenue.

The situation between Philo and RCA was growing worse, as Sarnoff continued ambushing Farnsworth in order to position RCA as the inventor of commercial television. While Farnsworth actively promoted his progress, Sarnoff made sure that RCA remained silent on the technical information about the company's progress on television. When Farnsworth gave presentations, the front rows were filled with engineers photographing his slides. These ideas would often make their way into patent applications by competitors, including RCA. Conversely, David Sarnoff insisted that he have final approval on any statement made by any member of the organization about the future of television.

Finally, Farnsworth decided he had had enough of RCA's espionage, delays, and propaganda. He needed the Patent Office to clarify the situation once and for all. With the help of Donald Lippincott, his trusted patent attorney, Farnsworth filed suit against RCA. This legal action became known as Patent Interference Number 64,027. At issue was nothing less than the big question: who invented electronic television? While Sarnoff was content to let this question linger as long as possible, in order to buy time for Zworykin, Farnsworth knew that the dispute had to be resolved before he could move ahead. The stakes couldn't be higher. The winner of the case would be granted controlling rights to the invention of television.

To establish the chronology of events, RCA brought in a former Westinghouse engineer named Joseph Tykociner to testify that Zworykin had described, constructed, and demonstrated his television idea to him long before Farnsworth's patent applications. Of course, this testimony, lacking any written record, was dubious. Additionally, Tykociner and Zworykin had been in contact throughout the period when Zworykin began working on television for RCA. Tykociner must have been coached to revise his story, charged the Farnsworth team.

When it came to establishing the Farnsworth chronology, Lippincott and his team faced a big problem. Upon conceiving his idea, Farnsworth only disclosed it to two people: to his father, now deceased, and to his high school science teacher, Justin Tolman, who had since left Rigby, Idaho. Farnsworth hadn't been in touch with Tolman since moving away from Rigby, and he had no idea of his whereabouts or whether the teacher remembered much about the matter in question. If they could not produce a witness, no court could possibly believe that a farm boy at the tender age of fourteen could have come up with an invention as complicated as electronic television.

Luckily, Farnsworth's legal team was able to locate Tolman, who clearly remembered the description Philo gave to him long ago. In court, he was able to replicate the sketch that his student had drawn on the blackboard. While it was a much simplified version, the elements matched all of those in Farnsworth's patent application. What happened next was truly remarkable. Asked whether he could show written evidence, Tolman reached into his breast pocket and produced a folded-up, well-worn sheet of notebook paper. When he unfolded it, Tolman revealed a shockingly simple sketch of the image dissector. "This was made for me by Philo in early 1922," he said. The teacher had saved the drawing all these years.

This testimony, coupled with the accusation that RCA had engaged in an act of corporate espionage, sending Zworykin to the Green Street lab in 1930, seemed to leave no doubt about who the true inventor of television was. Still, the court took several months to decide the issue. The court eventually affirmed Philo's controlling patent, officially anointing him as the father of television.

Of course, Sarnoff was not going to leave the decision solely up to the courts. As luck would have it, Sarnoff's old friend Joe Kennedy was appointed by President Roosevelt to be the first chairman of the new Securities and Exchange Commission. Under Kennedy's leadership, the SEC investigated about 2,300 cases of possible securities fraud. He didn't go after any major members of the New York Stock Exchange. Rather, almost all the cases involved manipulation of small-time, over-the-counter stocks. At this point, Farnsworth Television was one such creature. Faced with a whopping $30,000 legal bill from the trial and $5,000 per month in salaries and lab costs, Everson and company president McCargar were living on company expenses in New York, selling as much stock as they could to pay bills. This coincided with a run-up in the price of company shares, which was fortunate. But such activity could also smell fishy to Sarnoff's friend at the SEC.

In the months preceding the court ruling Philo decided to do some showing off. He agreed to do a ten-day demonstration of his invention at the Franklin Institute, a prestigious science museum in Philadelphia. When the exhibit opened, Farnsworth staged a surprise at the main entrance. He pointed a mobile camera at the incoming stream of visitors, while a receiver just inside the door televised their faces, allowing people to watch their friends and family members. The demonstration was a huge success, with a line quickly forming of people waiting to pay seventy-five cents to see Philo's amazing machine. Yet the demonstration was not financially successful for the Farnsworth Television Company and left the entire staff exhausted.

Narrow Escape

Two years later, in 1936, Sarnoff arranged for RCA's first public television demonstration, an event that would end up being referred to as the first TV dinner. All of RCA's major licensees were invited to a complementary dinner at the new Waldorf-Astoria Hotel in New York City. Broadcast on television were speeches by several members of the RCA leadership, followed by entertainment fare including a fashion show, monologues, comics, and several film clips. Unlike Farnsworth's show at the museum, the RCA demonstration served as a wake-up call to the entire radio industry. Never mind that the screens were much smaller and of much lower resolution than the ones Farnsworth had displayed two years earlier.

Meanwhile, Farnsworth now controlled an impressive array of more than twenty-five patents, plus at least seventy-five pending applications. He had largely achieved his goal of building up a formidable patent structure around the art of electronic television. Licensing revenue was bound to pick up at some point, but now was the time to shift gears from research to development and become a full-fledged manufacturing company. The Farnsworth team arranged to take over a high-end radio manufacturer called Capehart Company, of Fort Wayne, Indiana. Farnsworth's company needed to raise funds to begin a lab at the new location, but could not do so until the SEC approved its public offering plan. With World War II on the horizon, the stock market took a plunge. Raising funds seemed impossible.

In Philadelphia Farnsworth was getting depressed and drinking heavily. To get away from his problems, Philo, Pem, and two friends went on a trip to Maine. While there, Farnsworth fell in love with a rundown old farmhouse. He insisted on buying it on the spot. Pem thought he was mad, but realized that the project would at least get his mind off the company's financial woes.

In 1939 Farnsworth was summoned to testify before Congress in what would be called the "Monopoly Investigation." FDR had become convinced that concentration of economic power was a structural problem that was preventing economic recovery and urged an investigation. Consisting of members of the House, the Senate, and various executive branch departments, the officially named Temporary National Economic Committee had begun its investigation in the summer of 1938. Its mission was to scrutinize industries ranging from insurance to banking, from finance to manufacturing, looking for instances of systematic anticompetitive behavior harmful to workers and consumers, then coming up with legislation to address antitrust loopholes. The centerpiece of the hearings was a probe into patents. Since patents by definition grant the holder a limited monopoly over an invention, committee members had great hopes that they would find smoking guns buried in patents. Some of the biggest industrial behemoths in the country drew much of their power from pools of patents. Foremost among these companies were General Electric, AT&T, and RCA, which was known simply as the radio monopoly.

Here was Farnsworth's big chance to get back at RCA. None of the top executives from the radio monopoly were invited to appear at the hearing, and they were distraught over the fact that Farnsworth could launch into specific monopoly charges. Farnsworth could have described the constant harassment from RCA and its many attempts to interfere with his patent applications. He could have recounted how Vladimir Zworykin appeared at his laboratory under false pretenses, then reported back to David Sarnoff with what he learned. He could have told how RCA was spreading misinformation about the validity of Farnsworth's patents, and how he had to endure years of expensive litigation to clear it up. He could have exposed Sarnoff's unfair relationships with radio manufacturers who were contemplating getting into television. He could have told how RCA had intimidated Philco during the time Farnsworth was its partner. He could have complained about how RCA had been influencing the FCC to delay television until it had come up with its own quality system.

Instead of attacking RCA, Farnsworth acted as if had just come straight off the potato farm. He gave the committee his life story complete with the technical details about obscure scientific matters. Things began to get interesting when a committee member asked why television usage was at a more advanced stage in England and Germany than in the United States. Farnsworth offered a vague explanation of how the governments in those countries were footing much of the cost of programming. In addition, he said, the FCC has been slow in its effort to adopt a unified broadcasting standard for the United States. Then he switched to his optimistic view that television would be in the American home before very long.

He offered virtually no unkind words for the patent process in general, mainly because he truly believed the U.S. system was excellent and deservedly was the envy of the world. RCA's anticompetitive business tactics that had haunted Farnsworth for a decade were left unexamined, in part because the committee members didn't know what to ask about.

There were several reasons Farnsworth failed to speak up when he had the chance. He was certainly naive about how the game of business and politics really worked, but the idea of seeking assistance from the government also went against his self-image as a self-reliant individual. What's more, he believed that things were going pretty well and that television was close to becoming a commercial reality. He didn't know that he'd be proven wrong by events in the immediate future.

All's Fair, World's Fair

In 1939 New York City was to host the World's Fair. The theme of this event was Building the World of Tomorrow. Sarnoff saw the fair as the ideal stage on which to promote RCA as the leader of the new television age. The publicity leading up to the opening of the fair reinforced the stature of RCA. *Life* magazine pictured RCA executives huddled around their newest model television, which was to debut at the fair, not mentioning, of course, that it had been built illegally, infringing the patents of someone else. RCA spent millions to build and operate a 9,000-square-foot pavilion where it could showcase its new television technology. Shaped like a colossal radio tube, the immense yellow structure was branded with bright red RCA logos. As visitors entered, they walked past the TV cameras, which entitled them to an "I was televised" wallet card with spaces for printing their name and the date. The Radio Living Room of Tomorrow exhibit featured an immense wall unit that housed a combined radio, record player, television, music recorder, film projector, and facsimile machine.

On display were RCA's first commercial TV sets, housed in cabinets that projected straight up through a lens that magnified and reflected the image to be viewed indirectly on a mirror built into the unit's lid. To avoid the appearance of visual trickery, RCA designed transparent Lucite plastic cabinets for these sets, which exposed the innards of the apparatus.

RCA also used the World's Fair as an opportunity to officially bring their televisions to market. "The corporate sales force stocked all the major stores in the New York City area with enough inventory to respond to the expected demand. Promotional dollars ensured that RCA televisions were placed in street-level store windows at all of the city's famous department sores, including Macy's, Bloomingdales, and Wanamaker's. These sets carried luxurious $600 price tags, although less expensive models as low as $150 were soon added to the line.

At a press conference just before the opening of the fair, David Sarnoff made a grand announcement to the press.

> It is with a feeling of humbleness that I come to this moment of announcing the birth in this country of a new art so important in its implications that it is bound to affect all society. Television is an art which shines like a torch of hope to a troubled world. It is a creative force which we must learn to utilize for the benefit of mankind. Now ladies and gentlemen, we add sight to sound!

He also announced that the NBC radio network would begin to operate as a television network too.

In doing all this, Sarnoff not only was violating Farnsworth's patents but also was bypassing the sovereignty of the FCC. "Without FCC adoption of commercial standards, Sarnoff was gambling that public enthusiasm would stampede the industry and the commission behind the RCA system," wrote RCA's Kenneth Bilby. While Philco and Zenith did object loudly, the FCC remained indecisive, neither condoning nor condemning Sarnoff's plan. Technically, Sarnoff may have been bending various rules and laws, but at this special moment, he was able to manufacture a little bit of extra authority to do so with impunity.

Philo T. Farnsworth was also in New York during the fair, though he refused to attend. He was only there to attend meetings of the Farnsworth Television Company. Having recently received the go-ahead from the SEC for its initial public offering, the company was deciding how to proceed with the three million dollars in capital it had raised. In light of RCA's guerilla tactics, they also had to decide whether or not they would sue for patent infringement.

On the afternoon of April 30, Farnsworth was walking back to his hotel from that day's board meeting. When he saw RCA televisions projecting the opening ceremony in a department store window, he stopped cold in his tracks. David Sarnoff was on the air, yielding the podium to President Roosevelt. Farnsworth stepped closer to the window and listened to the sounds that were being piped out to the streets. Other pedestrians were stopping to watch and listen too. Sarnoff was clearly taking credit for the invention in a way that Farnsworth knew he could never match, creating an impression that could never be erased. Sarnoff was doing this through the very power of television itself.

Farnsworth's entire existence seemed to be annulled in this moment. The dreams of a farm boy, the eureka moment in a potato field, the confession to a teacher, the confidence in him shown by businessmen and bankers and investors, the breakthroughs in the laboratory, all these years of work, the decisions of the official patent examiners, those hard-fought victories, all of those demonstrations that had come and gone, the entire vision of the future. All of this was being negated by Sarnoff's performance at the World's Fair.

Farnsworth couldn't believe what he was seeing. The agony set off sharp pains in his stomach. All along, television was supposed to bring pictures of reality to the people. It never occurred to him that his invention would be used to subvert reality, to manufacture impressions that were not true. He really had created a monster.

Breakdown, Breakout

With his introduction of television at the World's Fair, David Sarnoff had left RCA exposed to a patent-infringement lawsuit from Philo T. Farnsworth. RCA could have lost such a battle, given the fact that it had lost all its previous patent fights against Farnsworth. With RCA television sets for sale in department stores and with NBC broadcasting an extensive schedule of baseball, boxing, Broadway shows, and live dramas from Radio City, the risk of an embarrassing and expensive lawsuit was now too high for Sarnoff to endure. Faced with no alternative, he agreed in May 1939 to open serious negotiations to license the Farnsworth intellectual property his engineers were already incorporating into RCA products.

The negotiations proved a great victory for Farnsworth. He held strong in his refusal to sell his patents outright. RCA reluctantly agreed to pay $1 million plus continued royalties on every television sold. The jubilation about reaching an agreement was short lived. Shortly after, the United States entered into World War II. Upon entry, the government suspended all manufacturing of consumer electronics in order to divert capacity to the war effort.

With television now on hold, David Sarnoff became as determined to win the war as he was determined to win the television battle. He saw his military involvement as an honor of the highest degree and as tangible proof that he was an American patriot who had shed his immigrant heritage. In the early 1920s, he had joined the U.S. Army Reserves as a member of the Signal Corps, and RCA chairman James Harbord used his own military connections to win for Sarnoff the rank of lieutenant colonel, even though Sarnoff lacked the required experience.

RCA was rapidly converted into a military contractor, producing radar tubes, sonar systems, and radio transmitters for the Allied communications effort. In 1944, when Sarnoff was summoned for active duty, he reported directly to General Dwight D. Eisenhower. Without revealing the full details of the secret plan to storm the beaches of Normandy and free Europe from the Nazis, Eisenhower told Sarnoff to construct a powerful broadcasting station that could centralize all electronic communications in one place and relay information across the entire continent, an assignment that also brought Sarnoff into personal meetings with Prime Minister Winston Churchill. On D-day, June 6, 1944, the Allied Forces Network that Sarnoff had put in place worked as planned; Allied generals used the network to coordinate history's most massive military operation, and military journalists reported the news of the invasion to the rest of the world with unprecedented quickness. After France was liberated, Sarnoff played a key role in reconstructing war-torn French Radio, linking Paris once again with London and New York. Upon his return to the United States, Sarnoff was appointed an honorary brigadier general by President Roosevelt. When he returned to his post at RCA, he let the word spread that he was no longer "Mr. Sarnoff"; he was now to be called "General Sarnoff," or simply "General."

The war had not empowered Philo T. Farnsworth. He was convinced that his controlling patents would expire before his vision of television would be realized. This sent him into a deeply depressive state at a time when depression wasn't treated like the disease it is. He began drinking not just at night but during the day.

The move to Fort Wayne, Indiana, did not help with Philo's condition. The shift in focus from invention to manufacturing and from progress to profit was more than Farnsworth could handle. He had a nervous breakdown, couldn't get out of bed, and, at only one hundred pounds, appeared to be on the edge of death. A brief stay in a hospital revived his body, but not his spirit. Finally, in 1947, the day Farnsworth had been dreading arrived. His seventeen-year patents on the television camera and television receiver expired. Farnsworth still held more than one hundred other television-related patents, some of which were quite valuable, and many had up to ten years of life remaining, but the two golden ones had now lapsed into the public domain, and all promises of royalty payments for them ceased, just weeks before the sudden breakout of a nationwide television obsession that seemed at first like a fad but grew only more intense over time.

Postwar

Starting in the fall of 1947, television caught on even more ferociously than radio did a quarter of a century earlier. American consumers bought 1 million sets within two years, with 80 percent of the market controlled by RCA. In 1948, Milton Berle's *Texaco Star Theater* debuted on NBC, and CBS responded with a variety hour hosted by Ed Sullivan. The average television family was now watching for more than three hours each day, and early TV owners often had to set up numerous chairs in their living rooms to share their viewing with their neighbors. Restaurants, nightclubs, and movie theaters in major metro areas experienced a sharp drop in business. When an NBC drama series called *Kraft Television Theater* plugged a new product called Cheez Whiz, Americans bought tons of Cheez Whiz, and the meaning was clear: if television could sell Cheez Whiz, it could sell anything. Advertising dollars quickly shot past the $100 million mark, and RCA's total television investment to date was rapidly recouped many times over.

On January 7, 1949, RCA and Sarnoff officially laid claim to the invention of TV. NBC aired "Television's Twenty Fifth Anniversary Special." The program commemorated the date that Vladimir Zworykin filed his patent application. David Sarnoff told the story of television's invention and introduced Zworykin as the inventor of television. That broadcast probably reached a greater number of people in a half hour than all the people who had ever heard or read the name *Philo T. Farnsworth* over a lifetime. The following year, Sarnoff lobbied the Radio and Television Manufacturers Association to bestow on him the title "Father of Television." His effort was successful, and RCA memos informed employees that these designations were official: only David Sarnoff was to be called the Father of Television, and only Vladimir Zworykin was to be called the Inventor of Television. No one disputed it.

Despite the expiration of his patents, the Farnsworth Corporation still hoped to cash in on the television craze. The company designed a complete line of televisions, from small tabletop models to large consoles in wooden cabinets. The problem was that high demand had created a shortage in necessary parts. Many of these parts could only be obtained through RCA, and somehow the Farnsworth Corporation always ended up on the bottom of the priority list. With bank loans coming due, the company was forced to sell. The International Telephone and Telegraph Corporation (ITT) purchased the company and renamed it the Farnsworth Electronics Company. Of course, what ITT was really after was the brain of Philo T. Farnsworth.

Farnsworth got to work on various electronic components. However, at night he began to focus on a new invention that would occupy him for his remaining years, much as television had in his youth. Philo T. Farnsworth spent his remaining years trying to master the art of nuclear fusion. He was after one of the holy grails of modern science, a safe way to tap a virtually endless source of cost-free energy. While Philo turned his efforts to fusion, Sarnoff continued pursuing the potential of television. While he never quite got the grasp of entertainment programming, he did have a penchant for recognizing television's political potential. He worked as the unofficial image consultant for his old friend Ike Eisenhower during his presidential bid, producing twenty-second spots promoting "Ike for President."

Farnsworth largely separated himself from television, save an appearance on *I've Got a Secret*, where he stumped the panel as to his true identity as the inventor of television. Vladimir Zworykin, too, became disillusioned with his invention. When asked what specific feature of a television he was most proud of, he replied, "Da svitch, so I can turn the damn theenk off!"

Epilogue: Perceptions and Reality

When the FCC was formally launched in 1934, it said that broadcasting existed for the purpose of serving the public interest, as we all know. But that public interest doctrine began slowly eroding, especially when the television age began. It turns out that both Farnsworth and Sarnoff, toward the end of their lives in the 1960s, were disappointed with what television had become.

This story of the early days of television technology at first glance may appear to be a classic narrative pitting the reckless and idealistic young inventor against the older, world-weary and well-connected industrialist. But glance again. Both men were children of their times. Both struggled from humble beginnings, and both had to confront the harsh realities of raising capital and managing fundamental technical research. Both adventured gamely into public relations gimmicks and gambles. Both attempted to utilize the patent and court systems to their best advantage. In the end Sarnoff used his connections and superior economic resources more shrewdly and perhaps with fewer ethical reservations, but certainly with extraordinary competitive success.

The irony here is that both men began with strikingly similar dreams of what television could become as an institution of public service and education. Neither man ever abandoned his vision of such an institution. Neither man, in the hubbub of capitalization, invention, and marketing, had the time or energy to pursue these visionary purposes for television. The search for a balance between public needs and private enterprise remains with us still. Such stories are likely to be echoed in the days and years ahead as the Internet, a child of the public sector and academic and military research, becomes yet a new engine of capitalism and human aspiration.

This chapter includes material used by permission from the author's book, *The Last Lone Inventor: A Tale of Genius, Deceit and the Birth of Television* (HarperCollins)

The Cable Fables:
The Innovation Imperative of
Excess Capacity

HARMEET SAWHNEY

The edges of distance-spanning networks are interesting places where system order meets an unpacified zone of open-ended possibilities. As Bowman observes, "The end of a new railway line at the frontier of settlement is one of the most engaging places in the world. . . . The rails may be extended now or later, may go this way or that, a town will spring up here and not there" (1931, 64). More abstractly, there are three possibilities: system's expansion and the colonization of this zone of open-ended possibilities, a freeze in system's expansion and maintenance of status quo, and unexpected exploitation of open-ended possibilities by new actors.

While instances of the first two possibilities abound, those of the third have been few and far between. The development of rural telephony in the United States is a celebrated case. In the heyday of Bell patent monopoly, 1879–94, the telephone company refused to expand the network beyond urban areas, in spite of persistent demand by farmers, because it deemed the rural areas to be unprofitable. In effect there was a freeze in network expansion with little possibility of a public policy intervention because the telephone had not yet become a basic necessity. The status quo was shattered by farmers who created their own makeshift networks after Bell's patents expired in 1894. The so-called independent companies soon became a major competitive force that forced Bell to invest in rural areas. The ensuing competition fueled network expansion in rural areas.

The birth of cable is a particularly rare example because the new actors—cable entrepreneurs—started exploiting the open-ended possibilities at the edges while the dominant system—television—was still expanding. This chapter examines this process at two levels: one, with an eye on the realities on the ground, the particulars of the circumstances within which cable was born; two, with an eye on the theoretical plane, the insights the cable experience offers into the dynamics of network development in general.

Much has been written about the particular circumstances within which cable was born. While most of this literature is descriptive, there are notable studies that bring considerable conceptual power to the analysis (see especially Parsons 1989). The main contribution of this chapter is that it brings a different conceptual apparatus, developed over a series of studies on large-scale networks such as canals, railroads, highways, telegraph, telephone, and Internet, to the study of cable and in the process develops new insights into the dynamics of network development.

We start by considering the actual circumstances of the birth of cable. Since an extensive literature already exists on cable's history, the discussion presented here is bare bones. It lays out the basic elements of the cable story, from the earliest CATV systems to HBO's move to satellite delivery, which marked the transformation of cable from a local medium to a national one, leaving analysis for later sections. Subsequent sections operate at a higher conceptual plane. In particular we look at the cable story from the following conceptual lenses: system blind spot, excess capacity, and Agre's amplification model.

Cable Story: CATV to HBO

There is some dispute about where and when the first cable system was started (see Phillips 1972; Parsons 1996, Southwick 1998). But that is not important for our purposes. All that we need to note is that the first cable system was developed some time in the late 1940s. What makes the birth of cable in the 1940s remarkable is that it arrived on the scene while TV was still in its infancy. In the past the "feeder" networks, which extend the reach of the established networks, have tended to appear after the older technologies have achieved some maturity, for example, railroads that fed traffic into canals from areas, such as the hills, which the latter could not reach (see Sawhney 1992 for an extended discussion on feeder networks). As we will see, the "early" arrival of cable gave an interesting twist to the relation between the old and the new technologies.

The first TV stations, when the construction of a TV broadcasting system started, were located in major urban centers. Their signals typically traveled fifty to sixty miles. It was at the edges of this range, where the wonder of the day was teasingly "so close yet so far," that cable was born. Rural communities just out of range often found their access to TV blocked by a hill. They, much like rest of America, perhaps more so because of rural isolation, were very keen on accessing cable. These communities also had returning World War II veterans who had acquired technical savvy, including knowledge of coaxial cable technology, while serving in the army. Furthermore, coaxial cable and electronic components were then readily and cheaply available because of the sales of army surpluses. These elements came together to form the early cable systems, which were variations of an archetypal pattern wherein the signal was picked up by an antenna placed on the obstructing hilltop and then carried down to the local community over coaxial cables.

The TV networks were supportive of these early cable systems. Overall their impact was marginal. But still they extended the reach of TV signals and thereby increased the audience size. To most observers, the cable systems were little more than curious activity in the peripheral areas. The FCC[1] and the IRS[2] monitored their development but did not know what to make of them (Southwick 1998). The municipalities loved them. The telephone and other utility companies provided easy access to their poles and rights of way (Davis 1998; Southwick 1998). In effect, as Davis notes, "Early cable had almost no enemies" (1998, 14).

One of the reasons why our forebears were unable to anticipate the future development of feeder technologies, such as railroads displacing the canals, was that they saw them as mere appendages of the established systems. This tendency was accentuated in the case of cable by a peculiar circumstantial factor. Soon after the initial set of TV stations became operational at the end of World War II, a number of complications arose with regard to standards, and the FCC declared a "freeze" from 1948 to 1952 on new TV stations. It wanted to sort out the problems before proceeding further. Within this context, cable appeared to be even less than an appendage—a temporary patch that would go away as the TV broadcasting system's growth proceeded.[3] As Davis observes, in the mid-1950s "it seemed impossible that cable would ever get big; it was only a matter of time before the broadcasters built powerful transmitters in every city and town, and there would no longer be any need for the cable companies to import a signal" (1998, 13). So much so that the TV networks even saw cable as doing the marketing legwork for them by preparing rural audiences for the final arrival of over-the-air broadcasting (Davis 1998).[4]

The general expectation was that once a nationwide television system was in place, cable would be reduced to a niche business that served locales with peculiar problems, such as Manhattan, where over-the-air broadcast signals suffered from static because of spectrum clutter.[5] However, within a year and a half of the lifting of the freeze in 1952, it became clear that the expansion of TV beyond metropolitan areas would be slow because of the economics of setting up and operating transmitters. Later, the advent of color TV broadcasting in 1954 gave cable another boost. The static-free images of cable had a decided quality advantage over over-the-air reception. In effect, there was continued need for cable service (Phillips 1972). When it became clear that the vision of local UHF stations, which were seen as a more cost-effective way of extending TV to rural areas than the VHF stations in urban areas, blanketing the country would not pan out, the realization sank in that "cable would not die on the vine" (Parsons 1989, 21).

Till the mid-1960s cable was a mom-and-pop operation. Then the picture started changing. Big money discovered cable, and the government started getting involved.[6] The continued persistence of cable per se was not problematic. It basically extended the reach of existing TV stations. If cable had stayed within this mold, its status would have been upgraded from a temporary patch to an appendix, and little else would have changed. But that was not to be. The source of all the subsequent chaos in many ways can be traced to a single factor: availability of excess capacity.

The earliest cable systems carried a single channel, and that itself was a marvel. The channel carrying capacity of cable systems increased from one to three, and cable subscribers had a choice—they could view any one of the three major networks. Then the channel capacity of cable increased from three to five to twelve. "Cable technology had outrun the cable operator's ability to make use of it . . . there simply weren't enough signals that could be snatched out of the air and used to fill cable's growing capacity" (Davis 1998, 22). Now the cable operators were faced with a peculiar human dilemma. They simply could not let the excess capacity lie idle—in other words, waste it. They had to do something with it. At first, for the lack of new ideas, they did things that were highly unimaginative. One channel displayed a thermometer and wind gauge, another a wire-service news ticker, another a fishbowl and piped background music (DiStefano 2005).

It was the marriage of coaxial cable with microwave that brought about a revolutionary change. Microwave enabled cable operators to import signals from places other than the nearest town. Now cable systems were no longer simply serving as extensions of the local TV broadcasters. They were instead bringing competition to them.[7] It was an entirely different ball game. The local broadcasters screamed loud. The FCC, concerned that importation of distant signals by cable would undermine local TV franchisees, started imposing restraints on cable's growth, such as the restriction on entering the top one hundred markets.

Hungry for programming to fill their excess capacity, cable operators procured whatever footage they could get their hands on—old films, old programs, promotional films made by businesses and interest groups, freelancers who provided footage of sports and local events (Davis 1998). They would then share this programming with each other by physically transporting films and videotapes from one cable operator to another, or what was known in the industry parlance as "bicycling." Microwave enabled cable operators not only to import distant signals but also to interconnect with nearby cable systems to create regional networks for sharing programming. With the creation of these regional clusters, we saw the beginnings of companies like HBO that sought to provide content to cable operators. They remained regional operations because it was very expensive to go national with programming specifically created for cable. The main reason was that cable systems were geographically scattered.

HBO offered new uncut films, sports events, and original programming. More importantly, it offered a very different viewing environment—the programming was not interrupted by commercials and there were no censorship constraints of over-the-air broadcasting, which meant HBO's programming could include nudity, off-color language, and politically controversial topics. But the channel lost money in the first three years (Balio 1990).[8] HBO was not "successful until it was able to abandon the costly and inefficient microwave and make use of a new transmission system, one that could reach the entire nation with its signal: a satellite" (Davis 1998, 93).

The idea of satellite distribution had been around for quite sometime. The first satellite capable of transmitting television signals—AT&T's Telstar—was launched in 1962. There was much discussion in the 1960s about the potential of using satellites for broadcasting purposes. But the focus was largely on the possibilities of direct-to-home (DTH) broadcasting. The possibility of using satellites in conjunction with cable was at best a marginal thought (Parsons 2003). But it was there. In 1965, Leon Papernow, a cable executive, wrote that in the future "some CATV subscribers will view not only their local and nearby TV stations but additionally will have access to direct reception of New York and Los Angeles programs relayed to the CATV by a synchronous multi-channel space satellite" (1965, 31). But then he went on to reveal the limitations of his imagination by adding: "On an occasional basis, perhaps once weekly, CATV systems will offer to their subscribers, on a nationwide basis, a program especially created for CATV exhibition for which a special charge will be made" (31).

As Parsons (2003) notes, the next conceptual step was developing the understanding that the resulting network could be used for many specialty-programming networks. In 1967 the Carnegie Commission Report on Educational Television proposed interconnection of PBS stations via satellite. In an accompanying paper, J. C. R. Licklider presented multiple scenarios including one in which specialized networks served niche audiences via cable and satellite. He even coined the term *narrowcasting*. Similarly, in 1967, Leland Johnson of Rand Corporation in an address to the American Astronautical Society talked about channels catering to what he called "minority" tastes. A National Academy of Sciences study published in 1969 sketched out an actual plan for implementing the idea (Parsons 2003). So the idea was pretty much in the air.[9] Yet the actual implementation came as a surprise.

After the first satellite demonstration of a live satellite transmission to the 1973 National Cable Television Association convention, the cable operators were impressed with the capabilities of the new technology. But they could not see how it was relevant for their business, which was essentially retransmission of local broadcasts. Furthermore, the cost of a receiving dish, about $100,000, was a sizable amount for a cable operator (Southwick 1998).[10] Even if a cable company was willing to make this investment, it had no guarantee that other operators would follow suit. Thus, even though there was an awareness that satellite could bring about a paradigm shift, the industry seemed stuck in its entrenched ways. The situation was ripe for bold action. Jerry Levin of HBO delivered this bold action.

In 1975 Levin somehow managed to convince Time Inc., HBO's parent company, to lease transponders for six years on SATCOM 1 for 7.5 million even though HBO had been been in the red (Mair 1988). After getting his bosses on onboard, his next concern was getting FCC's approval. He feared that a single objection from TV networks, a rival pay service, the theater owners, or any other player would stall his plans. According to Levin, "I assumed the networks, particularly CBS, would object. All they had to do was object and it would have been held up by a year. Time Inc. would have lost its nerve" (quoted in Southwick 1998, 116). To his surprise, nobody objected even though FCC had notified the industry of HBO's plans and given everybody an opportunity to file objections. He got his approval (Mair 1988).

Levin's challenge was to show how the industry could make money from a satellite-based system. Levin made the first major demonstration on September 30, 1975, when he used a satellite to deliver the Muhammad Ali–Joe Frazier "Thrilla in Manila" fight to paying customers in Vero Beach and Fort Pierce, Florida, and Jackson, Mississippi (Davis 1998).[11] After this demonstration, TelePrompTer Inc. signed on for over eighty systems, and other cable operators followed (Parsons and Frieden 1998). There were the inevitable hiccups in the development of business, especially in the procurement of programming, but the overall growth was rapid (Mair 1988). Advances in earth-station technology and FCC's relaxation in 1976 of its requirements and approval of smaller, less expensive dishes worked in HBO's favor. Within three years of going onto the satellite, HBO was beaming its programming to more than 700 cable systems, serving 2 million subscribers (Balio 1990). HBO first turned a profit in 1977 and thereafter became a cash cow for Time Inc., eventually surpassing even the magazine division (Mair 1988).

Since HBO offered creative freedom that was unimaginable on broadcast TV, it was able to attract top Hollywood talent even when the money was less than that offered by TV networks (Southwick 1998). Grumbles noted: "We were the entertainment industry, and we took what was essentially a retransmission business and transformed it into an entertainment business" (quoted in Southwick 1998, 121).

Until HBO went on the satellite, cable was largely a local phenomenon. The cable systems were scattered across the landscape and "taken together or viewed separately, they did not constitute a television juggernaut, and they still appeared to be part of a self-limiting, temporary phenomenon" (Davis 1998, 50). It was satellite transmission that transformed cable from an appendage of an old system to a system in its own right.

HBO inspired the launch of Christian Broadcasting Channel (CBN) by Pat Robertson, Cable-Satellite Public Affairs Network (C-SPAN) by Brian Lamb with help from John Evans and others, Entertainment and Sports Programming Network (ESPN) by Scott and Bill Rasmussen with the help of Chet Simmons and others, WTBS and Cable Network News (CNN) by Ted Turner, and other new channels. The media landscape was radically changed.

Through the Conceptual Lens

The cable story becomes even more interesting when it is viewed through a conceptual lens. We are able to garner valuable insights into the network development process. We will now use three different conceptual lenses to analyze cable's development.

The case of cable prompts us to think beyond the concepts employed in the literature on the development of large-scale systems—especially reverse salient, momentum, and crisis of control. Hughes (1983) developed the first two concepts and Beniger (1986) the third one.

Hughes borrowed the term *reverse salient* from military historians, who use it to identify a segment of an advancing battle line that has not been able to keep pace with other sections of the front. Hughes believes that this "metaphor is appropriate because an advancing military front exhibits many of the irregularities and unpredictable qualities of an evolving technological system" (1983, 14). In the case of technological systems, the reverse salients arise whenever there is uneven growth between the different components of a system. The resulting imbalance leads to dysfunctional system development. The growth of the entire system is hampered, and there is a need for an innovative solution if the expansion is to proceed. Thus reverse salients induce technological innovations by attracting institutional attention and resources and also independent inventors and entrepreneurs seeking fame and fortune.

Momentum, the second metaphor Hughes employs, deals with the direction and pace of system development. According to Hughes, as the system grows, its span expands beyond technical objects to include the institutions that maintain and operate it, government agencies that regulate it, educational institutions that supply skilled professionals, and other "institutional components" that sustain it. While discussing the development of the polyphase universal electric supply system, Hughes observed, "The systematic interaction of men, ideas, and institutions, both technical and nontechnical, led to the development of a supersystem—a sociotechnical one—with mass movement and direction. An apt metaphor for this movement is 'momentum'" (1983, 140). In other words, as more and more institutions and groups get aligned and invested in the system, it becomes difficult to change the direction of its development.[12]

According to Beniger (1986), crises of control in a complex society energize the development of information technologies. Whenever the complexities of managing a large-scale system outstrip the ability of the existing coordination and control mechanism to manage it, a crisis of control occurs. The resolution of the crisis of control typically depends on a technological or organization innovation that either increases the speed and volume of information processing or reduces the need for information flows. The development of telegraph, which enabled railroads to coordinate fast-moving traffic, and of optical scanners, without which today's supermarkets would be unmanageable, are examples of the former. Interchangeable parts, time zones, and decentralization are examples of the latter. The development and adoption of a new control technology temporarily resolves the problem until the system reaches the next level of complexity. Then there is once again a need for a new round of technological innovation. The process continues in an ever-rising spiral. "Only through the dynamic tension between crisis and control, with each success at control generating still new crises, has the revolution in technology continued into the twentieth century and into the emerging Information Society" (Beniger 1986, 220).

While the three concepts—reverse salient, momentum, and crisis of control—focus on different aspects of the network development process, they are oriented toward the forward movement or the growth of a system. The case of cable, on the other hand, begs the formulation of a nonkinetic concept—*system blind spot*. Often new technologies, as was the case with cable, grow in spaces neglected by the incumbent system.

System blind spots develop where system growth marked by reverse salients, momentum, and crises of control does not proceed. The reasons are more often than not economic—corporations do not venture into areas they deem to be not profitable. System blind spots occur when this perception is wrong. The development of rural telephony in the United States is a classic case. As mentioned earlier, Bell's management refused to invest in rural areas in spite of persistent demand from rural populations because it could not see how rural areas could generate the level of demand necessary to justify the expense of stringing wires across thinly populated expanses. Soon after the Bell patents expired in 1894, farmers took matters into their own hands and developed their own telephone networks, often using barbed wires as transmission lines.

The "independents" became a major competitive threat and by 1900 they controlled 38 percent of all the telephones in operation in the United States (Brock 1981). Bell's blind spot was that it did not realize the nature of rural demand. While population density was low in rural areas, the intensity of usage was much higher. On one level, rural isolation made the use of telephones especially attractive. On another level, rural households, unlike urban households, were not just places of residence but also centers of production—the telephone was used for both personal and business reasons (Fischer 1987).

The system blind spot could also occur for conceptual reasons. The development of radio provides a classic example. When radio was first developed, it was seen as a point-to-point technology—a "wireless" extension of telegraph. Even at the time of the GE-AT&T-Westinghouse agreement,[13] the institutional forces guided by the telegraph analogy were working toward casting radio as a point-to-point technology. In fact broadcasting was not even within the realm of imagination (Brock 1981). It was the stubborn refusal of renegade amateurs to comply with the larger institutional framework that resulted in the identification of broadcasting as a new means of communication. Frank Conrad, in early 1920, started transmitting phonograph music as part of his ongoing experiments over a radio transmitter. His signal was picked up by amateur radio buffs, and their enthusiastic response led Conrad to schedule regular concerts, which set the stage for development of broadcasting. Audiences grew at a phenomenal rate, and broadcasting became a big business. People in the wireless industry could not help but wonder why they did not see something as obvious as the potential for broadcasting. William C. White, a scientist at the General Electric research laboratory, later recalled, "[I was] amazed at our blindness . . . we had everything except the idea" (Barnouw 1966, 73–74).

Thus we see that system blind spots occur not only in physical spaces, such as rural areas, but also in conceptual spaces, such as point-to-multipoint communication or broadcasting. In the case of cable, the system blind spot was temporal. The grand plan was to roll out TV from the metropole to the periphery. But the periphery proved to be impatient.

Metaphorically speaking, it is in these system blind spots that the proverbial barbarians gather. They form a peculiar subculture that generates an unexpected innovation, especially a technological one. The farmers with their grassroots networks demonstrated pent-up latent demand. The radio amateurs, with their very distinctive culture akin to that of today's hackers, developed broadcasting. The cable-entrepreneurs too were a very peculiar breed. While the earliest pioneers were tinkerers of sorts, their successors were fleet-footed businesspersons with an eye on quick returns. Certain provisions in the tax code allowed cable operators to write off the cost of setting up their businesses over a three- to five-year period. This gave cable operators an incentive to sell off their systems at the end of each write-off period and then buy another one. "This legal tax avoidance set the tone for the industry. It favored freewheeling dealmakers over small-town chamber of commerce types, quick-buck financiers and quick-and-dirty technicians over old-school engineers and media visionaries" (DiStefano 2005, 33).

Christensen (1997) observes that the disruptive technologies whose emergence brings down the established market leaders often grow within a subculture. While the established firms tend to ignore these technologies because they underperform mainstream products, they often appeal to fringe groups because of their low cost and simplicity, for example, personal computers and small off-road motorcycles. The upstart companies that develop these technologies refine them within subcultures that do not register on the radar of established firms. Later, when these technologies become the cutting edge, the fringe culture brings them into the mainstream market with a vengeance. A similar phenomenon occurs at the system blind spots. But there is an important contextual difference.

The subcultures Christensen talks about tend to be internally referential. They do what tickles their imagination. In the case of communications networks, the subcultures that gather in the system blind spot tend to be externally referential. The established system dominates their imaginations. Their efforts go toward extending it or tapping into its resources.

Excess Capacity

One of the biggest spurs to innovation seems to be the presence of excess capacity in a communications system. It is a particularly strong stimulant of innovation when its usage is available for free or at a very marginal cost. Consider the following examples.

New Brunswick prospered during the Napoleonic Wars, 1803–15, by exporting timber and shipbuilding. The ships that carried square-hewn timber from New Brunswick had excess capacity on their return journey. They carried back immigrants, and by 1824 the colony's population increased to 75,000 (AAA 1999).

In 1920s the idea of linking WEAF, New York, and other "stand-alone" radio stations owned by AT&T "came about originally almost as an accident" (Hedges 1930, 39). It was triggered by the availability of excess capacity over AT&T's long-distance lines. These facilities were used primarily during the day and considerable capacity was available in the evenings. It occurred to AT&T that it could use this capacity to distribute WEAF programming to its radio stations in other cities. This initiative led to the development of the networking concept in broad-casting (Hedges 1930). In the 1960s the excess capacity on the network Lockheed built for NASA subcontractors led to the creation of Dialog, among the first online global information retrieval systems (Ventresca 1995). In the 1970s the availability of excess capacity in ATMs led to the development of ATM networks. The banks realized that they would reduce their costs and increase their reach by sharing their ATMs with one another. In the 1990s Star TV realized that it could use the unused capacity in its transponder on AsiaSat for broadcasting purposes. As Jaya-kar notes, "It was the lack of demand for Asia Sat's transponders that provided the immediate incentive for the development of a broadcasting service based on the satellite" (1994, 53). We soon had the birth of the phenomenon called Star TV, which has changed the face of broadcast-ing all over Asia.

In the case of cable, Mullen makes an interesting observation:

On the fringes of cities with television, enterprising technological amateurs (many with military training) devised methods for extend-ing broadcasting signals into communities not served by television. These included booster or translation stations, as well as community antenna systems (CATV). While boosters and translators continued quietly as retransmitters of broadcast signals, CATV grew into much more. (2003, 33)

It is indeed interesting to note that boosters and translators stayed as appendages of broadcasting while CATV grew into "much more." While Mullen does not provide an explanation, we know from the preceding analyses that excess capacity on CATV systems made the decisive differ-ence. It led to a series of innovations—local origination, importation of signals, satellite delivery—that made cable what it is today.

Amplification Model

Agre (2002) argues against using technology as the starting point of analysis. For example, researchers who study virtual communities typically start with the Internet. Agre points out that while the Internet can connect anyone to anyone else, the connections that are actually established are rarely random. People connect with others with whom they have something in common. These commonalities may be interest in the same hobbies, a struggle against the same medical condition, or a shared diasporic culture. If we look at any issue that people find important today, we are likely to find a corresponding virtual community on the Internet. But the "communities of practice should not be identified analytically with the technologies that support them" (Agre 2002, 320). The desire to connect should exist a priori. What the Internet has done is create connectivity and reduce the cost of information sharing and thereby provide the material basis for actualizing the preexisting desire to be part of a particular community. In earlier times, geographically dispersed networking was limited to writers, artists, and scientists who were willing to invest the effort required to connect with their compatriots in far-flung places. Today the Internet has drastically reduced the threshold of effort required to create and maintain such networks for topics both serious and frivolous.

Agre uses this and other examples to illustrate his amplification model, which posits that the Internet basically amplifies the social and institutional forces that are already operating in a society before the introduction of a new technology. What makes the process unpredictable is that not all forces are amplified equally. Accordingly, Agre emphasizes, "In analyzing new uses of information technology, the forces are analytically prior to the tools" (2002, 319).

Agre's dictum that "forces are analytically prior to the tools" cautions us against getting fixated on the satellite in our understanding of the development of HBO. In fact, when we trace the genesis of HBO, we see that the impulse for what became HBO has been around for quite some time.

Mullen (1999) shows that HBO was essentially the culmination of the effort over five decades to develop pay TV. She traces the notion of pay TV all the way back to the theater television developed by Hollywood studios in the late 1940s for special-event programming. Just like movies, audience watched special programming in theaters, uninterrupted by commercials. This experiment did not succeed for a variety of reasons, including FCC's refusal to allocate frequencies on a permanent basis. From the late 1940s onward there were experiments with different methods of delivering pay TV. They usually involved over-the-air transmission of scrambled broadcast signals. Various projects experimented with arrangements such as IBM punch cards for program selection and billing, coin boxes for payments on a per program basis, and flat rate pricing. While the focus was on over-the-air delivery of pay TV, cable was also in play from the very beginning, with the first experimental project launched in 1953. As the channel capacity of cable increased, the interest in pay TV increased on the part of both cable and pay TV companies. There were numerous experiments to deliver programming, especially sporting events, over cable. In 1960 TelePrompTer used an intercity closed-circuit network to broadcast a boxing match to thirteen CATV systems it had acquired—an early prototype of the Muhammad Ali–Joe Frazier "Thrilla in Manila" that launched HBO into the major leagues.

For over half a century before the advent of HBO, pay TV interests had been struggling with the development of an economically viable model that would provide an alternative to broadcast TV. But their efforts met with little success. It was the advent of satellite that allowed the development of a national market, and with it, the economics of pay TV became viable. While satellite was a critical technological piece in the development of the overall system, Agre's amplification model reminds us that it basically amplified the impulse for development of pay TV, which has been around for several decades.

Conclusion

Over the years much has been written about the development of cable. This chapter retells the old story but in a new way. Accordingly, it is in the "new way" and not the "old story" that its contributions lie.

The most patent contribution is the conceptual apparatus employed to analyze the development of cable. Instead of the theories typically used to analyze cable's development (e.g., structuration theory, diffusion of innovations, industrial organization), this chapter employs concepts and vocabulary developed out of research on large-scale networks such as canals, railroads, highways, telegraph, telephone, and Internet. This approach sharpens the analytical focus on the evolution of the relationship between cable, new technology, and TV—the old one. The case of cable, in turn, prompts the formulation of the notion of system blind spot and provides a crystallizing case of the role of excess capacity in facilitating innovation. In addition, Agre's amplification model, drawn from the literature on politics and the Internet, is integrated into the framework. Thus there is an element of cross-fertilization between bodies of knowledge that had not been brought together before.

The other element of the "new way" is the analysis of the cable case at dual planes—ground reality and conceptual plane. The new technology studies rarely rise above the descriptive level. The end result is that they have a very short shelf life. When the next new technology arrives, which we can be assured will happen as long as our present civilization lasts, researchers start afresh from more or less the same point and produce another series of descriptive studies. There is a need for a cumulative buildup of theoretical knowledge so that we approach each new technology with an increasingly sophisticated conceptual apparatus. This chapter provides one example of how we can proceed. It also adds, I hope, to the cumulative buildup of theoretical knowledge in a notable way.

NOTES

1. *Television Digest* on January 13, 1951, reported that the "FCC *is not involved*—in fact gave go-ahead—because no radio transmissions are employed. State utility commission has said installations aren't public utilities. So legal barriers are few" (quoted in Phillips 1972, 38).

2. Later the IRS wanted to impose an 8 percent excise tax on subscriber fees. But the U.S. Circuit Court of Appeals ruled that the excise tax was not applicable because cable systems were not even around when Congress passed the law imposing the tax on utilities (Southwick 1998).

3. Looking back in history, one can easily eulogize pioneers. For instance, DiStefano says:

> As long as it was relegated to places like Pennsylvania coal country and Mississippi's Delta country, cable would remain a marginal business. But cable attracted visionaries who thought big almost from the start, and they were soon at work hatching big plans to bring cable to the nation's cities and metro areas where most TV watchers lived. (2005, 44)

But in all fairness, even some cable operators saw cable as a temporary solution. Consider the following July 26, 1949, report in the *Times Herald* (Washington, DC) on Ed Parsons's pioneering network in Astoria, on the outskirts of Seattle:

> The Seattle station okayed the rebroadcasts because it broadened the audience and the Federal Communications told him to go ahead—although doubting it could be done. He did it—and kept the FCC advised.
>
> Parson expects soon to be able to rebroadcast the original signal directly and do away with the cable. He has asked the FCC for approval. (Quoted in Phillips 1972, 16)

4. There was a general concern that some new invention would put cable out of business. As Southwick notes, "There were plenty of candidates to put cable under. As the TV frenzy swept the nation, entrepreneurs, backyard electronics buffs, inventors, crackpots and broadcasters themselves considered a wide array of techniques to extend the broadcast signals. Boosters on broadcast towers and construction of mini broadcast towers (known as satellites) were the two most commonly suggested solutions" (1998, 30). In more conceptual terms, rural connectivity was seen as a reverse salient, a concept explained in a later section of this chapter, which was bound to attract resources and creative talent for the development of an effective solution.

5. There were a few perceptive observers who had a sense that cable would become something bigger than a temporary patch. For instance, *Television Digest* noted in its January 13, 1951, issue: "A sort of 'antidote to the freeze'—limited, to be sure, but possessing intriguing possibilities—is the 'community' receiving antenna" (quoted in Lockman and Sarvey 2005, 3). It went on to say three months later, "Don't kiss off the community antenna idea as a mere flash-in-the-pan novelty—not yet, at any rate" (quoted in Lockman and Sarvey 2005, 3).

6. Among other changes, telephone companies, which started seeing cable as a threat, made it increasingly difficult to access their poles and rights of way (Davis 1998).

7. ABC, in a filing, asked FCC to "provide for coordinated development of free television and cable" (quoted in Southwick 1998, 61). This is a typical ruse of incumbent systems. After they are unable to crush a new system, they seek to locate it within the established framework. For instance, the canal interests in the late nineteenth century lobbied the State of New York to prohibit railroads from carrying freight on lines located near the Erie Canal. Later, the railroads were allowed to carry freight but only if they charged the same toll as the Erie Canal (Ringwalt 1966).

8. It lost $1 million in 1973, $4 million in 1974, and $3 million in 1975 (Mair 1988).

9. In fact in January 1972 Charles Dolan, founder of Sterling Manhattan Cable. which later spawned HBO after acquisition by Time Inc., wrote the famous "Green Memo" to Time's board:

> In the long run, we may think of ourselves as the Macy's of television, shopping everywhere for programs that some public, large or small, will buy. If we are successful in meeting these retail program needs of the region we are attempting to serve we will later use whatever efficient transmission systems become available, from microwave to satellite, to sell television programs worldwide to any public that signals its specific demand to us. (Quoted in Mullen 2003, 107)

10. Initially it was thought that there would be a few dishes and multiple systems connected to them. But technological advances and declining costs changed the equation. It was now simpler to duplicate dishes. In addition, unlike microwave, once the capital costs of the dish had been recovered, there were no ongoing costs (Southwick 1998).

11. Levin's choice of the Muhammed Ali–Joe Frazier fight was an inspired one because the "Thrilla in Manila" had receive much publicity but the TV networks were not in a position to show it because they were not on satellite. By showing it live, HBO was able to create quite a sensation (Mair 1988).

12. This paragraph has been excerpted from Sawhney and Wang 2006.

13. The intense rivalry between AT&T, General Electric, and Westinghouse led to a situation where none of them could commercialize radio because the patents for key components were controlled by different corporations. The resulting impasse was resolved in 1920–21 via a patent-sharing agreement between the three corporations. Each corporation had access to a pool of about 1,200 patents, but their areas of operations were restricted to specific applications. Very broadly, AT&T could use any of these patents for applications related to the public telephone network, while General Electric and Westinghouse could use them for private networks and amateur markets. The interesting thing about this agreement is that it was based on the notion that radio is essentially a point-to-point technology. Therefore no provision whatsoever was made for the emergence of broadcasting. The agreement collapsed once broadcasting became a reality. Each rival claimed that broadcasting fell within the area earmarked for it. The agreement was eventually renegotiated in 1926. As a result of the second agreement, AT&T decided to quit broadcasting in exchange for financial compensation and guarantees safeguarding its monopoly over the public telephone network. On the other hand, General Electric and Westinghouse were allowed to dominate broadcasting (Brock 1981).

REFERENCES

AAA. 1999. *Tour Book: Atlantic Provinces and* Quebec. Heathrow, FL: AAA Publishing.

Agre, Philip E. 2002. "Real-Time Politics: The Internet and the Political Process." *The Information Society* 18 (5): 311–31.

Phillips, Mary A. M. 1972. *CATV: A History of Community Antenna Television*. Evanston, IL: Northwestern University Press.

Balio, Tino. 1990. "Introduction to Part II." In *Hollywood in the Age of Television*, ed. Tino Balio, 259–96. Boston: Unwin Hyman.

Barnouw, Erik. 1966. *A Tower in Babel: A History of Broadcasting in the United States to 1933*. New York: Oxford University Press.

Beniger, James. 1986. *The Control Revolution: Technological and Economic Origins of the Information Society*. Cambridge: Harvard University Press.

Bowman, Isaiah. 1931. *The Pioneer Fringe*. New York: American Geographical Society.

Brock, Gerald W. 1981. *The Telecommunications Industry: The Dynamics of Market Structure*. Cambridge: Harvard University Press.

Christensen, Clayton M. 1997. *The Innovator's Dilemma: When New Technologies Cause Great Firms to Fail*. Boston: Harvard Business School Press.

Davis, L. J. 1998. *Billionaire Shell Game: How Cable Baron John Malone and Assorted Corporate Titans Invented a Future Nobody Wanted*. New York: Doubleday.

DiStefano, Joseph N. 2005. *COMCASTed: How Ralph and Brian Roberts Took Over America's TV, One Deal at a Time*. Philadelphia: Camino Books.

Fischer, Claude S. 1987. "The Revolution in Rural Telephony: 1900–1920." *Journal of Social History* 21 (1): 5–26.

Hedges, William S. 1930. "The Business of Broadcasting." In *Radio and Its Future*, ed. Martin Codel, 38–49. New York: Harper and Brothers.

Hughes, Thomas P. 1983. *Networks of Power: Electrification in Western Society, 1880–1930*. Baltimore: Johns Hopkins University Press.

Jayakar, Krishna P. 1994. "Star over Asia: Governments and Policy Making in the Era of International Satellite Broadcasting." Master's thesis, Department of Telecommunications, Indiana University.

Lockman, Brian, and Don Sarvey. 2005. *Pioneers of Cable Television: The Pennsylvania Founders of an Industry.* Jefferson, NC: McFarland.

Mair, George. 1988. *Inside HBO: The Billion Dollar War between HBO, Hollywood, and the Home Video Revolution.* New York: Dodd, Mead.

Mullen, Megan. 1999. "The Pre-history of Pay Cable Television: An Overview and Analysis." *Historical Journal of Film, Radio, and Television* 19 (1): 39–56.

Mullen, Megan. 2003. *The Rise of Cable Programming in the United States.* Austin: University of Texas Press.

Papernow, L. 1965. "One Man's Opinion." *Television Magazine,* December, 30–31.

Parsons, Patrick R. 1989. "Defining Cable Television: Structuration and Public Policy." *Journal of Communication* 39 (2): 10–26.

Parsons, Patrick R. 1996. "Two Tales of a City: John Walson, Sr., Mahanoy City, and the 'Founding' of Cable TV." *Journal of Broadcasting and Electronic Media* 40 (3): 354–65.

Parsons, Patrick R. 2003. "The Evolution of the Cable-Satellite Distribution System." *Journal of Broadcasting and Electronic Media* 47 (1): 1–17.

Parsons, Patrick R., and Robert M. Frieden. 1998. *The Cable and Satellite Television Industries.* Boston: Allyn and Bacon.

Ringwalt, J. L. 1966. *Development of Transportation Systems in the United States.* Philadelphia: Published by the author, 1888; reprint, New York: Johnson Reprint Corporation.

Sawhney, Harmeet. 1992. "Public Telephone Network: Stages in Infrastructure Development." *Telecommunications Policy* 16:538–52.

Sawhney, Harmeet, and Xiaofei Wang. 2006. "Battle of Systems: Learning from Erstwhile Gas-Electricity and Telegraph-Telephone Battles." *Prometheus* 24 (3): 235–56.

Southwick, Thomas P. 1998. *Distant Signals: How Cable TV Changed the World of Telecommunications.* Overland Park, KS: Primedia Intertec.

Ventresca, Marc. 1995. "Organizational Approaches to Industry Emergence: Institutional and Political Dynamics in Electronic Data Services, 1967–1992." Paper presented at the "Telecommunications Infrastructure and the Information Economy: Interactions between Public Policy and Corporate Strategy" conference, Ann Arbor, Michigan, March.

Some Say the Internet Should Never Have Happened

PAUL N. EDWARDS

Nobody who reads this book will need to be told that the Internet is among the modern wonders of the world, a technological marvel that now underpins much of global commerce, communication, and knowledge. Like all wonders, and precisely because of its pervasive presence in every corner of modern life, the Internet's history lies shrouded in myth. The truth-value of such *founding myths* rarely matters as much as their dramatic and moral qualities, and the Internet is no exception.

Good myths need lonely heroes, visionaries embarked on long and arduous journeys in search of sacred grails, which they win through struggle and ordeal. The Internet's origin myth does not disappoint. Once upon a time, it goes, a tiny cadre of computer scientists at elite universities and think tanks realized that connecting computers into a giant network would bring untold benefits, all the way from sharing machines, files, data, and programs to serving as a new Alexandrian library. They knew it would take decades, but they persevered against all odds. Enduring great resistance, they built the first computer networks and then linked them together into the Internet. Funded by the U.S. Defense Department's Advanced Research Projects Agency (ARPA), and blessed by enlightened project managers who trusted their brilliance, their project survived and progressed only because of their dedication and persistence. Their community thrived on an open, meritocratic philosophy, which they embedded in the Internet's technology. In the 1980s, their hard-won victories faced a final peril, when international standards negotiations threatened to recentralize networking and subject it to government control. In the 1990s, our heroes' generation-long struggle was finally rewarded. The Internet's crown jewel, the World Wide Web, shone forth, bringing a new age of enlightenment in which billions could access the sum of human knowledge. The exponential growth of the Internet and the World Wide Web was unprecedented, unique in human history, world-transforming.

In this story, the Internet should never have happened. The forces arrayed against these lonely heroes seemed invincible. No commercial firm would have invested in internetworking, since it would undermine companies' interests in securing a customer base. Yet in the end, through stealth, persistence, and brilliant ideas, the heroes prevailed at last. According to this myth, without ARPA's long-term vision and massive financial support, computer networking might have been locked into a much more restrictive, centralized form, controlled by byzantine bureaucracies and giant corporations, preventing the flowering of innovation.

Like all good myths, this one has some basis in reality. Brilliant scientists really did spend decades working out Internet protocols and software. Enlightened managers at ARPA really did invest enormous sums and permit researchers to work almost without constraint. Early ARPANET, Internet, and web communities really did enshrine open and meritocratic (if not democratic) principles. Today's descendants of those principles guide the most vital, energetic forms of information technology, especially open-source software (Linux, Firefox), open-access knowledge (Wikipedia), and social networking (MySpace, Facebook). The Internet really has grown explosively, now reaching over a billion people—given a very generous definition of "reach"—and changing the way we live and think.

But all good myths also sacrifice details of reality in the service of exciting plots. There is always more to the story, and the Internet story is no exception.

So I will tell a different version. This tale places the ARPANET and Internet in the wider context of their times: the computing environment and the prevailing beliefs about the economics, the purpose, and the technology of computing and networking. This is not a story of technological determinism, in which one technology begets another as a matter of pure technical logic. Instead, my tale is driven by the conflicting motives of computer users and manufacturers; the incentives (financial, social, etc.) that led to sociotechnical change; visions and principles that differed from those of the ARPANET's designers; and the striking parallels between the Internet and earlier network technologies. Adding missing pieces reveals a surprisingly different picture—perhaps less exciting, but fuller, more complex, and more useful as a model for future socio-technical systems. In my story, the Internet (or something much like it) *had* to happen, sooner or later.

The Internet Origin Myth

Before we go further, let me briefly recap the details of the Internet origin myth for readers who spent the last decade or so asleep or on Mars. Usually it goes something like this. Starting around 1960, J. C. R. Licklider, an MIT psychoacoustician turned computer geek, published seminal papers on "Man-Computer Symbiosis" (1960) and "The Computer as a Communication Device" (1968). Licklider's visionary ideas about a "library of the future" and a "galactic network" of computers (1965) led to his appointment as first head of the Information Processing Techniques Office (IPTO) of the Defense Department's Advanced Research Projects Agency (ARPA, later known as DARPA). At ARPA, Licklider found himself in a unique position to promote these visions, which he passed on to IPTO successors Ivan Sutherland, Robert Taylor, and others. Unlike virtually any other funding agency, ARPA's mandate was to promote research whose payoffs might not arrive for ten to twenty years or more. Operating outside the scientific peer review system and generally under the radar of congressional oversight, the agency created "centers of excellence" at a handful of institutions such as MIT, Stanford, and SRI International, bringing the country's best minds together in a few lavishly funded laboratories (Reed, Van Atta, and Deitchman 1990; Norberg and O'Neill 1996).

Meanwhile, also around 1960, Paul Baran at the RAND Corporation envisioned packet switching in decentralized communication networks to avoid network "decapitation" during a nuclear war (Baran 1964; Reed, Van Atta, and Deitchman 1990). In the mid-1960s, Donald Davies independently developed similar ideas for a civilian network sponsored by the British National Physical Laboratory (Davies et al. 1967). When ARPA initiated a major network project, Larry Roberts, the project's manager, rediscovered Baran's ideas by way of Davies. Bolt, Beranek and Newman (BBN)—Licklider's former employer—won the contract to build a packet-switched ARPANET linking all the ARPA laboratories across the country.

The ARPANET's purpose, in the minds of its designers, was to permit ARPA researchers to share data and programs residing on the computers of other ARPA research centers, with a view to both intellectual productivity and efficient resource use. Today this sounds easy, but at the time, ARPA centers had dozens of different, incompatible computers. No one knew how to link them. To solve this problem, the BBN team developed the Interface Message Processor (IMP)—what we would now call a router. IMPs were small computers whose only job was to encode messages from the host computer into packets for distribution through the network, and to decode incoming packets for the host computer. Leased long-distance telephone lines linked the IMPs. By 1969, the ARPANET linked four ARPA labs. Two years later the network spanned the continent, and by 1973 the forty-node network included satellite links to Hawaii and Norway.

Much of the ARPANET protocol development was carried out by the Network Working Group (NWG), initially made up mainly of graduate students. Fearing they might offend their senior colleagues, they published early protocol proposals under the heading "Request for Comments" (RFC). This approach led to a tradition in which all protocols were published initially as proposals, up for discussion by anyone with the technical knowledge to make an intelligent comment:

> The content of a NWG note may be any thought, suggestion, etc. related to the HOST software or other aspect of the network. Notes are encouraged to be timely rather than polished. Philosophical positions without examples or other specifics, specific suggestions or implementation techniques without introductory or background explication, and explicit questions without any attempted answers are all acceptable. . . . These standards (or lack of them) are stated explicitly for two reasons. First, there is a tendency to view a written statement as ipso facto authoritative, and we hope to promote the exchange and discussion of considerably less than authoritative ideas. Second, there is a natural hesitancy to publish something unpolished, and we hope to ease this inhibition. (Crocker 1969)

As the tradition evolved into the Internet era, RFCs had to be implemented at least twice on different machines before being formally adopted as Internet standards. This procedure made for rapid, robust, and relatively consensual development.

With the ARPANET working, attention quickly turned to how other computer networks might be linked to the ARPANET in an *internetwork*, or network of networks. By the early 1970s, ARPA program manager

Robert Kahn had initiated an internetworking project with a handful of others, among them Vint Cerf. Kahn and Cerf would come to be known as the fathers of the Internet. With many others, they developed and extended the ARPANET's Network Control Program (NCP) into the more powerful Transmission Control Protocol and Internet Protocol (TCP/IP), standards for linking computers across multiple networks. The ARPA internet evolved from 1974 onward, becoming known simply as "the Internet" in the early 1980s. In the mid-1980s, the U.S. National Science Foundation took on a major role when it linked NSF-funded supercomputer centers via high-speed "backbones" using TCP/IP and encouraged academic institutions to join the network.

But the Internet faced fierce challenges from competing approaches. By the mid-1970s other networking concepts were working their way through the tangled, bureaucratic structures of the International Standards Organization (ISO). The ISO's X.25 network standard (1976) and its successor, the Open Systems Interconnection initiative (OSI), were dominated by large, powerful interests such as corporations and government PTTs (post-telephone-telegraph agencies). The X.25 network model assumed that only a handful of operators would provide networking services, and early versions of OSI took X.25 as a basis. Had these other standards been adopted, the Internet might have been still-born and all networking dominated by a few large operators. But the negotiations moved slowly. By the time the OSI standard was released in 1983, thousands of systems had already adopted TCP/IP, and a few manufacturers (such as Sun Microsystems) began building TCP/IP into their equipment. TCP/IP had become so entrenched among grassroots users that instead of destroying TCP/IP, the ISO standard was eventually forced to conform to it (Abbate 1999).

In the Internet origin myth, this was a great victory. Small and simple had won out over big and complex. Open, meritocratic, consensus-based development had defeated closed, proprietary, bureaucratic systems supported by huge, powerful entities. Ingenuity had beaten money. Had the ISO standards been finished sooner, goes this tale, TCP/IP might have been crushed, and the Internet would never have happened.

Early uses of the Internet, such as e-mail and (later) Usenet newsgroups, came to embody a libertarian, meritocratic, free-speech philosophy, widely celebrated by the counterculture as an "electronic frontier" where laws and government were unnecessary (Rheingold 1993; Turner 2006). In 1992 David Clark summed up the Internet engineering community's philosophy in a battle cry: "We reject: kings, presidents, and voting. We believe in: rough consensus and running code" (Russell 2006). Many link the Internet's libertarian culture to its decentralized technical structure, which makes it very difficult to censor or block communication.

This culture-technology link is the principal source of the origin myth's power. It's a strong *technological determinism,* which sees Internet culture as directly and causally linked to such technical characteristics as packet switching and TCP/IP. Had computer networks evolved as more hierarchically organized systems, the wild cyber frontier might have looked more like a cyber subdivision, with cookie-cutter houses and lawn-care rules set up for the profit of a few huge corporations.

Homogeneous Networks and the "Computer Utility"

It's a powerful myth—and as I have said, much of it is actually true. But consider: if ARPA and its network were really the visionary hero of our tale, what about the other networks that needed to be joined to form the ARPA Internet? Where did they come from, and what were they for? How did contemporaries see the future of computing and networks in the early days of ARPANET development? Would the Internet have happened anyway, with or without ARPA?

To understand this crucial piece of context, we need to look back to the 1960s, when the computer industry first came to maturity. In that era, two "laws" of computing competed for the status of common sense. Moore's law, first articulated in 1965, predicted that the number of transistors on a silicon chip would double approximately every twenty-four months. Moore's law still holds today.[1] But in the 1960s—before microprocessors, personal computers, and the Internet—another prediction known as Grosch's law held sway.

Working with some of the earliest computers at Columbia University in the 1940s, Herbert Grosch devised a dictum initially phrased as "economy [increases] only as the square root of the increase in speed—that is, to do a calculation ten times as cheaply you must do it one hundred times as fast" (Grosch 1953, 310). This somewhat puzzling assertion later morphed into the more useful claim that "the performance of a computer varies as the square of its price," or alternatively that "the average cost of computing decreases as the square root of the power of a system" (Ein-Dor 1985). Whatever its formulation, Grosch's law essentially held that computers displayed dramatic economies of scale. Double your spending on a computer system and you could buy four times as much "power." Triple it, and you could get nine times as much power, and so on.

Economists had considerable trouble finding a real-world metric for "computer power," and some writers occasionally wondered whether Grosch's "law" originated in IBM's marketing department (Hobbs 1971). But in its day the principle was very widely accepted. Larger contexts mattered; similar arguments about economies of scale dominated much corporate thinking in the 1950s and 1960s. Analogies to electric power plants, automobile companies, and other examples produced a "bigger is better" mentality that seemed to apply equally to computing. As a result, corporate data-processing departments typically sought both organizational and technological centralization, buying ever-larger, ever-faster computers. Reviewing the literature in 1983, King noted that "until the end of the 1970s . . . articles on computing centralization were nearly unanimous: . . . centralization saves money" (1983, 322).

When time-sharing technology arrived, in the early 1960s, it seemed to vindicate Grosch's law. Time-sharing allowed several people to use the same computer simultaneously. Previously, computers could run only one program at a time ("batch processing"). With time-sharing, the computer could run many programs at once, cycling from one user to the next so quickly that users never knew that someone else was using the same machine—at least in principle. Teletype and, later, CRT terminals, either directly connected or using modems, untethered users from direct proximity to the machine. Time-sharing's proponents sought to end the tyranny of batch processing and its necessary evil, the computer operator who stood between users and the machine. In an age when most computers cost $50,000 or more, time-sharing promised an experience much like today's personal computing: the feeling, at least, that the machine was yours and yours alone. Furthermore, time-sharing maximized the CPU's value; before time-sharing, the CPU spent most of its time idle, waiting for slower input-output devices to do their work.

Time-sharing made a particular path to personal computing seem obvious and inevitable. Because of Grosch's law, a relatively small incremental investment would bring time-shared computing to a much larger number of users. Maybe one day a single giant computer could be shared by everyone. Between 1965 and 1970, every major U.S. manufacturer announced plans to market time-sharing computers.

These arguments convinced many people that computers should be treated like power plants. It made no sense to put an electric generator in every household, when a single giant power plant could do the job for a whole city more reliably and far more cheaply. By analogy, it made no sense for individuals to have their own computers if a single giant computer could do the job for everyone—better, faster, more reliably, and more cheaply. In 1964, in a widely read *Atlantic Monthly* article, MIT professor Martin Greenberger wrote that "an on-line interactive computer service, provided commercially by an *information utility,* may be as commonplace by 2000 A.D. as the telephone is today."

Superficially, this sounds a lot like the World Wide Web. Yet beneath the surface of the computer utility model lay a completely different imagining of networked computing:

> Computation, like electricity and unlike oil, is not stored. Since its production is concurrent with its consumption, production capacity must provide for peak loads, and the cost of equipment per dollar of revenue can soar. The high cost of capital equipment is a major reason why producers of electricity are public utilities instead of unregulated companies. A second reason is the extensive distribution network they require to make their product generally available. This network, once established, is geographically fixed and immovable. Wasteful duplication and proliferation of lines could easily result if there were no public regulation (Greenberger 1964, 65).

In Greenberger's vision, users would interact with the central computer through "consoles" or other dumb terminal equipment, sharing programs, resource libraries, and other information via the central computer. Following the power company analogy, "the distribution network" would be like power lines, a cable system for delivering the centralized resource to the end user. Thus the earliest popular notion of a computer "network" referred to a computer center accessed by remote terminals.

These early systems can all be classified as *homogeneous networks.* Organized in hub-and-spoke fashion around one or a few central nodes (computers), this network model assumed a single type of computer and a single system for communicating among them. And indeed many such systems quickly emerged. The earliest were transaction-processing systems such as the SABRE airline reservation system, which allowed remote clients to access centrally maintained databases and carry out transactions such as making a travel reservation or entering a check into a banking system. In the mid-1960s, computer service bureaus sprang up around the world, renting computer time directly and offering value-added data-processing services. As time-sharing technology matured, some systems allowed users to access the computers directly via remote terminals, adding interactivity to the list of features.

By 1967 some twenty firms, including IBM and General Electric, had established computing service bureaus in dozens of cities. In a preview of the 1990s dot-com bubble, these firms' stocks swelled on the can't-lose promise of the computer utility:

> Dallas-based University Computing Company (UCC) . . . established major computer utilities in New York and Washington. By 1968 it had several computer centers with terminals located in thirty states and a dozen countries. UCC was one of the glamour stocks of the 1960s; during 1967–68 its stock rose from $1.50 to $155. (Campbell-Kelly and Aspray 1996, 218)

By 1969 Tymshare's TYMNET, Control Data's CYBERNET, CompuServe, and numerous other firms had entered this exploding market. TYMNET—in a move that originated with an ARPA-sponsored project—began centralizing its network along exactly the lines envisioned by Greenberger, with the goal of "consolidating its computers into one location and transfer[ring] the computer power from that location to where it was needed" (Beere and Sullivan 1972, 511). In the language of the day, these networks were known as RANs, for remote-access networks.

The computer utilities sought economies not only in scale, but also in homogeneity. Each computer center would operate only one or a few computer models, all made by a single manufacturer, using a standard package of software and a single operating system. This aspect of the computing environment of the 1960s can hardly be overemphasized: in those days, making computers from different manufacturers work together required major investments of time, money, and training, so much that in practice most computer users did not even attempt it.

Unfortunately for most of the computer service bureaus, the technology of time-sharing never worked in quite the way that Grosch's law implied. IBM's initial foray, the System 360/67 with TSS (Time-Sharing System), sold sixty-six exemplars by 1971, but endured innumerable software problems, leading to losses of $49 million on the 360/67 line (O'Neill 1995, 53). Similar difficulties marred all other early time-sharing projects. Though MIT's famous MULTICS project of the mid-1960s envisioned 1,000 remote terminals and up to 300 concurrent users, writing software for managing so much simultaneous activity proved far more difficult than anticipated. Constant crashes and reboots led to wails of agony from frustrated users. In the end, no matter how big and powerful the computer, time-sharing simply did not scale beyond a limit of around fifty users. Ultimately, as Campbell-Kelly and Aspray note, Grosch's law failed because Moore's law applied. The price of computer power dropped like a stone, rapidly wiping out the economic rationale behind the time-sharing service model. UCC's stock crashed in 1971 (Campbell-Kelly and Aspray 1996, 218).

The fantasy of a single giant computer serving the entire country never materialized. Yet the computer utility model failed to die. Many of the 1960s network services, including TYMNET and CYBERNET, survived for decades, albeit in a remodeled form. The information utility model eventually morphed into a consumer product, under corporate giants such as CompuServe, Prodigy, and America Online. Grosch's law, too, experienced a long afterlife. In the 1970s and beyond, the inherent logic of the homogeneous, centralized network remained obvious, beyond dispute for many.

> Users with nothing more than a terminal and access to the telephone may select from a large number of potential suppliers [of basic computing services]. Since geography is no longer of major concern . . . a sufficiently large complex, wherever located, may offer basic services to users anywhere in the country at prices lower than they can obtain locally. (Cotton 1975)

Computer manufacturers proceeded to develop proprietary homogeneous networking systems, among them IBM's SNA (System Network Architecture) and Digital Equipment Corporation's DECNET. These homogeneous networks could be decentralized, but they remained linked to a single manufacturer's proprietary standards and could not be connected to those of others. Well into the 1980s, the vast majority of computer networks remained homogeneous and proprietary. As we will see, not only did this not represent a failing on their part, it was a principal reason for the Internet's success in the 1990s.

The ARPANET, Packet Switching, and Heterogeneous Computing

The ARPANET project faced two basic problems: how to get the widely dispersed labs to communicate efficiently over long distances, and how to get the labs' computers to work together. These may sound like two versions of the same difficulty, but in fact they are completely different issues.

In the standard origin story, communication between the ARPA labs gets most of the attention. Both cost and reliability mattered. Connecting every lab directly to every other one using expensive leased phone lines would drive costs upward exponentially. If direct connections were required, this would also make the network less reliable, with each new connection a potential point of failure.

Famously, the ARPANET solved both cost and reliability problems through a technique known as packet switching. In this system, each lab was directly connected to a few others, but not to all. Outgoing messages were divided into "packets," small units of data. The IMPs (Interface Message Processors) assigned each packet a message header containing its destination and its place in the bitstream of the overall message. IMPs then "routed" each packet individually, to another IMP closer to the destination. Using the address in message header, the receiving IMP would forward the packet onward until it reached its final destination. There, the receiving IMP would reassemble the bitstream into its original order to make up the entire message. The IMPs could sense when a connecting circuit was overloaded and use another one instead; every packet might conceivably take a different route. In principle, at least, no longer did each computer have to be directly connected to every other one. Nor would a down IMP delay an entire message; instead, the routers would simply choose another of the many possible paths through the network. Less busy circuits could be used more efficiently. In practice the IMP system proved far less reliable than anticipated (Abbate 1999). In the long run, though, packet switching made completely decentralized communication networks nearly as efficient as, and far more reliable than, alternative hub-and-spoke or hierarchical network designs.

Packet switching also advanced a key military ambition: building a command-and-control network that could survive a nuclear war. Since destroying even a large number of nodes would not prevent packets from reaching their destinations, a packet-switched network could endure a lot of damage before it would fail, as Baran's early RAND studies had shown. Depending on which version of the Internet story you consult, you will read either that designing survivable command and control was the ARPANET's main goal, or that this motive had absolutely nothing to do with it. In my view, *both* stories are true. ARPANET packet switching ideas came in part from Baran's work, communicated to Larry Roberts via Donald Davies (though Roberts himself credited Leonard Kleinrock with the earliest and most influential concepts [Roberts 2004; Kleinrock 1961, 1964; Abbate 1999]). In interviews, Licklider repeatedly noted that solving military command-control problems was IPTO's original purpose. He himself wrote about these problems in a number of places, including his seminal "Man-Computer Symbiosis" (Lee and Rosin 1992; Licklider 1960, 1964, 1988).

Still, once the project really got rolling, four years after Licklider left ARPA in 1964, the data- and program-sharing, community-building, and efficiency-improving goals drove ARPANET's designers, who mostly cared little about military applications. Nor did the agency ask those designers to think about military potential, at least at first. Yet as I have argued elsewhere, in the Cold War climate many military goals were accomplished not by directly ordering researchers to work on something, but simply by offering massive funding for research in uncharted areas of potential military interest (Edwards 1996).

By the early 1970s ARPA directors *were* starting to demand military justifications for ARPA research. Unclassified military computers were connected to the ARPANET early on, and by 1975 ARPA had handed over ARPANET management to the Defense Communication Agency (DCA). In the early 1980s, nervous about potential unauthorized access and hacking, the DCA physically split off the ARPANET's military segment to form a separate network, MILNET. In the event, nuclear command and control networks never physically linked to either ARPANET or MILNET.

This half of the ARPANET problem—how to build a large, geographically dispersed, fast, reliable network—represented what historians of technology call a *reverse salient:* a major problem, widely recognized, that held back an advancing technological system and drew enormous attention from firms, scientists, and engineers as a result (Hughes 1983, 1987). By 1968 numerous corporate research laboratories and academic research groups were working on it (many with ARPA support), and solutions very similar to the ARPANET were emerging. Packet switching itself had already been tested in Davies' small UK pilot project.

Furthermore, the IMP solution exactly mirrored the dominant network concept of its day. Since the IMPs were identical minicomputers, the "network" part of the ARPANET (in which only the IMPs were directly connected) was a homogeneous one very much like its numerous corporate cousins. TYMNET, for example, also used small minicomputers to link remote sites with its mainframes. The same can be said for the

ARPANET's goals: sharing data and programs was also the principal idea behind the commercial networks. (Alex McKenzie, an early manager of the ARPANET's Network Control Center, saw the project precisely as a "computer utility" [Abbate 1999, 65].) Though often described as revolutionary, in these respects the ARPANET, while important, did not constitute a major innovation.

Instead, the ARPANET's most significant technical achievements occurred around the other half of the problem: making the labs' incompatible computers speak to each other. By the mid-1960s the agency—having left purchasing decisions to the labs—found ARPA research centers using dozens of incompatible computers. This was a deeply hard problem; as anyone who has wrestled with connecting Macs, Windows, Linux, and Unix machines knows, it remains hard even today. Some directly involved in the ARPANET project failed to see the point of even trying:

> We could certainly build it, but I couldn't imagine why anyone would want such a thing. . . . "Resource sharing" . . . seemed difficult to believe in, given the diversity of machines, interests, and capabilities at the various [ARPA] sites. Although it seemed clear that with suitable effort we could interconnect the machines so that information could flow between them, the amount of work that would then be required to turn that basic capacity into features useful to individuals at remote sites seemed overwhelming—as, indeed, it proved to be. (Ornstein 2002, 165–66)

But ARPA had the money to pay for it, and (crucially) the ability to force its labs to try the experiment.

The ARPANET's "host-to-host" protocols required separate, unique implementation on each host computer, a long, painful effort. Initial host-to-host protocols concentrated simply on "direct use," such as allowing remote users to log in and run programs on the host computers as if using a terminal (the TELNET protocol). Direct-use protocols required that the remote user know the language and conventions of the host computer. Since few users had mastered more than one or two different machines and operating systems, by itself this remote login capability did little to improve the situation.

By 1971 the first protocol for "indirect use" had emerged: file transfer protocol (FTP), which permitted a remote user to download a file from the remote machine, or to upload one (Bhushan 1971). FTP was a simple, modest initial step toward cross-platform communication (as we would call different computer/operating systems today). Depending on what it contained, the user still had to work out how to decode the file and potentially convert it into a format usable on his or her own machine. A few standards already existed, such as those defining text files (the ASCII character set), so plain text could be sent from computer to computer with relative ease. As a result, FTP became the basis of ARPANET e-mail (which simply transmits a text file from one computer to another). As many have pointed out, this very simple innovation proved a key to the ARPANET's growth. Within a year, e-mail made up half the traffic on the ARPANET. Further, much of the e-mail had nothing to do with sharing data and programs; it was social and informal. No one had planned for this use of the system, which directly challenged the ARPA managers' resource-sharing model.

Popular accounts make much of e-mail's surprise emergence, as another supposedly revolutionary feature of the network. Yet e-mail long predated the ARPANET, existing under other names in time-sharing systems from at least 1965 (at MIT). And while it is true that the explosion of e-mail traffic made the ARPANET into the phenomenon it became, similar developments have occurred in all other communication technologies. Tom Standage's *The Victorian Internet* showed how telegraph operators—who could communicate with each other over the international telegraph network at will—developed a remarkably similar culture of informal communication (1998). And the same thing happened again with early radio, and yet again with telephone chat (Fischer 1988, 1992). In all of these cases, *users rapidly co-opted media initially developed for formal, official, or institutional purposes,* turning them instead toward informal social communication.

A similar phenomenon occurred again in 1979, when users adapted another file transfer program, uucp (Unix to Unix copy), to create Usenet newsgroups. Usenet depended on the Unix operating system, then becoming popular in academia but not yet a mainstay of business or government computing (Hauben and Hauben 1997). Early newsgroups primarily treated technical topics, but they soon expanded to included discussions of virtually anything, from *Star Trek* to sex. Like e-mail, Usenet rapidly became a dominant feature of the evolving global computer network.

As a result, Usenet has been absorbed into the Internet myth, often as Exhibit A in the argument for a special Internet culture. Yet for a number of years Usenet had virtually nothing to do with either the ARPANET or the Internet. As late as 1982, only a handful of Usenet hosts were even linked to the ARPANET:

> Can anybody tell me how to send mail from this uucp node (cwruecmp) to a user at an ARPANET node (specifically, HI-Multics) and back? I have tried every path I know, and they all get returned from Network:C70. Help! (Bibbero 1982; see McGeady 1981)

Indeed, the Usenet community experienced the ARPANET not as an open, meritocratic space, but as an elite system available only to a chosen few (as in fact it was [Hauben 1996, chap. 9]).

By the early 1980s, computer networking had already exploded on many fronts, but very few of them connected to the ARPANET or used the TCP/IP protocols (adopted as the ARPANET standard in 1982). With personal computing emerging as a major force, e-mail, listservs (mailing lists), and bulletin board systems had sprung up on many scales, from local operators providing homegrown dial-up connections in small towns to gigantic national firms. France deployed its nation-wide Minitel network in 1981; within a couple of years, the *messageries roses* (semipornographic chat and dating services, much like bulletin boards) became a colossal business (De Lacy 1989). CompuServe had built its own, nationwide packet-switched network in the 1970s, providing e-mail and bulletin board services to both consumers and corporate clients (including Visa International, for which its network handled millions of credit card transactions each day). BITNET, an academic network founded in 1981, initially used IBM networking software: "By the end of the 1980s [BITNET] connected about 450 universities and research institutions and 3000 computers throughout North America and Europe. By the early 1990s, BITNET was the most widely used research communications network in the world for e-mail, mailing lists, file transfer, and real-time messaging," including listservs similar to the Usenet newsgroups (Stewart 2000). All of these and numerous other computer networks deployed a wide variety of networking schemes, including the much-maligned X.25 and proprietary schemes. Furthermore, some, such as BITNET, created their own protocols for linking to other networks—ignoring TCP/IP, but forming internetworks of their own. Although censorship did occur to varying degrees, in virtually all of these systems a culture of freewheeling, unconstrained online discussion emerged that had absolutely nothing to do with the Internet. The most celebrated of these, the Whole Earth 'Lectronic Link

(WELL) bulletin board system, was founded in 1985. If in these early years BITNET had continued to use IBM proprietary software rather than switch over to TCP/IP after just two years, would the now *path dependent* QWERTY inevitability of TCP/IP and its celebrated culture have prevailed?

In 1984, after more than ten years of development, the Internet counted only about 1,000 hosts. That was the year William Gibson coined the term *cyberspace* in his novel *Neuromancer*. If the Internet inspired him, it shouldn't have, because only after that did really serious Internet growth begin, reaching 10,000 hosts by 1987; 100,000 by 1989; and 1,000,000 hosts by 1991. The reason for this explosion, then, was simple: when other networks "joined" the Internet through TCP/IP links, each one added hundreds or thousands of hosts. By the mid-1980s, Unix had become a de facto standard in academic computing and high-end workstations (e.g., Sun Microsystems); since it provided built-in IP support, Unix networks could easily join the Internet. TCP/IP made it easy, but the thing that made the Internet explode was—other networks.

Conclusion: From Systems to Networks to Webs

Far from being unique, the Internet story has striking analogues throughout the history of technology. The problem it represents has occurred over and over again in the history of network technologies. In the nineteenth century, differing track gauges, car linkages, and other mechanical features of early railroads prevented one company from using another's track or rolling stock. Only after standards were agreed on (or forced) did railroad transport become a true national network in which multiple railroad companies could use each other's tracks and rolling stock. Similarly, early electric power networks used different voltages—dozens of them—as well as both alternating current (AC) and direct current (DC). Yet eventually these differences were settled and the many individual networks linked into gigantic national and international power grids. Rail, highway, and shipping networks formed separately according to their own dynamics. Yet the ISO standard container—along with railroad cars, trucks, ships, and ports all adapted to fit it—now links these networks, so that a container can travel from one to the next in a virtually seamless process much like packet switching (Egyedi 2001). Examples from telephone, telegraph, television, and many other technical systems can be multiplied ad infinitum.

All of these stories follow a similar pattern. They begin with proprietary, competing, incompatible systems. Then someone creates a *gateway*
that allows these systems to interoperate, as networks. Finally, incompatible networks form internetworks or webs. This process is driven not by
technology itself, but rather by the demands of users, who frequently
lead the process through direct innovation (technical, social, political)
of their own.

Gateways—converters or frameworks that connect incompatible systems—are the key to the transition from systems to networks to webs.
For example, in the late nineteenth century the AC/DC power converter
formed a gateway between AC- and DC-based electric power networks,
enabling competing utilities to work together or merge (David and
Bunn 1988). Devices like the AC/DC converter, however, are neither
the only nor necessarily the most important form of gateway: standards
(such as track gauge or the ISO container), rules/laws (such as the NSF
prohibition on commercial use of the Internet, lifted in 1991), institutions (money, the stock market), languages (pidgins, lingua francas),
and virtually anything else can serve the gateway function, depending on
the circumstances (Edwards et al. 2007).

The history of computing follows this pattern precisely. Initially, computers were little more than stand-alone calculators. Within a few years,
people started trying to connect them; the result was networks. But just
as no system can provide every function a user might need, no network
could provide all of the connectivity a user might desire. Linking the
networks into internetworks was not a stroke of genius, but a straightforward, entirely logical step. This story *seems* unique mainly because people
forget too easily.

Yet it is also true that this case of the system-to-network-to-web transition represented an extremely difficult case. Computers gain their awesome power from awesome complexity; linking heterogeneous computers, and then linking heterogeneous networks, were exceptional feats of
engineering, rightly celebrated.

The end of my story, then, is this. It's all true: the Internet really is a
revolution, the product of a generation-long effort by thousands of brilliant and dedicated people. It should never have happened. Yet despite
its difficulty, it was completely and utterly inevitable. Both the facts of the
case and the example of the past belie the notion that government PTTs
or big commercial networks might have dominated networking forever.

I see two reasons why this had to be true. First, more than in almost
any other network technology, computing's designers are also its heavi-

est users. This fact is arguably responsible for many computer usability problems (Landauer 1995), but it has also produced a virtuous cycle in which designers keep finding new ways to improve how computers work (Castells 2001). The second reason is that Moore's law (with a lot of help from ingenious engineers) has created a world chock full of ever-smaller, ever-cheaper computers. Computers are language machines. So are people. Our most human feature—our need to communicate, about anything and everything, all the time—would eventually have produced the "galactic network" on whose doorstep we now stand.

NOTE

1. Moore actually revised his prediction a number of times after the original 1965 article (Moore 1965). The historical course of chip development has varied, sometimes widely, from the smooth curve usually depicted in discussions of the "law." Nonetheless, taken as a heuristic rather than a precise constant, it has proven remarkably accurate for more than fifty years (Mollick 2006).

REFERENCES

Abbate, Janet. 1999. *Inventing the Internet*. Cambridge: MIT Press.
Baran, Paul. 1964. *On Distributed Communications*. RAND Memorandum Series. Santa Monica, CA: RAND Corporation.
Beere, Max P., and Neil C. Sullivan. 1972. "TYMNET—a Serendipitous Evolution." *IEEE Transactions on Communications* 20 (3, pt. 2): 511–15.
Bhushan, Abhay. 1971. "A File Transfer Protocol." Network Working Group, RFC-114.
Bibbero, I. 1982. arpa-uucp mail. Republished in Usenet Oldnews Archive: Compilation. Retrieved April 5, 2009, from http://quux.org:70/Archives/usenet-a-news/NET.arpa-uucp/82.04.08_cwruecmp.65_net.arpa-uucp.txt.
Campbell-Kelly, Martin, and William Aspray. 1996. *Computer: A History of the Information Machine*. New York: Basic Books.
Castells, Manuel. 2001. *The Internet Galaxy: Reflections on the Internet, Business, and Society*. New York: Oxford University Press.
Cotton, I. W. 1975. "Microeconomics and the Market for Computer Services." *ACM Computing Surveys (CSUR)* 7 (2): 95–111.
Crocker, Steve. 1969. Documentation Conventions. Network Working Group, RFC-3.
David, Paul A., and Julie Ann Bunn. 1988. "The Economics of Gateway Technologies and Network Evolution: Lessons from Electricity Supply History." *Information Economics and Policy* 3:165–202.
Davies, D. W., K. A. Bartlett, R. A. Scantlebury, and P. T. Wilkinson. 1967. "A Digital Communication Network for Computers Giving Rapid Response at Remote Terminals." *Proceedings of the First ACM Symposium on Operating System Principles* 2.1–2.17.

De Lacy, Justine. 1989. "The Sexy Computer." In *Computers in the Human Context*, ed. Tom Forester, 228–36. Cambridge: MIT Press.

Edwards, Paul N. 1996. *The Closed World: Computers and the Politics of Discourse in Cold War America*. Cambridge: MIT Press.

Edwards, Paul N., Steven J. Jackson, Geoffrey C. Bowker, and Cory P. Knobel. 2007. *Understanding Infrastructure: Dynamics, Tensions, and Design*. Ann Arbor: Deep Blue.

Egyedi, Tineke. 2001. "Infrastructure Flexibility Created by Standardized Gateways: The Cases of XML and the ISO Container." *Knowledge, Technology and Policy* 14 (3): 41–54.

Ein-Dor, P. 1985. "Grosch's Law Re-revisited: CPU Power and the Cost of Computation." *Communications of the ACM* 28 (2): 142–51.

Fischer, Claude S. 1988. "'Touch Someone': The Telephone Industry Discovers Sociability." *Technology and Culture* 29 (1): 32–61.

Fischer, Claude S. 1992. *America Calling: A Social History of the Telephone to 1940*. Berkeley and Los Angeles: University of California Press.

Greenberger, Martin. 1964. "The Computers of Tomorrow." *Atlantic Monthly* 213 (5): 63–67.

Grosch, H. A. 1953. "High Speed Arithmetic: The Digital Computer as a Research Tool." *Journal of the Optical Society of America* 43 (4): 306–10.

Hauben, Michael, and Ronda Hauben. 1997. *Netizens: On the History and Impact of Usenet and the Internet*. Los Alamitos, CA: IEEE Computer Society Press.

Hauben, Ronda. 1996. *The Netizens' Netbook*. http://www.columbia.edu/~hauben/netbook/.

Hobbs, L. C. 1971. "The Rationale for Smart Terminals." *Computer*, November–December, 33–35.

Hughes, Thomas P. 1983. *Networks of Power: Electrification in Western Society, 1880–1930*. Baltimore: Johns Hopkins University Press.

Hughes, Thomas P. 1987. "The Evolution of Large Technological Systems." In *The Social Construction of Technological Systems*, ed. Wiebe Bijker, Thomas P. Hughes, and Trevor Pinch, 51–82. Cambridge: MIT Press.

King, J. L. 1983. "Centralized versus Decentralized Computing: Organizational Considerations and Management Options." *ACM Computing Surveys (CSUR)* 15 (4): 319–49.

Kleinrock, L. 1961. "Information Flow in Large Communication Nets." *RLE Quarterly Progress Report*, July.

Kleinrock, Leonard. 1964. *Communication Nets: Stochastic Message Flow and Delay*. New York: McGraw-Hill.

Landauer, Thomas K. 1995. *The Trouble with Computers: Usefulness, Usability, and Productivity*. Cambridge: MIT Press.

Lee, John A. N., and Robert Rosin. 1992. "The Project MAC Interviews." *IEEE Annals of the History of Computing* 14 (2): 14–35.

Licklider, J. C. R. 1960. "Man-Computer Symbiosis." *IRE Transactions on Human Factors in Electronics* HFE-1 (1): 4–10.

Licklider, J. C. R. 1964. "Artificial Intelligence, Military Intelligence, and Command and Control." In *Military Information Systems: The Design of Computer-Aided Systems for Command*, ed. Edward Bennett, James Degan, and Jospeh Spiegel, 119–33. New York: Frederick Praeger.

Licklider, J. C. R. 1965. *Libraries of the Future*. Cambridge: MIT Press.

Licklider, J. C. R. 1988. "The Early Years: Founding IPTO." In *Expert Systems and Artificial Intelligence,* ed. Thomas C. Bartee, 219–27. Indianapolis: Howard W. Sams.

Licklider, J. C. R., and R. W. Taylor. 1968. "The Computer as a Communication Device." *Science and Technology* 76 (2): 1–3.

McGeady, S. 1981. Usenet Network Map. Republished in Usenet Oldnews Archive: Compilation. Available from quux.org:70/Archives/usenet-a-news/NET.general/82.01.06_wivax.1043_net.general.txt.

Mollick, E. 2006. "Establishing Moore's Law." *IEEE Annals of the History of Computing* 28 (3): 62–75.

Moore, Gordon E. 1965. "Cramming More Components on Integrated Circuits." *Electronics* 38 (8): 114–17.

Norberg, Arthur L., and Judy E. O'Neill. 1996. *Transforming Computer Technology: Information Processing for the Pentagon, 1962–1986.* Baltimore: Johns Hopkins University Press.

O'Neill, Judy E. 1995. "'Prestige Luster' and 'Snow-Balling Effects': IBM's Development of Computer Time-Sharing." *IEEE Annals of the History of Computing* 17 (2): 51.

Ornstein, Severo M. 2002. *Computing in the Middle Ages: A View from the Trenches, 1955–1983.* 1st Books Library.

Reed, Sidney G., Richard H. Van Atta, and Seymour J. Deitchman. 1990. *DARPA Technical Accomplishments: An Historical Review of Selected DARPA Projects.* Alexandria, VA: Institute for Defense Analyses.

Rheingold, Howard. 1993. *The Virtual Community: Homesteading on the Electronic Frontier.* Reading, MA: Addison-Wesley.

Roberts, Lawrence. 2004. Internet Chronology, 1960–2001. Available from www.packet.cc/internet.html.

Russell, A. L. 2006. "'Rough Consensus and Running Code' and the Internet-OSI Standards War." *IEEE Annals of the History of Computing* 28 (3): 48–61.

Standage, Tom. 1998. *The Victorian Internet: The Remarkable Story of the Telegraph and the Nineteenth Century's On-Line Pioneers.* New York: Walker and Company.

Stewart, Bill. 2000. Bitnet History. Retrieved from www.livinginternet.com/u/ui_bitnet.htm.

Turner, Fred. 2006. *From Counterculture to Cyberculture: Stewart Brand, the Whole Earth Network, and the Rise of Digital Utopianism.* Chicago: University of Chicago Press.

Privacy and Security Policy in the Digital Age

AMITAI ETZIONI

This may be in sharp contrast with the conventional wisdom, but I have come to conclude that privacy is better protected now by technical means than it ever has been in human history. How could this be so?

If you think about how messages have been traditionally sent by messenger, by carrier pigeon, by phone or fax—all before encryption—they were easily intercepted. These messages could be read by a casual observer, a postmaster and, of course, the police. Strong encryption, however, typically used in day-to-day communication, prevents routine violation of privacy. The capacity of strong encryption technologies to protect communication represents a significant factor of change—increasing the individual's power to protect privacy by a factor of a thousand, perhaps a million. This same principle applies as well to databases. Take health records, for example, databases often full of intimate details. Until rather recently, most patient medical records were kept on paper in file folders protected only by the lock on the file room door—a level of security easily overcome with a little effort. Now with the transfer to digital records, when encryption is engaged and the data is protected by access audit trails, the information is much more secure. The electronic audit trail provides an important level of security by identifying who entered the data as well as who accessed it and when it was accessed. It is not a matter of *technological determinism,* of course; it represents a technical affordance. In order to take advantage of the protective shield of encryption, one has to take the initiative to encrypt one's communication, whether routine or otherwise.

In the wake of 9/11, however, some of this new potential for privacy has been diluted. The reasons for this are complex and require us to carefully examine the trade-offs between privacy, clearly an important and fundamental right, and other important values and rights. I have argued elsewhere that the implicit assumption that personal privacy trumps all other claims needs to be carefully examined. It may require a carefully crafted balance among core values. Perhaps it is best to understand this as a dynamic process akin to an arms race between technologies. Every year new technical means for invading privacy are invented as are new countermeasures. Government agencies such as the National Security Agency may become more intrusive, but private citizens have new and sophisticated security techniques available to them as well—it's a tug of war. The war has not been won or lost by either side; it is ongoing and that is the focus of this chapter. I will review the technical developments related to personal privacy in several technical domains—three that enhance personal privacy (I refer to them as liberalizing technologies): cellular phones, Internet communications, and strong encryption; and two developments that enhance surveillance (I label them public protective): technologies for intercepting digital communication, and technologies for intercepting actual computer keystrokes.

I argue that both individual rights and public safety must be protected. Given that on many occasions advancing one requires some curtailment of the other, the key question is what the proper balance between these two cardinal values should be. The concept of balance is found in the Fourth Amendment. It refers to the right not to be subjected to unreasonable search and seizure. Thus, it recognizes a category of searches that are fully compatible with the Constitution—those that are reasonable. Historically, courts have found searches to be reasonable when they serve a compelling public interest, such as public safety or public health.

The counterclaims of advocates on both sides are best understood within a historical context. Societies tend to lean excessively toward the public interest or toward liberty. Corrections to such imbalances then tend to lead to overcorrections. For example, following the civil rights abuses that occurred during the years J. Edgar Hoover was the director of the FBI, the attorney general imposed severe limitations on the agency in the 1970s. These limitations excessively curbed the agency's work in the following decades. The public safety measures enacted after September 11 removed many of these restrictions and granted law enforcement agencies and the military new powers. These changes arguably tilted excessively in the other direction. This overcorrection was soon followed by an attempt to correct it (for example, by limiting the conditions under which military tribunals can be used and spelling out procedures not included in their preliminary authorization). Historical conditions also change the point at which we find a proper balance. The 2001 assault on America and the threat of additional attacks have brought about such a change. This chapter argues that we should strive to achieve a balance by focusing on accountability.

Liberalizing Technologies

In 1980, communication surveillance could be carried out easily by attaching simple devices to a suspect's landline telephone. In the following decades, millions of people acquired several alternative modes of convenient, instantaneous communication, most significantly cellular telephones and e-mail. According to CTIA Wireless estimates, by 2007 there were over 250 million cellular phone subscribers in the United States, a penetration of about 83 percent. E-mail and Internet usage are similarly pervasive.[1]

By 2007 Nielsen//Net Rating estimates, 216 million people in the United States were online, representing a penetration of about 72 percent of the population.[2] These technological developments greatly limited the ability of public authorities to conduct communications surveillance using traditional methods.

Attempts were made to apply the old laws to new technologies, but the old laws did not fit the new technologies well. The law governing full intercepts, contained in Title III of the Omnibus Crime Control and Safe Streets Act of 1969, originally required that court orders for intercepts specify the location of the communications device to be tapped and establish probable cause that evidence of criminal conduct could be collected by tapping that particular device. Hence, under this law, if a suspect shifted from one phone to another or used multiple phones, the government could not legally tap phones other than the one originally specified without obtaining a separate court order for each. Once criminals were able to obtain and dispose of multiple cellular phones like "used tissues," investigations were greatly hindered by the lengthy process of obtaining numerous full intercept authorizations from the courts.[3]

The rise of Internet-based communications further limited the ability of public authorities to conduct communications surveillance under the old laws. Title III did not originally mention electronic communications. Similarly, the language of the Electronic Communications Privacy Act of 1986 (ECPA) that governed pen/trap orders (recording the telephone numbers of the caller and called party but not the content of the call) was not clearly applicable to e-mail. To determine how to deal with this new technology, courts often attempted to draw analogies between e-mail and older forms of communication. Because electronic communication used to travel largely over phone lines, courts extended laws governing intercepts or traces for telephones to electronic messages as well. However, reliance by the police on such interpretations was risky because there was a possibility that a court would rule that e-mail did not fall under a pen/trap order.

Extending laws that were written with telephones in mind to e-mail was an imperfect solution because e-mail messages differ from phone conversations in important ways. Unlike phone conversations, e-mails do not travel in discrete units that can be plucked out. Each e-mail is broken up into digital packets, and the packets are mixed together with those of other users. This makes it difficult to intercept individual e-mails. Law enforcement agents attempting to intercept or trace the e-mail of just one user may violate the privacy of other users.

The decentralized nature of the Internet created additional complications in carrying out wiretap orders. When the old legislation was enacted, a unified phone network made it easy to identify the source of a call. E-mail, by contrast, may pass through multiple Internet service providers (ISPs) in different locations throughout the nation on its way from sender to recipient. As a result, public authorities would have to compel information from a chain of service providers. Thus, until recently, if a message went through four providers, four court orders in four different jurisdictions would be needed to find out the origin of that message.[4]

Similarly, agents faced jurisdictional barriers when they tried to obtain search warrants for saved e-mail. Under old laws, a warrant had to be obtained from a judge in the jurisdiction where the search would take place. E-mail, however, is not always stored on a personal computer but often is stored remotely on an ISP's server. This means that if a suspect in New Jersey had e-mail stored on a server located in Silicon Valley, an agent would have to travel across the country to get a warrant to seize the e-mail.

In short, the introduction of both cellular phones and e-mail made it much more difficult to conduct communications surveillance, even in cases in which the court authorized such surveillance. The old laws and enforcement tools were not suited to deal with these new technologies.

Public authorities were also set back by the development of strong encryption. Although ciphers have existed for thousands of years, programmers have only recently developed 128-bit key length and higher levels of encryption that are extraordinarily difficult to break, even by the National Security Agency (NSA). Moreover, software that uses strong encryption is readily available to private parties at low cost. Today, manufacturers routinely prepackage these programs on computers. Thus, encrypted messages are more private than any messages historically sent by mail, phone, messenger, or other means. Similarly, now data stored on one's own computer is protected much better than analogous data stored under lock and key. Despite court orders, strong encryption has frustrated the efforts of law enforcement in a growing number of cases.

The impact of the development of strong encryption is qualitatively different from the impact of the other privacy-enhancing technologies. The main factor that constrained public authorities in the area of new modes of communication was the obsolescence of laws. In the case of strong encryption, on the other hand, the technology imposes its own barrier. Updating the law was sufficient to enable law enforcement to handle the challenges posed by the other new technologies. By contrast, no court order can enable strong encryption to be broken (Russell and Gangemi 1995, 11; Denning and Baugh 1997).

These technological developments have provided all people—law-abiding citizens and criminals, nonterrorists and terrorists—greater freedom to do as they choose. In this sense, these technologies are "liberalizing." At the same time, they have significantly hampered the ability of public authorities to conduct investigations. Some cyberspace enthusiasts welcomed these developments, hoping that cyberspace would be a self-regulating, government-free space. In contrast, public authorities clamored for the laws to be changed in order to enable officials to police the new "territory" as they do in the world of old-fashioned, landline telephones. Such pressures led to some modifications in the law before the 2001 attack on America, but the most relevant changes in the law have occurred since.

One provision of ECPA attempted to make the laws governing communications intercepts more effective by providing for "roving wiretaps" in criminal investigations. Roving wiretaps are full intercept orders that apply to a particular person rather than to a specific communications device. They allow law enforcement to intercept communications from any phone or computer used by a suspect without specifying in advance which facilities will be tapped.

The process for obtaining a roving intercept order is more rigorous than the process for obtaining a traditional phone-specific order. The Office of the United States Attorney General must approve the application before it is even brought before a judge. Originally, the applicant had to show that the suspect named in the application was changing phones or modems frequently with the purpose of thwarting interception. After the Intelligence Authorization Act for Fiscal Year 1999 changed the requirement, the applicant merely had to show that the suspect was changing phones or modems frequently and that this practice "could have the effect of thwarting" the investigation. Although roving intercepts have not yet been tested in the Supreme Court, several federal courts have found them to be constitutional.

Prior to September 11, the FBI could not gain authorization to use roving intercepts in gathering foreign intelligence or in investigations of terrorism. The Uniting and Strengthening America by Providing Appropriate Tools Required to Intercept and Obstruct Terrorism Act of 2001 (USA PATRIOT Act) amended the Foreign Intelligence Surveillance Act of 1978 (FISA) to allow roving intercept orders. FISA provides the guidelines under which a federal agent can obtain authorization to conduct surveillance for foreign intelligence purposes. Agents who wish to conduct surveillance under FISA submit an application first to the attorney general's office, which must approve all requests (as with roving intercepts under ECPA). If the attorney general's office finds the application valid, the application will be taken to one of seven federally appointed judges, who together make up the Federal Intelligence and Security Court (FISC), for approval. The FISC allows no spectators, keeps most proceedings secret, and hears only the government's side of a case.[5]

There has been some debate in the courts and among legal scholars about the application of the Fourth Amendment to the new technologies and to the new legislation governing these technologies. Before 1967, the Supreme Court interpreted the Fourth Amendment in a literal way to apply only to physical searches. In *Olmstead v. United States,* the Court ruled that telephone wiretaps did not constitute a search unless public authorities entered a home to install the device. The Court held that the Fourth Amendment does not protect a person unless "there has been an official search and seizure of his person, or such a seizure of his papers or his tangible material effects, or an actual physical invasion of his house."[6]

In 1967, the Court replaced this interpretation of the Fourth Amendment with the view that the amendment "protects people, not places."

In *Katz v. United States*, the Court established that an individual's "reasonable expectation of privacy" would determine the scope of his or her Fourth Amendment protection. Justice Harlan, in his concurring opinion, set out a two-part test: the individual must have shown a subjective expectation of privacy, and society must recognize that expectation as reasonable.

Although legal scholars have criticized this test, *Katz* still represents the state of the law. However, the emergence of new technologies requires a reexamination of what constitutes a reasonable expectation of privacy. In *United States v. Maxwell*, the court determined that there was a reasonable expectation of privacy for e-mail stored on America Online's "centralized and privately-owned computer bank." However, the court in *United States v. Charbonneau*, relying on *Maxwell*, held that an individual does not have a reasonable expectation in statements made in an Internet chat room.[7]

Additionally, there is some question as to whether roving intercepts are constitutional. The Fourth Amendment states, "No warrants shall issue, but upon probable cause, supported by oath or affirmation, and particularly describing the place to be searched, and the persons or things to be seized." Because roving intercepts cannot name the location to be tapped, they may violate the particularity requirement of the Fourth Amendment.

The argument in favor of their constitutionality is that the particularity of the person to be searched is substituted for the particularity of the place to be searched. In *United States v. Petti*, the Ninth Circuit Court of Appeals upheld the use of roving intercepts. It explained that the purpose of the "particularity requirement was to prevent general searches." As long as a warrant or court order provides "sufficient particularity to enable the executing officer to locate and identify the premises with reasonable effort," and there is no "reasonable probability that another premise might be mistakenly searched," it does not violate the Fourth Amendment. In other words, a court order to tap all phones used by a specific person does describe particular places but in an unconventional way. Public authorities cannot use the order to tap any location they wish. They can only tap a set of specific locations, namely those used by a specific person.

Additional questions may arise regarding differential application of the laws to various classes of people. Should noncitizens be treated the same as citizens? Terrorists the same as other criminals? International terrorists the same as domestic terrorists? These are significant issues that go to the heart of the debate about the rights of noncitizens. These issues raise potential problems, such as how to define terrorism and whether that definition should extend to citizens, as well as the danger that a loose definition might allow ordinary criminals to be encompassed by terrorism laws.

Public Protective Technologies

The liberalizing technologies already addressed enhance individuals' liberties but hinder public authorities. The following technologies are public protective technologies, which enhance the capabilities of government authorities and accordingly may curtail individual rights.

In July 2000 the FBI unveiled a new resource awkwardly labeled "Carnivore" to signal the breadth of its power to capture online communication. It was designed to capture a suspect's e-mail messages or trace messages sent to and from a suspect's account. To do so, it sorts through a stream of many millions of messages, including those of many other users. Carnivore has a filter that can be set to scan various digital packets for specific text strings or to target messages from a specific computer or e-mail address. The program can operate in two different modes: "pen" or "full." In pen mode, it will capture only the addressing information, which includes the e-mail addresses of the sender and recipient as well as the subject line. In full mode, it will capture the entire content of a message. Carnivore was designed to copy and store only information caught by the filter, thus keeping agents from looking at any information not covered by the court order. In response to ongoing negative press coverage the technology was renamed a more innocent "DCS1000" and the special-purpose Carnivore package was shelved in 2002 in favor of commercial off-the-shelf products that function similarly and are known as "packet sniffers." The use of this digital traffic-monitoring software generally requires the cooperation of a suspect's Internet Service Provider, which may be voluntary or by court order.[8]

Because packet sniffers still cannot overcome the protective power of strong encryption, security authorities sought means to track actual physical computer keystrokes to capture passwords and text before encryption. The FBI has developed two technologies, the Key Logger System (KLS), which requires physical installation on a computer, and the software-based Magic Lantern that can be surreptitiously downloaded and installed on a computer.

Once agents discover that they have seized encrypted information, they can seek a warrant to install and retrieve KLS. In the case of Nicodemo Scarfo, a suspected racketeer, agents had to show both probable cause that Scarfo was involved in crime and probable cause that evidence of criminal activity was encrypted on his computer before installing KLS. As in other warrants, the FBI had to specify the exact location of the computer on which KLS would be installed.

Once installed, KLS uses a "keystroke capture" device to record keystrokes as they are entered into a computer. It is not capable of searching or recording fixed data stored on the computer. Moreover, KLS is designed so that it is unable to record keystrokes while a computer's modem is in operation because intercepting electronic communications would require an intercept order that is more difficult to get than a warrant.

Because KLS must be manually installed on a suspect's computer, it requires breaking and entering into a suspect's home. In contrast, Magic Lantern allows the FBI to put software on a computer to record keystrokes without installing any physical device. Like KLS, Magic Lantern cannot decrypt e-mail by itself but can retrieve the suspect's password. The details of how it does this have not been released. It is said to install itself on the suspect's computer in a way similar to a Trojan horse computer virus. It disguises itself as an ordinary, harmless message, then inserts itself onto a computer. For example, when someone connects to the Internet, a pop-up box could appear, stating "Click here to win!" When the user clicks on the box, the virus will enter the computer.[9]

Groups like the Electronic Privacy Information Center (EPIC) and the Center for Democracy and Technology (CDT) have raised multiple arguments for why packet sniffers should not be used at all. They are skeptical that these programs operate as the FBI claims and are troubled by the degree of secrecy the FBI maintains about the way they work. Furthermore, they argue that separating addressing information from content is more difficult for Internet communications than for phone calls. Therefore, Carnivore, they say, will not allow the FBI to do a pen/trap without seizing more information than authorized. Privacy advocates also worry that packet sniffers violate the Fourth Amendment because they scan through "tens of millions of e-mails and other communications from innocent Internet users as well as the targeted suspect." The ACLU compares a Carnivore search to the FBI sending agents into a post office to "rip open each and every mail bag and search for one person's letters."

Officials at the FBI respond that when used properly, packet sniffers will capture only the targeted e-mails. Additionally, Carnivore's use is subject to strict internal review and requires the cooperation of technical specialists and ISP personnel, thus limiting the opportunities an unscrupulous agent might have to abuse it.

A review of the original Carnivore program conducted by the Illinois Institute of Technology concluded that although it does not completely eliminate the risk of capturing unauthorized information, Carnivore is better than any existing alternatives because it can be configured to comply with the limitations of a court order. However, the report also determined that failure to include audit trails makes the FBI's internal review process deficient. Specifically, the operator implementing a Carnivore search selects either pen or full mode by clicking a box on a computer screen, and the program does not keep track of what kind of search has been run. Therefore, it is difficult, if not impossible, to determine if an operator has used the program only as specified in the court order. Furthermore, it is impossible to trace actions to specific individuals because everyone uses the same user ID. The head of the review panel commented, "Even if you conclude that the software is flawless and it will do what you set it to do and nothing more, you still have to make sure that the legal, human, and organizational controls are adequate."[10] This focus on accountability will be explored below.

The oversight of these surveillance activities has traditionally been conducted under the ground rules of the Foreign Intelligence Surveillance Act of 1978. The act set up a special court to review wiretap or corresponding digital surveillance activities. The court routinely approved about 500 warrants a year, rising to 1,758 in 2004. The court also oversees efforts to minimize the collection of information about American citizens, given the focus on foreign agents. Since 2001 there has been an escalating controversy between the administration and the courts and Congress over the minimization procedures and the practice of issuing "national security letters" as an alternative to court-approved warrants. One estimate reports that the FBI may issue over 30,000 national security letters a year, indicating a high level of warrantless surveillance. Further, the Bush administration pressed for legislation that provides immunity from litigation for telephone and Internet companies that cooperate with authorities, a proposal not well received by the Democratic Congress. As of mid 2008 the controversy continues without clear resolution and is likely to continue as an issue for the next administration.[11]

Accountability—a Question of Balance

When homeland protection is discussed, it is often framed in terms of finding a legitimate balance between two competing public goods—safety and liberty. As Senator Ron Wyden (D-OR), put it in a December 2007 *Washington Post* op-ed considering the reauthorization and updating of FISA: "For nearly 30 years, the Foreign Intelligence Surveillance Act of 1978 (FISA) has represented the ultimate balance between our needs to fight terrorism ferociously and to protect the constitutional rights of Americans."[12] Senator Russ Feingold (D-WI), speaking on the Senate floor explaining his "no" vote on the PATRIOT Act in 2001, framed his decision to do so in similar terms: "I have concluded that this bill still does not strike the right balance between empowering law enforcement and protecting civil liberties."[13] Back in 2004, the *Economist* framed the debate between Democrats and Republicans on homeland protection again referring to this first balance:

> Since the terrorist attacks of September 11th 2001, the Bush administration has brought in a slew of law-enforcement and surveillance powers that critics fear is turning America into an Orwellian nightmare. The worriers are thinking of the all-seeing Big Brother of "1984," though so far the chaos of "Animal Farm" may be closer to it. Others—and they are still in a clear majority—feel that a few limits on their freedoms are a small price to pay for fewer terrorist attacks. But even they agree that a balance has to be struck between civil liberties and security. The argument—between Republicans and Democrats, George Bush and John Kerry—is over where exactly this balance should lie.[14]

Moreover, courts regularly use the terminology of balance, weighing the public interest against individual rights, and allowing the latter to be curtailed when they undermine a "compelling public interest," for instance, allowing the violation of privacy of sex offenders in order to protect children from sex abuse, authorizing wiretaps for suspected killers, and to enhance security.

The next step is to recognize that the point of balance changes throughout history, as domestic and international conditions change. Thus, in the wake of Prohibition more power was given to national police forces—to the FBI, after it was revealed that local law enforcement authorities were riddled with corruption. At that time, J. Edgar Hoover was a major positive force, bringing professionalism and integrity to police work. Over the decades that followed, the FBI accumulated more and more power and eventually itself became a major violator of individual rights and civil liberties, leading to the Church Committee reforms in the 1970s, which greatly curbed the bureau's powers—tilting the balance back toward stronger protections of individual rights. Following 9/11, the USA PATRIOT Act was introduced, followed by numerous other security-enhancing measures introduced by President Bush, which, as noted above, jerked the balance heavily in the opposite direction.

The question is, given the current conditions, which direction does the balance need to be pulled? Critics often argue that new security measures are excessive and demand that they be rolled back. But it is necessary to proceed with some caution here. Although there have been no successful terrorist attacks on the U.S. homeland since 9/11, there is good reason to assume that continued attempts will be made to inflict harm on the United States. Moreover, old and new security measures are best treated not as one bundle, but reviewed one at a time. One should avoid both holistic positions, the ones that claims that we are at war and hence must pull out all the stops, or the position that all new security measures are suspect. An unbundled review finds the following:

1. Some measures are fully justified, indeed overdue. These often entail a mere adaptation of the law for technical developments. For example, FISA provided guidelines under which a federal agent could obtain authorization to conduct surveillance for "foreign intelligence purposes." Prior to 9/11, wiretap warrants were limited to a given phone. Because of the increasing use of multiple cell phones and e-mail accounts over the last decades, federal officials engaged in surveillance under FISA found it much more difficult to conduct surveillance, as they could not follow suspects as they changed the instruments they were using unless they got a new court order for each communication device. The USA PATRIOT Act, enacted in October 2001, overcame this difficulty by amending the existing FISA law to allow what is called "roving surveillance authority"—making it legal for agents to follow one suspect, once a warrant is granted, whatever instrument he or she uses. Unless one holds that terrorists are entitled to benefit from new technologies but law enforcement is not entitled to catch up, this is an overdue and reasonable measure.

Similarly, before 9/11, the regulations that allowed public authorities to record or trace e-mails were interpreted by Department of Justice lawyers as requiring court orders from several jurisdictions through which e-mail messages travel.[15] This was the case because in the old days phone lines were local and hence to tap a phone, local authorization sufficed. In contrast, e-mail messages travel by a variety of routes. As of 2001 the USA PATRIOT Act permits national tracing and recording.

A third example of a measure that is overdue stems from another technological development. FISA warrants are not required for surveillance of foreign-to-foreign communications. Currently, however, many foreigner-to-foreigner communications (say from Latin America to Europe) are routed through the United States. Still, the law is interpreted as requiring a warrant for tapping these communications, as if they were between U.S. persons. A progressive should not oppose updating this interpretation of the law to adapt to new technological realities.

2. Some new security measures are reasonable. One should note that although the PATRIOT Act has become a sort of symbol for great excesses in hasty pursuit of security, only a small fraction, about 15 of its more than 150 measures, have been seriously contested. (Indeed, one of them reduces the penalty on hackers!) That is, most measures encompassed in the act are considered reasonable even by civil libertarians. Another example of a new security measure that seems reasonable is a tracking system of those who come to study, visit, or do business in the United States. Before 9/11, the United States did not check whether those who came into the country for a defined period of time, say on a student visa, left at the end of that period. Many did not leave, but there was no way of knowing how many there were, who they were, and above all what they were doing. The new Internet-based student tracking system requires colleges to alert authorities if a newly enrolled foreign student fails to show up for school or is otherwise unaccounted for. The system was initially plagued by a variety of problems (not the least of which was opposition by some college administrators, students, and others). One can argue whether or not such a measure is beneficial, but it is hard to see why it would be declared prima facie unreasonable, a system that is in place in practically all free societies.

3. Some measures such as torture and mass detention of people based on their social status are beyond the pale.

4. Many measures are neither inherently justified because enhanced security requires them nor inappropriate because they wantonly vio-

late rights. Instead, their status is conditioned on their being subject to proper oversight. In other words, the legitimacy of such measures depends on their place in what I call the second balance.

The Second Balance

Homeland protection requires drawing greatly on the second balance and not being limited to attempts to find the first one. The idea that underlies the second balance is that a measure that may seem tilted toward excessive attention to security may be tolerated if closely supervised by second-balance organs (discussed below), while a measure that is judged as tilting toward excessive attention to individual rights may be tolerated if sufficient exceptions are provided that are backed up by second-balance organs. That is, new measures can either be excessively privileged (undermining either security or the regime of rights) or excessively discriminated against both (leading to inaction on behalf of either element of a sound balance).

The second balance sought here is not between the public interest and rights, but between the supervised and the supervisors. Deficient accountability opens the door to government abuses of power, and excessively tight controls make agents reluctant to act or incapable of doing so.

Although the two forms of balance have some similarities and at some points overlap, they are quite distinct. For instance, the argument that the government should not be able to decrypt encoded messages is different from recognizing that such powers are justified—as long as they are properly circumscribed and their use is duly supervised.

A simple example of the idea at hand may serve to introduce this key point. On many highways drivers now have the option of using computerized toll-collection systems, such as the E-Z pass, whereby an electronic device deducts the toll from credit posted on a chip inside the person's car. The information gained by the computers of the toll booth—that a car owned by a given person passed a given point at a given time—can be treated in a variety of ways. At one extreme, it can be erased immediately after the computer deducts the proper amount from the credit stored in the car's chip. At the opposite extreme, such data can be kept on file for years, added to that person's dossier kept by a government agency or even private company, and made available for law enforcement, divorce lawyers, and even the media (a far from hypothetical situation). One extreme maximizes individual rights, especially privacy, while the second excessively privileges security and arguably other common goods. And one can readily conceive of a variety of intermediary positions.

If one approaches this device only within a first-balance frame of mind, one will ask how long and for what usages one should allow the said information to be stored. One then judges the use of E-Z passes—or any other such measure—as proper or as illegitimate per se. The second balance adds another major consideration: It asks how the arrangements worked out in terms of the first balance are reviewed and enforced. Different answers to this second question will lead one either to tolerate or reject a measure, whatever its standing according to the first-order balance. Thus, for instance, if we know that said information will be used only for curbing terrorism, and be available only if a proper search warrant has been issued by a court, one may find such storing of information more acceptable than if one learns that on many occasions the employees of toll agencies released the information to the likes of private investigators and the media. The same holds for all security measures but those that are tabooed.

The term *balance* is chosen because one can tilt excessively in either direction. Although most consideration is currently given to lack of adequate oversight, supervision, or accountability (from here on, to save space, I use the term *oversight* to refer to all such second-order processes: those that examine, review, and correct first-order processes), the opposite can also take place. For instance, FBI and CIA agents may again become reluctant to act if they believe that the acts they were authorized—indeed ordered—to carry out in the past can be retroactively defined as illegal and they can be jailed for having performed their jobs, or at least be forced to assume large personal debts to pay for legal representation. (True, as the famous Eichmann case illustrated, from a moral standpoint there are some acts that "everyone" should know are beyond the pale regardless of what their orders are, and should hence refuse orders to carry them out. However, one cannot run a security system based on the notion that people will rebel routinely. Instead, one should seek to ensure that as a rule those involved will be able to assume that orders are legitimate, in part because they are subject to proper oversight.)

Oversight is already in place in several forms and modes. And is it without the desired effect. However, a progressive approach recognizes that in the current circumstances it is essential to make oversight much stronger—in order to allow enhanced security.

Conclusion

Determining whether a specific public policy measure is legitimate entails more than establishing whether it significantly enhances public safety and minimally intrudes on individual rights. It also requires assessing whether those granted new powers are sufficiently accountable to the various overseers—ultimately to the citizenry. Some powers are inappropriate no matter what oversight is provided. However, others are appropriate given sufficient accountability. If accountability is deficient, the remedy is to adjust accountability, not to deny the measure altogether.

Whether the specific powers given to the government sustain or undermine the balance between rights and safety depends on how strong each layer of accountability is, whether higher layers enforce lower ones, and whether there are enough layers of accountability. I suggest that we should ignore both public authorities' claims that no strengthening of accountability is needed and the shrillest civil libertarian outcries that no one is to be trusted. Instead, we should promote reforms that will enhance accountability rather than deny public authorities the tools they need to do their work. This does not necessarily mean granting them all the powers they request, but in a world where new technologies have made the government's duties more difficult and in which the threat to public safety has vastly increased, we should focus more on accountability before denying powers to law enforcement.

NOTES

This chapter draws significantly on four sources: the author's videotaped remarks at the Media, Technology and Society conference at the University of Michigan, March 2006; and Etzioni 1999, 2002, and 2008.

1. www.ctiawireless.com.

2. www.nielsen-netratings.com.

3. 18 U.S.C. §§ 3122–23 (2000); *United States v. Giordano,* 416 U.S. 505, 549 n. 1 (1974); 18 U.S.C. § 2518 (2000); *Smith v. Maryland,* 442 U.S. 735 (1979); Swire 2001.

4. Schultz 2001, 1221–23; Berg 2000; Dempsey 1997; Dhillon and Smith 2001; Freiwald 1996; Taylor 2001; Department of Justice, Field Guide on the New Authorities (Redacted) Enacted in the 2001 Anti-Terrorism Legislation § 216A.

5. ECPA, Pub L. 99-508, § 106(d)(3), 100 Stat. 1848, 1857 (1986) (codified as amended at 18 U.S.C. § 2518(11) (2000)); Intelligence Authorization Act for Fiscal Year 1999, Pub. L. 105-272, § 604, 112 Stat. 2396, 2413 (1998) (codified as amended at 18 U.S.C. § 2518(11)(b) (2000)); *United States v. Petti,* 973 F.2d 1441, 1444–45 (9th Cir. 1992); see also Faller 1999; USA PATRIOT Act (2001), Pub. L. 107-56, 115 Stat. 272 (codified in scattered sections of U.S.C.); Foreign Intelligence Surveillance

Act of 1978, Pub. L. 95-511, 92 Stat. 1783 (codified as amended at 18 U.S.C. §§ 2511, 2518–19 (2000), 47 U.S.C. § 605 (2000), 50 U.S.C. §§ 1801–11 (2000)).

6. *Olmstead v. United States,* 277 U.S. 466 (1927).

7. *Katz v. United States,* 389 U.S. 347, 351 (1967); *State v. Reeves,* 427 So. 2d 403, 425 (La. 1982); Amsterdam 1974, 384–85; Laba 1996, 1470–75; Sundby 1994; Julie 2000, 131–33.

8. The "Carnivore" Controversy: Electronic Surveillance and Privacy in the Digital Age: Hearing Before the Senate Comm. on the Judiciary, 106th Cong. (statement of Donald M. Kerr, Assistant Director, Laboratory Division, FBI).

9. Affidavit of Randall S. Murch at 3–4, *United States v. Scarfo,* 180 F. Supp. 2d 572 (D.N.J. 2001) (No. 00-404); "Judge Orders Government to Explain" 2001, 3; *United States v. Scarfo,* 180 F. Supp. 2d 572, 577 (D.N.J. 2001).

10. Ted Bridis, "Congressional Panel Debates Carnivore as FBI Moves to Mollify Privacy Worries," *Wall Street Journal,* July 25, 2000, A24; Carnivore's Challenge to Privacy and Security Online: Hearing Before the Subcomm. on the Constitution of the House Comm. on the Judiciary, 107th Cong. (2001) (statement of Alan Davidson, Staff Counsel, Center for Democracy and Technology); ACLU, "Urge Congress to Stop the FBI's Use of Privacy-Invading Software."

11. Ron Wyden, "Rights That Travel," *Washington Post,* December 10, 2007, A19.

12. Wyden, "Rights That Travel," A19.

13. Russ Feingold, October 25, 2001, floor statement.

14. "The Enemy within; Liberty and Security," *The Economist* (London), October 9, 2004, 1.

15. Department of Justice, Field guide on the New Authorities (Redacted) Enacted in the 2001 Antiterrorism Legislation, § 216.

REFERENCES

Amsterdam, Anthony G. 1974. "Perspectives on the Fourth Amendment." *Minnesota Law Review* 58:349–477.

Berg, Terrence. 2000. "www.wildwest.gov: The Impact of the Internet on State Power to Enforce the Law." *BYU Law Review* 2000:1305–62.

Dempsey, James X. 1997. "Communications Privacy in the Digital Age: Revitalizing the Federal Wiretap Laws to Enhance Privacy." *Albany Law Journal of Science and Technology* 8:65–120.

Denning, Dorothy E., and William E. Baugh Jr. 1997. "Encryption and Evolving Technologies: Tools of Organized Crime and Terrorism." U.S. Working Group on Organized Crime, National Strategy Information Center.

Dhillon, Joginder S., and Robert I. Smith. 2001. "Defensive Information Operations and Domestic Law: Limitations on Government Investigative Techniques." *Air Force Law Review* 50:135–74.

Etzioni, Amitai. 1999. *The Limits of Privacy.* New York: Basic Books.

Etzioni, Amitai. 2002. "Implications of Select New Technologies for Individual Rights and Public Safety." *Harvard Journal of Law and Technology* 15:258–90.

Etzioni, Amitai. 2008. "Toward a Progressive Approach to Homeland Protection." *Democracy and Security* 4 (2): 170–89.

Faller, Bryan R. 1999. "The 1998 Amendment to the Roving Wiretap Statute: Congress 'Could Have' Done Better." *Ohio State Law Journal* 60:2093–2121.

Freiwald, Susan. 1996. "Uncertain Privacy: Communication Attributes after the Digital Telephony Act." *Southern California Law Review* 69:949–1020.

"Judge Orders Government to Explain How 'Key Logger System' Works." 2001. *Andrews Computer and Online Industry Litigation Reporter,* August 14.

Julie, Richard S. 2000. "High-Tech Surveillance Tools and the Fourth Amendment: Reasonable Expectations of Privacy in the Technological Age." *American Criminal Law Review* 37:127–43.

Laba, Jonathan Todd. 1996. "If You Can't Stand the Heat, Get Out of the Drug Business: Thermal Imagers, Emerging Technologies, and the Fourth Amendment." *California Law Review* 84:1437–86.

Russell, Deborah, and G. T. Gangemi Sr. 1995. "Encryption." In *Building in Big Brother: The Cryptographic Policy Debate,* ed. Lance Hoffman 10–14. New York: Springer-Verlag.

Schultz, Christian D. H. 2001. "Unrestricted Federal Agent: 'Carnivore' and the Need to Revise the Pen Register Statute." *Notre Dame Law Review* 76:1215–59.

Sundby, Scott E. 1994. "'Everyman''s Fourth Amendment: Privacy or Mutual Trust between Government and Citizen?" *Columbia Law Review* 94:1751–1812.

Swire, Peter P. 2001. "Administration Wiretap Proposal Hits the Right Issues but Goes Too Far." October 3. Retrieved April 6, 2009, from http://www.brookings.edu/papers/2001/1003terrorism_swire.aspx.

Taylor, Paul. 2001. "Issues Raised by the Application of the Pen Register Statutes to Authorize Government Collection of Information on Packet-Switched Networks." *Virginia Journal of Law and Technology* 6:4.

Theoharis, Athan G., ed. 1999. *The FBI: A Comprehensive Reference Guide.* Phoenix, AZ: Oryx Press.

Who Controls Content?
The Future of Digital Rights Management

GIGI SOHN AND TIMOTHY SCHNEIDER

In *The Wealth of Networks,* Yochai Benkler describes two "parallel shifts" experienced by advanced societies. The first shift is nearly a century old: the transition to an information economy centered on cultural production and the manipulation of data. The second is more recent: the rise of the modern Internet, a pervasive network linking inexpensive, powerful processors and cheap storage (Benkler 2006, 3). A necessary third shift unites these two: the transformation of traditional analog formats—the printed book, the pressed LP—to 1s and os that can be inexpensively created, flawlessly copied, and instantly distributed between devices and around the world. Digital media place the raw material of the information economy on the pervasive network.

An economy that generates great wealth by selling information and culture to millions of consumers now faces a fundamental inversion. "The declining price of computation, communication, and storage have, as a practical matter, placed the material means of information and cultural production in the hands of a significant fraction of the world's population" (Benkler 2006, 3). The same consumers now possess the tools to create their own culture and sell it or give it to one another. This change threatens centuries-old businesses like newspapers and encyclopedias, and comparative newcomers like video rental and commercial software development.

Old models of content production and dissemination don't just disappear, nor are they likely to any time soon. The content production industry—movie studios, book publishers, and the recording industry—has struggled to adapt business models based on capital-intensive production, reproduction, and dissemination to the new digitally networked reality, in which the price of all three has plummeted. Content industries face threats from new competitors created by the dramatic reduction in barriers to entry, and from widespread noncommercial reproduction and distribution by private actors. The fundamental changes that make Wikipedia and open-source software development possible also facilitate the widespread copyright infringement of peer-to-peer networks such as Napster and BitTorrent. We confront a classic case of an energetic *suppression of radical potential.*

The content industries responded to a problem created by technology with a technological solution: digital rights management (DRM). DRM technologies are technical measures that give content creators unprecedented control over the use of media by private actors, preempting the legal default rules—copyright law—that have traditionally governed relations between consumers and producers of copyrighted works. At their most basic, DRM technologies attempt to limit consumers' ability to copy and distribute protected works. More advanced forms of DRM use access controls to dictate use with greater precision and broader scope, creating works that can only be played on a specified device, or that phone home for authorization by the copyright holder prior to playback. These technologies transform the content creator's government-granted "copy right" into an ever-widening right of control.

Unwilling to rely on technology alone, over the last two decades the content industries have attempted to make DRM itself law. The Audio Home Recording Act (AHRA) required certain digital media devices to include government-mandated copy protection technology. The Digital Millennium Copyright Act, passed in 1998, gave privately implemented DRM restrictions the force of law by creating criminal and civil penalties for circumventing access controls. For almost two decades, DRM has dominated copyright policy debates, as the content industries pushed ever broader technology mandates to protect digital media. In response, a growing chorus of consumer advocates, academics, and businesses have questioned both the efficacy of DRM in preventing infringement, and the implications of increasingly widespread DRM, both government mandated and government supported.

There is much at stake in this debate. If the direst predictions are to be believed, without government intervention and DRM, the future existence of the content industries themselves may be in jeopardy. The *resilience of the interpretive schemes* associated with the traditional business model is striking. Mandated technologies to enforce copyright threaten innovation in the vibrant information technology and consumer electronics industries by placing design control in the hands of government regulators. The private transactions embodied in DRM's restrictions trump established norms of copyright and criminalize actions that were legal for prior forms of media. The "enclosure" of the information commons by DRM may have a dramatic impact on how we experience, record, and share culture (Benkler 1999).

This chapter explores in some detail the content industries' proposed use of DRM in the United States, exploring the rationale for its use, the reasons for its frequent failures, and the legal developments that give DRM technologies power even in defeat. We track government technology mandates from the AHRA to the current battle over the "broadcast flag," and offer lessons learned and predictions for the future.

DRM and Digital Media

Microsoft, a longtime supporter and developer of DRM technologies, defines DRM as "any technology used to protect the interests of owners of content and services."[1] This definition embraces a wide array of technologies. Current forms of DRM can prevent users from copying a protected work, distributing it over the Internet, viewing it for longer than a preset time, pausing, watching it without viewing previews, transferring it between devices, and much more (Godwin n.d.). The content industry describes DRM as an enabling technology that benefits consumers by allowing them to enjoy digital versions of a copyrighted work.[2] For most consumers DRM is anything but beneficial, crippling many of the potential advantages of digital media formats.

Consider, for example, Mpeg-1 Audio Layer 3, also known as MP3. A digital audio encoding and compression format, it stores music in a small file size with audio quality good enough for most users: a three-minute, 32-megabyte song off a CD can be converted to a 3-megabyte MP3.[3] Most MP3 encoders incorporate metadata that allow searching and organizing by artist, genre, and even volume level, and the encoding algorithm is licensed on terms that make it accessible to both commercial and open-source software developers. MP3s can be copied endlessly without degradation, played on multiple devices, and streamed over the Internet or a home network. They can be modified easily using freely available software, and last as long as the media on which they are stored. This rich functionality and the small file size have fueled the MP3's enormous popularity.

The audio formats with which the MP3 competes, such as Microsoft's WMA and the AAC/mp4 used by the iTunes Music Store, include DRM that removes or constrains these features, restricting users' ability to make copies, edit tracks, burn to CD, or transfer and play back on other devices.[4] The extra processing power required to negotiate DRM-protected content may even shorten the battery life of playback devices (Kim 2006). This is the central problem of DRM for the content industries: how to convince consumers to buy new media that let them do *less*.

DRM and Copyright

The restrictions on reproduction and distribution imposed by many forms of DRM seem to mirror the constraints imposed by copyright law; the "rights" in *digital rights management* evokes the "rights" of copyright holders. This is a false congruence: DRM protects far more than copyrights. Copyright is a government monopoly granted to authors for certain uses of creative works. These rights, guaranteed by the Constitution[5] and codified in federal law,[6] include exclusive rights to reproduction, distribution, the creation of derivative works, and, for certain works, public performance or display.[7] If the government does not grant the right, then it does not exist.

Once granted, these rights are limited by the terms of copyright, and by the exceptions and exemptions found within copyright law. The First Sale doctrine limits the copyright holder's distribution right to the first sale, after which purchasers may share or resell the work at their discretion.[8] The religious services exemption[9] waives the public performance right for works performed "in the course of services at a place of worship or other religious assembly." The broadest and most important of these exceptions is fair use,[10] a multifactor test that allows for legal flexibility in the face of new technologies and new uses.[11]

DRM inverts the copyright model, by taking all the rights for the copyright holder, even rights not granted by copyright law. The "rights" managed by DRM are not in fact rights at all. Where the law granted rights holders the right to *some* of the value of the copyrighted works, DRM potentially grants them *all*. These rights can then be subdivided and sold to users piece by piece. Adobe's eBook format allows a retailer to offer a different price based on whether a user would like to be able to print or copy all or part of a purchased eBook, share it with a friend, or have it read aloud using specialized software (Oestreicher-Singer and Sundararajan 2005; see also Lessig 2004a). For those rights that copyright *does* grant, no DRM yet invented effectively encompasses the complexity and the flexibility of copyright law.

DRM gives copyright holders an unprecedented degree of control over the uses of media by end users, control that increasingly bears little relation to copyright law. This does not mean that DRM is inherently bad. It simply means that DRM is never simply about enforcing copyright: DRM is about control, and the debate over DRM is about control. How much control should we grant to authors and rights holders? What should they be able to control and under what conditions?

Copying: Private Infringement and the AHRA

DRM is arguably a rational response to the dramatic increase in the ease of reproduction and distribution created by digital media and the Internet, changes that pose a very real threat to the traditional business models of the content industries. But the use of DRM and the first government DRM mandates preceded the modern Internet and began with the need to control copying. Earlier, analog forms of media were protected from widespread copying by the technical difficulty of duplication. There was little risk of private, noncommercial duplication supplanting the market for most content: few consumers could afford to copy and rebind their own books or press their own vinyl: the real threat to the content industries was large-scale commercial copying. Copyright law evolved to prevent these forms of infringement, while private use and private copying went unnoticed and unimpeded.

The introduction of the audiocassette marked a shift in attention from commercial, public copying to noncommercial private copying.[12] The audiocassette enabled home users to make private copies of copyrighted audio recordings, activity that, unlike large-scale commercial infringement, was nearly impossible for copyright holders to detect. The recording industry feared that shared copies of purchased music or music recorded off the radio would supplant the sale of original recordings. While record companies chose not to litigate the issue, they pursued legislation that would have required royalties on blank media and experimented with technologies that would interfere with the ability to record off of the radio.[13] When these efforts failed, they launched a massive public relations campaign, with the brilliantly overstated tagline "Home Taping is Killing Music."

Home taping failed to kill "music," or the recording industry, for that matter. If anything, the flexibility and portability of the audiocassette expanded the market for prerecorded music. The impact of home taping on the primary market for recordings was limited, in part, because analog copies were not lossless. While the first copy made of an original tape might be of fairly high quality, subsequent copies degraded significantly. The advent of recordable digital media and digital media recorders for private use threatened this technological check on serial copying.

While costly professional digital recording equipment and media were available as early as 1976, in the mid-1980s Sony and Philips introduced the digital audio tape (DAT), which offered the prospect of affordable digital recording and copying for consumers. MiniDiscs and digital compact cassettes followed in the early 1990s. These new digital formats could be copied again and again without degradation: the tenth serial copy was identical to the first. With these new tools, consumers now had the ability to make unlimited perfect duplicates.

The threat of infringement suits delayed the launch of DAT in the United States, and led to negotiations between the recording industry and consumer electronics industry as early as 1982.[14] After nearly a decade of private negotiation with the recording industry, Sony and Philips agreed in 1990 to include content restrictions—DRM—that would restrict serial copying in all consumer DAT and MiniDisc players sold in the United States.[15] The agreed-upon standard, the Serial Content Management System (SCMS), loosely followed the limitations of the media format that preceded it, the audiocassette, allowing first-generation copies but disabling copies of copies (serial copies) using information encoded on the media itself.

Music publishers were not included in these negotiations, and they sought royalties on devices and media to compensate for the copies the new media allowed. Four music publishers led by Sammy Cahn eventually filed suit for contributory infringement against Sony,[16] forcing a legislative compromise: the Audio Home Recording Act, passed by Congress in 1992.[17] The act codified the private agreement reached two years earlier. It required SCMS or its functional equivalent in all "digital audio recording devices" manufactured, sold, or imported into the United States: the first government-mandated DRM.[18] In exchange for dropping their suit against Sony, the act granted music publishers, record companies, and recording artists' royalties on all such devices and their media.[19]

DAT, MiniDisc, and DCC never gained much market share in the United States except in some niche markets. It is tempting now, when digital audio and video offerings compete on the basis of DRM, to link the failure of DAT, MiniDisc, and DCC to limitations imposed by SCMS, but history is littered with failed media formats. The additional costs imposed by royalties, consumers' reluctance to adopt another format in the midst of the transition from cassette or vinyl to compact disc, and the recording industry's apathy toward even a restricted recordable digital format were at least as responsible for these formats failure as the restrictions imposed by SCMS. The United States' first experiment with DRM technology mandates does, however, show the difficulty of enshrining a technological solution in the midst of rapidly changing technology. On the eve of the explosion of the modern Internet, the AHRA explicitly excluded computers from its DRM restrictions.[20]

Distribution

SCMS prevented copies in order to prevent distribution. Owners of prerecorded MiniDiscs already paid for their copies, so in order for copying to impact record company sales, those owners had to *distribute* copies to their friends and neighbors via the mails or the "sneakernet." Dramatic changes in distribution, however, were just over the horizon. Within two years of the AHRA's passage, the Clinton White House would support the creation of the National Information Infrastructure, an "Information Superhighway" that promised to be the most efficient media distribution network ever. Digital media—not just music and software, but soon books and movies as well—came conveniently preformatted for distribution over this network. SCMS, with its focus on physical distribution, quickly became irrelevant as the focus of DRM moved to preventing electronic distribution.

The trouble is, limiting this kind of distribution is extraordinarily difficult. The simplest way to prevent distribution is to prevent copying, but this may not be possible or even desirable, as the recording industry quickly discovered. The compact disc had been the primary format for commercial music distribution since the mid-1990s: individual tracks are unencrypted and easily convertible into file formats like the MP3 that can then be distributed quickly and efficiently over the Internet. Attempts to add copy protection to CDs can render existing players or media obsolete, and consumers are unlikely to reward a company for stripping their digital media of its functionality.[21] Many consumers expect, based on practice and legal doctrine, that they will be able to make backup copies of their recorded music, or create mix tapes and CDs.

Even if a content provider is capable of preventing most users from copying and distributing a copyrighted work themselves, they may still fail at preventing those users from gaining access to a copy of the work. A single unauthorized copy placed on a peer-to-peer network can be accessed and shared by millions of users all over the globe (Biddle et al. 2002). To limit unauthorized distribution entirely, copy controls must be complete, preventing one perfect copy from ever being made. In addition, the Digital Millennium Copyright Act permits the circumvention of copy controls for lawful uses of works under copyright. The content industries therefore turned to something completely different: access controls.

Access Controls

The move to digital media formats such as the compact disc and the DVD still encouraged consumers to obtain a physical copy of the work. But the combination of digital media, new distribution tools and new performance platforms has made the physical copy less relevant: the shift to digital media formats is increasingly a shift from hard to evanescent copies, from the book to the e-book, the LP to the streaming MP3. In the presence of a ubiquitous network, media can theoretically be always available on demand, the "celestial jukebox" (Goldstein 2003).

In this new context, physical ownership is just one of many ways to *access* content. As consumer demand has begun to move to access over physical possession, the content industries' DRM technologies have increasingly focused on access control: the use of digital locks and digital keys that allow the copyright holder to determine when and how their works may be seen, heard, and experienced. DRM does not require the legal backing of copyright law to control most users; the code does the work that law would have done (Lessig 2004a).

At their best, DRM technologies can be used to create new business models, or port existing business models to the Internet while limiting the threat of private infringement. For example, the reincarnated Napster uses DRM to allow users to pay a flat monthly fee for access to an expansive library of music.[22] CinemaNow and MovieLink offer Windows–DRM protected movie downloads that can be viewed either on a personal computer or networked TV set. Ideally, a diverse array of business models and DRM restrictions allow consumers to choose what works best for them and vote with their wallet. These market-based negotiations potentially offer consumers greater leverage than the interest group negotiations that traditionally characterize copyright legislation.

At their worst, DRM technologies can be used to enforce copyrights on, license, or otherwise monetize uses that were previously unaddressed by copyright law, or encroach on consumers' privacy rights under the guise of protecting copyrighted works. Works in the public domain, including the U.S. Constitution, are sold encumbered with DRM, though they are no longer subject to copyright law (Lessig 2004a, 2004b). In 2005, researchers discovered that DRM software bundled with over one hundred Sony Music titles installed hidden software on a consumer's computer without permission when the CD was inserted.[23] The software used a "rootkit" to conceal itself while running, a tactic commonly used by malicious software, but poor implementation potentially opened up users' computers to other malicious software. Sony was eventually forced to recall the CDs, and settled a class action lawsuit brought on behalf of consumers.[24]

The line between best and worst DRM is often difficult to draw. The Sony rootkit scandal raised questions about the lengths the content industries are willing to go to prevent unauthorized copying of copyrighted works, but there is no consensus on the principles that should guide the use of DRM technologies. This lack of consensus suggests a more basic critique of access control DRM. Individual consumers' intended uses of purchased works, expectations of privacy, and technological savvy vary as widely as their tastes in music, movies, and books. The effort to extract all value from a copyrighted work by slicing and selling each use assumes the ability to predict and price each use and preference accordingly. This is an impossible task, and faced with high prices or insufficient flexibility, some consumers will inevitably choose to opt out of the DRM regime altogether.

Cracking DRM

The history of most forms of DRM is a history of failure. Like real-world locks, digital locks can be picked, broken, or circumvented. All forms of DRM suffer from an essential weakness: the people who copyright holders want to keep their content from are the same people they are giving it to (Doctorow 2004). As a DRM format becomes more widely used, the incentive to circumvent it grows; when a proprietary DRM format is cracked, it is often an indication that the model has gained a toehold in the market.

Apple's Fairplay DRM, used on the songs sold through the popular iTunes Music Store, is a good example of this phenomenon (Doctorow 2004). Fairplay encrypts the songs sold on iTunes so that only devices owned or authorized by the purchaser can play them back. Introduced with the iTunes store in April 2003, Fairplay was defeatable by a reliable method six months later. Norwegian software engineer Jon Lech Johansen, aka "DVD Jon,"[25] released QTFairUse, which bypassed Fairplay by using Apple's software to decrypt the file and then copying the unencrypted copy of the file from the computer's random access memory (RAM). While effective, this method required users to play each song back individually to remove the encryption. This problem was solved shortly thereafter, when Johansen released playfair, which decrypted iTunes songs using the secret key stored on the iPod and in the iTunes software itself. Real Networks then released their own iTunes hack called Harmony, which allowed iTunes songs to be played on MP3 players other than the iPod, but reencrypted them with similar restrictions using their Helix DRM technology.[26] Finally, programmers developing a Linux client for the iTunes music store created PyMusique. Since Apple's music store relies on the purchaser's version of iTunes to add encryption, PyMusique allows the user to browse and purchase songs from the iTunes store, then conveniently neglects to add the Fairplay restrictions. Efforts by private individuals and commercial actors, reflecting a wide variety of motivations, defeated the iTunes encryption scheme four different ways. All this to avoid relatively mild restrictions that could be removed by simply burning individual songs to a (unencrypted) CD and converting them back to MP3.

Each time Fairplay was cracked, Apple released an updated version of its iTunes and iPod software to its users, disabling the crack temporarily (sometimes for only a few days).

Video content providers still rely on DRM. In 2005 Apple basically gave up on DRM, and after a passionate argument against the use of DRM by its CEO Steve Jobs, now sells DRM-less versions of songs. New Blu-ray DVD formats include the ability to revoke compromised encryption keys, and the ability to update consumer devices to repair breached DRM schemes. Meanwhile, stronger encryption means that encryption-based forms of DRM are less and less likely to fall to brute force decryption attacks (using computers and sophisticated forms of trial and error to defeat the encryption). The battle between content providers and DRM circumvention rages on, but the stakes of failure for content providers remain high. DRM must only be defeated once before the methods of circumvention and the protected content itself are made available on the network (Biddle et al. 2002).

This one-copy weakness ensures that, for sophisticated users, whether a given form of DRM has been cracked is irrelevant (Slater 2006). The primary media format for both the music and motion picture industry lack any effective content protection: CDs were unencrypted from the start, and the encryption scheme protecting DVDs has offered little real protection since it was first cracked in 1999. Most content available on current online music and video distribution outlets is also available on peer-to-peer networks. Though the new Blu-ray and HD-DVD video formats may be more secure,[27] their immense file sizes and the slow broadband speeds available to most consumers will discourage piracy at least as effectively as the accompanying DRM. Those determined to gain access to a work will inevitably find a way around the content protections, either through their own circumvention or by obtaining a copy from online sources.

If sophisticated, dedicated infringers occupy one extreme, and law-abiding, artist-friendly content industry executives the other, DRM increasingly aims for those people somewhere in between, lacking the motivation or the technical know-how to circumvent DRM. For these people, DRM provides a "speed bump" that "keeps honest people honest" by making copying just difficult enough that they are willing to purchase that additional copy.[28] If the relationship between unauthorized copies and legitimate copies is one to one, then every unauthorized copy deterred is a purchase gained.[29] The rhetoric of the content industries has gradually moved from the impossible dream of preventing a single unauthorized copy to the pragmatism of the speed bump. The key to defending DRM—and boosting sales—lies not in the DRM arms race alone, but in keeping the tools for circumvention out of the hands of the average user.

DRM Gets Legal Backing: The DMCA

While the AHRA missed the Internet entirely, the Digital Millennium Copyright Act was designed with the Internet—or at least something like it—specifically in mind. The "Information Superhighway" was an early nineties buzzword, a metaphor that captured the tremendous transport capacity of new fiber optic networks. Most observers envisioned something more like today's digital cable, a fat pipe with thousands of channels, video-on-demand, and an interactive element consisting primarily of the ability to shop. A *Time* magazine article from 1993 describes the future:

> But to focus on the number of channels in a TV system is to miss the point of where the revolution is headed. When the information highway comes to town, channels and nightly schedules will begin to fade away and could eventually disappear. In this postchannel world, more and more of what one wants to see will be delivered on demand by a local supplier (either a cable system, a phone company or a joint venture) from giant computer disks called file servers. These might store hundreds of movies, the current week's broadcast programming and all manner of video publications, catalogs, data files and interactive entertainment. Remote facilities, located in Burbank, California, or Hollywood or Atlanta or anywhere, will hold additional offerings from HBO and Showtime, as well as archived hits from the past: I Love Lucy, Star Trek, The Brady Bunch. Click an item on the menu, and it will appear instantly on the screen. (Elmer-Dewitt 1993)

The Clinton administration embraced the Information Superhighway, rechristened the "National Information Infrastructure" (NII), and formed a series of working groups to figure out just how to make this vision a reality (Litman 2001, 90). Since the Superhighway and digital media posed some challenges to traditional copyright law, one of those working groups was to focus on intellectual property.[30]

The IP Working Group's final white paper, issued in 1994, drew a connection between strengthened intellectual property protections and the success of the Information Superhighway. After outlining the NII's many potential benefits to authors, the report sounded the alarm:

> The availability of these benefits is by no means assured, however. Authors are wary of entering this market because doing so exposes their works to a higher risk of piracy and other unauthorized uses than any of the other traditional, current modes of dissemination. Therefore, authors may withhold their works from this environment. . . . Thus, the full potential of the NII will not be realized if the education, information and entertainment products protected by intellectual property laws are not protected effectively when disseminated via the NII. . . . What will drive the NII is the content moving through it. (Information Infrastructure Task Force 1995, 10)

As Jessica Litman points out, even at the time this was a dubious claim, as a number of major media outlets, including the *New York Times,* CNN, and all of the major networks, had already placed their content online (2001, 102). Consumer-generated content such as e-mail and personal web pages was at least as powerful a driver of the Internet: content would fuel the modern Internet, but not necessarily industries' content.

The white paper recommended two legal changes to enhance the rights of copyright holders. First, it advanced an interpretation of existing copyright law that transformed transmission into distribution by classifying ephemeral copies inherent in the manipulation and transmission of digital media as actionable copies for the purposes of copyright.[31] Second, it embraced content creators' use of DRM, and recommended legislation prohibiting the circumvention of DRM technologies.[32]

With backing from the content industries, and amid bipartisan support, in 1995 legislators introduced bills in both the Senate and the House of Representatives implementing the white paper's recommendations. The bill seemed destined for an easy passage, so much so that the commissioner of the United States Patent and Trademark Office (USPTO), Bruce Lehman, began using the imminent legislation to push for similarly expansive treaty language at the World Intellectual Property Organization (WIPO).[33] But an unlikely coalition of opponents rallied in opposition to the bill—U.S. Internet service providers, online services, telephone companies, and computer hardware and software manufacturers all had something to lose from a bill that imposed liability for the ephemeral copies made as content moved through their networks and devices. Legal academics, librarians, the Home Recording Rights Coalition, and consumer and civil liberties groups grew concerned about the fair-use implications of the working group's expansive vision of intellectual property and prohibition on circumvention of DRM. These groups joined together to create the Digital Future Coalition, and brought the bill to a standstill in the House and Senate (Litman 2001, 122–29).

Initially stymied in Congress, Lehman and the content industries pushed for inclusion of the white paper's recommendations in the next WIPO treaty, but with limited success. The final treaty passed by WIPO refused to consider temporary copies actionable, and exempted from liability companies that acted only as conduits for information. The WIPO treaty did, however, contain language backing the use of DRM, requiring signatory countries to ensure "adequate legal protection and effective legal remedies against the circumvention of effective technological measures."[34] Congress began work on bringing U.S. law into compliance with the terms of the WIPO treaty. Arguably, U.S. law already complied with this rather vague language: copyright infringement that circumvented DRM was already illegal, and the legal doctrine of contributory infringement had already been used successfully against manufacturers of products designed specifically to defeat DRM (Litman 2001, 131). Nonetheless, backers of the bill insisted that specific language was needed to fulfill the treaty's provisions regarding "technical measures." Content providers introduced legislation to Congress containing strong anticircumvention provisions, framed now as necessary to reconcile U.S. law with the treaty obligations from the WIPO's Copyright Treaty.[35]

The WIPO treaty gave the content industries' bills new life. Opponents of the bill who wielded significant power earned significant concessions. Telephone companies and Internet service providers received a "safe harbor" provision that exempted Internet service providers from liability if they removed copyrighted content upon notification by the copyright holder.[36] The bill was silent on the status of ephemeral copies and the distinction between transmission and distribution, leaving this debate to the courts.[37] Despite urging by some in Congress, the content industries refused to agree to any significant exceptions to the anticircumvention provisions, leaving librarians and consumer advocates an unwieldy bureaucratic process to create further exemptions as needed. One concession to consumer electronics makers was language stipulating that they were not required to update their hardware to conform to new DRM standards. The Digital Millennium Copyright Act passed both houses in early October, and President Clinton signed the bill into law on October 28, 1998 (Litman 2001, 134–43).

Provisions of the DMCA

The DMCA has four main provisions relevant to the use of DRM technologies. Section 1201(a)(1)(A) states that "no person shall circumvent a technological measure that effectively controls access" to a copyrighted work. Section 1201(c)(2) imposes penalties on those who "manufacture, import, offer to the public, provide, or otherwise traffic in any technology, product, service, device, component, or part thereof" that is designed or marketed for the purpose of circumventing *access* controls. An additional ban, 1201(b)(1)(A), mirrors 1201(c)(2) for a technological measure that protects a *right* of a copyright holder. Finally, 1201(k)— added in conference committee apparently without debate (Litman

2001, 140)—requires that "automatic gain control copy control technology"[38] be included on VHS and other analog videocassette recorders manufactured or imported in the United States.

The blanket bans are enforced by stiff civil and criminal penalties. The DMCA grants a civil cause of action to anyone injured by a violation of 1201 for actual damages (including any profits attributable to the violation) or statutory damages of up to $2,500 per act of circumvention, with treble damages for repeat violations.[39] The act imposes *criminal* penalties for willful violations "for purposes of commercial advantage or private financial gain."[40] Criminal penalties can be up to $500,000 or five years in jail for first offenders, and $1 million and up to ten years in jail for repeated offenses.[41]

Congress included six narrow statutory exemptions to 1201(a)'s ban on circumventing access controls. Nonprofit libraries, archives, and educational institutions may circumvent access controls for the sole purpose of determining whether they wish to purchase authorized access.[42] Users may also legally circumvent technological measures that collect or disseminate personally identifying information,[43] or if circumvention is necessary to "technology that prevent access of minors to material on the Internet."[44] The act includes additional exemptions for security testing,[45] encryption research,[46] and reverse engineering software for interoperability.[47] A final, rolling exemption creates the Triennial Review, an administrative rulemaking conducted by the librarian of Congress to consider the exemption of classes of works from the anticircumvention provisions of the DMCA.[48] Though the savings clause of the DMCA, section 1201(c) (1), insists that "Nothing in this section shall affect the rights, remedies, limitations, or defenses to copyright infringement, including fair use," the act contains no exemptions for the purposes of fair use.[49]

Aftermath of the DMCA

A great deal of ink has been spilled about the unintended consequences of the anticircumvention provisions of the DMCA (Electronic Frontier Foundation 2006), but in some ways the DMCA's effect on DRM was exactly what content makers intended. The DMCA dramatically raised the stakes of circumvention for both consumers and manufacturers. The civil and criminal penalties eliminate commercial circumvention tools and make such tools much more difficult to obtain for ordinary consumers. Even if they obtain or create their own circumvention tools, individual circumventers are potentially subject to harsh penalties, and must balance the gains from circumvention against the protections afforded by obscurity; content industries must weigh the cost of locating and prosecuting individual offenders.[50] By making DRM circumvention technologies harder to get and riskier to use, the DMCA enhanced the "speed bump" effect of DRM.

The speed bump is not the end of the road, however. The DMCA applies to manufacturers as well as consumers. Prior to the DMCA, consumer electronics and software manufacturers were free to reverse-engineer their competitors' media formats to enable cross platform compatibility. This is what enables, for example, Open Office or Apple's Keynote software to read presentations made in Microsoft PowerPoint (Lee 2006). The DMCA's reverse engineering exemption does not apply to these practices, so manufacturers potentially face *criminal* penalties if they create devices or software that circumvent DRM to allow playback of DRM-protected formats. This locks consumers of DRM-protected media into a single format, device, or service, imposing huge switching costs because purchased works will not necessarily play on other devices. Purchased content is locked in DRM "silos" that link content distributors and device manufacturers.

Under ordinary circumstances, content companies have as little to gain from DRM silos as consumers, but anticircumvention provisions also mean that if the content industry controls the DRM, it controls the terms on which access to its works may be granted. The DVD Copy Control Association, a consortium led by the major movie studios, retains strict licensing provisions for the Content Scrambling System (CSS) used to prevent copying and unauthorized playback in DVDs. The license for a DVD player that can play commercial DVDs (all of which are encrypted using CSS) dictates precisely the type of outputs the device may have and the additional copy protection measures (region coding, Macrovision, and CGMS-A on the analog outputs) with which the device must comply. While reverse engineering—or outright cracking—the CSS encryption and creating your own DVD player is technically feasible, doing so would be a violation of the DMCA.[51] By preventing reverse engineering, the DMCA allows the content industries to control access to content.

Onward to technology mandates

The DMCA did not solve the problem of unauthorized consumer copying, nor did it signal the end of the content industry's legislative efforts. Just as individuals prior to the DMCA could choose to circumvent DRM to violate copyright law, after the DMCA they could circumvent DRM to violate both traditional copyright law and the newly minted access restrictions. While the DMCA made the latter choice more difficult to exercise, some still chose to break the law by developing, sharing, and using methods of circumvention to gain access to copyrighted works. Those works—and the methods of circumvention used to obtain them—were then placed on peer-to-peer networks, and infringement continued unabated.

The content industries next worked to remove this choice from consumers altogether, by embedding the content protection in devices themselves. Hardware-based solutions are considered more robust than software-based DRM, but content makers have traditionally had a hard time convincing device manufacturers to embed content protection in their devices. Consumer electronics and consumer hardware makers compete on functionality, so there is little incentive to create devices that do less. The relative ease with which they were able to defeat traditional foes like libraries and the consumer electronics industry in Congress convinced the content industries to set their sights on broader, even more ambitious legislation. Government-mandated DRM, like that established by the AHRA, would bring device manufacturers—and by extension, consumers—to heel.

In 2001, three years after the passage of the DMCA, Senator Hollings of South Carolina introduced the Consumer Broadband and Digital Television Promotion Act (CBDTPA).[52] The bill required "digital media device manufacturers, consumer groups, and copyright owners" to reach an agreement on "security systems standards" within twelve months of enactment. If the groups reached an agreement, the Federal Communications Commission (FCC) would adopt those rules in a rulemaking. If not, the FCC was to adopt them on its own. These standards, a government-mandated DRM, would then be mandatory for any "digital media device" sold or transported in interstate commerce. Sale of digital media devices without such "security technology," removal or alteration of the technology, or even *knowing transmission* of works missing government-mandated identifiers would be punishable with the stiff civil and criminal penalties of the DMCA.[53]

The bill was truly astonishing in its scope, covering everything from televisions to cell phones to MP3 players to personal computers and the software running on them, though a lobbyist for the bill's main backer, Disney, declared that it was "an exceedingly moderate and reasonable approach (McCullagh 2001). The bill's curious structure—allowing par-

ties one year to negotiate a standard before the FCC imposed one—
was a transparent effort to use legislation to force interested parties to
the bargaining table to "solve" the DRM problem once and for all by
establishing a single standard that would literally apply to everything.
"I believe the private sector is capable—through marketplace negotiations—of adopting standards that will ensure the secure transmission of
copyrighted content on the Internet and over the airwaves," said Hollings in a statement introducing the bill. "But given the pace of private
talks so far, the private sector needs a nudge."[54]

From the content industries' perspective, a unified standard held several advantages. First, it removed the loophole in the AHRA that allowed
MP3 players—which lacked SCMS—to flourish, by ensuring that everything would include DRM. In theory, there would no longer be competition between new DRM-encumbered and DRM-free copyrighted content, since every new device and all new software would encode and obey
the mandatory standards. Second, it eliminated competition between
competing DRM formats, solving the nascent problem of content silos,
and preventing services and content makers from competing on the
basis of control granted to users. Finally, the bill's tight timeline reflected
the content industry's growing sense that time was of the essence in forcing adoption of DRM. Consumers accessing content on peer-to-peer networks were growing accustomed to the freedom of media that was not
subject to DRM restrictions.

As the installed base of next-generation devices not subject to the
mandates grew, government technology mandates would become increasingly ineffective at limiting the infringement that was the bill's primary
justification. Hilary Rosen, CEO of the Recording Industry Association
of America (RIAA) at the time, argued if the bill failed to pass, "online
piracy will continue to proliferate and spin further out of control."

The Senate Judiciary Committee held hearings on the bill in 1999.
Opposition to the bill was immediate and intense. Facing fierce opposition from consumer groups, the telecommunications industry, computer
software and hardware makers, and the consumer electronics industry,
the CBDTPA never made it out of the Judiciary Committee. But that
didn't mean it was over. The fight just switched venues.

The Broadcast Flag

The CBDTPA is often overlooked, but its unpronounceable acronym
provides an insight into how the content industries pitched their next

technology mandate. Like Lehman's working group before them, the bill's proponents argued that stricter intellectual property protections were necessary to entice consumers to utilize a new medium: content drives consumer demand, and without content there would be no consumer demand. Proponents of the Hollings bill argued that the CBDTPA was necessary to promote adoption of consumer broadband and the changeover to digital television. While this failed to move Congress, it was very effective at the FCC, where digital television was very serious business indeed.

Digital television (DTV), at its most basic, is a means of encoding a television signal using 1's and 0's. Until June 2009, U.S. televisions received "analog" television signals, which encoded information by varying the amplitude or frequency of the broadcast signal. Digital transmission is more efficient, enabling broadcasters to send much more information over the same amount of spectrum. For consumers, this means better picture quality, better sound quality, and potentially more channels, since broadcasters can offer as many as six different channels in the same spectrum allocation. It also requires new equipment, since analog tuners cannot process digital signals, and the wider motion picture aspect ratio (shape of the picture) for DTV.

This created a chicken-and-egg problem that lasted more than two decades. Broadcasters would not convert to digital TV without an audience; consumers would not invest in receivers without signals to receive. The Telecommunications Act of 1996 addressed this problem by giving each incumbent broadcaster a whole other station for free, enabling them to broadcast in both digital and analog until the transition was complete.[55] The initial deadline of 2006 set by the FCC was then amended in a 1997 spending bill to the date on which 85 percent of U.S. households had access to DTV.[56] This standard was repealed in 2006, and Congress set a new transition date of February 17, 2009.[57] Under pressure from the new Obama administration, which feared that millions of Americans would not be ready for the February 17 deadline, Congress extended it to June 12, 2009.

Digital television presents a familiar conundrum for the content industry, a formally analog medium suddenly become digital, theoretically enabling users to record and make perfect reproductions of content that could then be distributed to millions via the Internet. Hollywood argued that government-mandated content protection—a "broadcast flag"—was necessary because if the threat of indiscriminate redistribution of "high value" digital television content was not reduced, broadcasters would not make that content available, thus further slowing the country's transition to digital TV.[58] One of the most vocal proponents of this argument was Viacom,[59] which told the FCC in 2002 that "if the broadcast flag is not implemented and enforced by next summer, CBS will cease providing any programming in high definition for the 2003–2004 television season. And without the security afforded by a broadcast flag, Paramount will have less enthusiasm to make digital content available."[60] Under pressure from the broadcasters and Hollywood, and anxious to avoid any perceived roadblocks to the long-delayed DTV transition, the FCC took steps to implement the broadcast flag.

The broadcast flag scheme consisted of two main parts. The flag itself has already been added to the digital television standard, a one-bit field in the signal that can be set to either on or off, alerting receiving devices whether or not technological control of consumer distribution should be applied. Since the digital television signal is transmitted unencrypted, the flag is not self-enforcing, allowing device manufacturers to choose whether or not to enforce any restrictions upon recognizing the flag, or even to recognize it at all. Device manufacturers, understandably, were reluctant to add features that restricted functionality.

The second part of the broadcast flag scheme gave it teeth. The FCC's 2003 broadcast flag order mandated that every device capable of demodulating or receiving a DTV signal recognize the flag and impose technological measures to prevent unauthorized copying and redistribution. These measures, dictated by the MPAA and ratified with limited changes by the FCC, required devices with DTV demodulators (such as TVs or HD tuner cards for PCs) in them to immediately encrypt flagged content using only technologies approved by the FCC. This content can then only be passed to "approved outputs." Analog outputs, which would strip the flag and any encryption, could only receive downgraded images, equivalent to the outputs from a standard (predigital) television. Flag-compliant devices' only digital connections would be via "approved output content protection technology," again subject to mandatory preapproval by the FCC. Importation of devices that did not comply with the FCC's flag order was prohibited.[61]

These requirements applied not only to DTV demodulators, but any so-called downstream devices that connect to a DTV demodulator, including DVD recorders, PVRs, and now iPods and cell phones. These devices would have to obey restrictions on the ability to copy and distribute flagged content set by the FCC. In addition, the FCC's report and order imposed robustness requirements to prevent user modification of devices that might allow access to the unprotected DTV signal. Since almost every consumer electronics device could conceivably connect to a DTV receiver, the "downstream device" requirement transformed the flag order into the CBDTPA.

Unlike the CBDTPA, which required a unified standard, the FCC broadcast flag order initiated a "certification process" to preapprove television sets, computer software, digital video recorders, cell phones, game consoles, iPods, and any other device that could potentially receive a digital television signal.[62] The FCC approved thirteen different (and non-interoperable) content protection standards. Several manufacturers removed legal and consumer-friendly features of their devices before submitting them to the FCC, largely at the behest of the movie studios.[63] The broadcast flag was essentially a backdoor CBDTPA, a wide-ranging government-mandated DRM dictated by the content industries. Congress rejected this approach,[64] but the FCC willingly went along.

There are a lot of reasons for consumers and the consumer electronics industry to dislike the broadcast flag. The flag's restrictions would devastate fair use of digital television content, and criminalize (under the DMCA) many customary public uses, such as recording and retransmitting programming for distance learning. The thirteen specifications approved by the FCC are not interoperable, creating a huge potential for consumer confusion and problems of vendor lock-in. The robustness requirements essentially ruled out any open-source software implementations of the flag, which by very definition would allow user modification. The flag order would have effectively frozen technological innovation for scores of devices at the pace of FCC rulemakings, which in the case of digital television, had lasted for nearly twenty years.

Perhaps most importantly, there was no evidence of any problem of unauthorized copying of over-the-air digital television content. The first barrier to redistribution of DTV content was a simple lack of bandwidth. Even using peer-to-peer protocols designed for large file sizes like Bit-Torrent,[65] the sheer size of a high-definition television[66] program and the low bandwidth of U.S. consumer broadband connections (1 megabit per second) made download times prohibitively long, and wide-scale piracy impractical at best. Much "high value" broadcast television content derives its value from timeliness: the demand for the Super Bowl drops off sharply hours after broadcast. Movies and popular television shows were already available on DVD, which utilized a compromised DRM scheme that offered no functional protection.[67] Flag-less HD tuners were already being sold, which in combination with readily available hardware provided a legal way to record and store DTV content, some of which, inevitably, would arrive on peer-to-peer networks. Despite Viacom's threats, the broadcast networks offered almost all of their most sought-after content over their DTV networks. The flag would likely have had no impact on infringement or the types of content broadcast in digital form.

But in the end, it was not policy arguments that derailed the broadcast flag scheme, it was jurisdiction—the FCC's power under the Communications Act of 1934 to implement the flag regime. The broadcast flag was an end run around Congress, which had refused the tech mandate of the CBDTPA; by going to the FCC, the content industries hoped to find a more receptive audience. But administrative agencies need congressional authorization to act, and it was not at all clear that the FCC's legislative mandate allowed it to impose the flag (Center for Democracy and Technology 2003, 26–28). The FCC claimed "ancillary" jurisdiction to implement the flag mandate over equipment manufacturers on the basis of its power to regulate digital broadcasting.[68]

Immediately after the FCC issued its flag order, nine public interest and library groups challenged the FCC's video broadcast flag rules in the United States Court of Appeals for the District of Columbia Circuit. Public Knowledge (with which the authors are associated) financed and coordinated the case, *American Library Association v. FCC.*[69] The court ruled that the FCC lacked the authority under the Communications Act to require technology manufacturers to build their devices to read and obey the broadcast flag. In a harsh rebuke, the court declared that "there is no statutory foundation for the broadcast flag rules, and consequently the rules are ancillary to nothing."[70]

Aftermath

Defeat in the DC Circuit did not settle the fate of the broadcast flag. The following year, as part of a much larger telecommunications reform bill, Senator Ted Stevens (R-AL) introduced legislation that would grant the FCC authority to implement the flag.[71] While the bill was voted out of the Senate Commerce Committee, it died before reaching the floor. Meanwhile, fighting the flag has become a lonely battle indeed. After the FCC issued its broadcast flag order in November 2003 and in the midst of ongoing litigation, companies developed and implemented flag-compliant technologies out of sheer necessity. With the up-front costs of compliance already paid, some early opponents of the flag dropped their opposition.

Folding on the flag created a problem, since the flag was just the leading edge of a raft of similarly ill-inspired technology mandates sponsored by the content industries: analog hole and audio broadcast flag legislation. So-called analog hole legislation would prevent consumers from using the analog outputs of video devices to copy DRM-protected content.[72] To accomplish this, the bill requires that all consumer devices with analog outputs detect, protect, and obey embedded watermarks that dictate what consumers may do with protected content.[73] The audio broadcast flag is a tech mandate for audio devices modeled on the video broadcast flag. Like the video flag, it is a combination of watermark and mandatory copy protection standard that would apply to all devices capable of receiving digital audio broadcasts.[74] The consumer electronics makers who supported the broadcast flag but oppose the audio broadcast flag find themselves in a difficult position, explaining why the arguably further-reaching video flag is reasonable and the audio flag is not.[75]

Lessons Learned and the Future of Technical Mandates

Given the sheer lobbying heft of the content industries, coalitions of opportunity with industry groups are absolutely essential. But the aftermath of the broadcast flag litigation shows why coalitions of industry allies are no substitute for genuine voices representing the public interest. Corporations and their lobbyists don't fight these battles on principle, nor should they be expected to: by their very nature they have a price. The content industries, meanwhile, have shown little inclination to negotiate.

Policymakers have only begun to recognize the existence of a public interest in questions of copyright that have historically been settled by negotiations between industry players. Advocates for the public in this particular fight must deal with the perception that the law-breaking, copyright-infringing public is itself the problem. Ironically, one of the biggest unintended consequences of the DMCA was the explosive growth of the modern copyright reform movement, and the emergence of a viable public voice in copyright policy.

Two high-profile cases brought the DMCA to national prominence. In 2000 the Secure Digital Music Initiative, an industry consortium developing a consumer DRM standard, issued an open invitation to the "Digital Community" to crack their digital watermarking scheme (Chiariglione

2000). Princeton professor Ed Felten and his team of graduate students took up the challenge, and within three weeks successfully removed all four of SDMI's watermarking techniques.[76] When Felten went to present his results at an academic workshop, SDMI and the RIAA threatened him with prosecution under the DMCA.[77] Russian programmer Dmitri Sklyarov was arrested for violating the DMCA in 2001 shortly after a presentation at a hacker conference describing his successful effort to crack the DRM protecting Adobe's eBook format.[78]

In both cases public response forced the content industries to back down. The tremendous outcry following Sklyarov's arrest included outdoor protests and a boycott of Adobe products. Sklyarov was released and a subsequent prosecution of his employer was unsuccessful. Professor Felten eventually presented his research at a later conference. But the cases awakened a community that had viewed government regulation as an annoyance that could easily be avoided, and drew attention to the DMCA's effect on academic research and innovation.

While the DMCA is widely reviled by those who form the "grass roots" of the copyright reform movement, the broadcast flag and analog hole legislation don't seem to incite the same passion. Rallying the grass roots on government technology mandates is a difficult task. In this sense, the content industries' strategies of indirect control, controlling devices to control consumers, is an effective tactic. Those who care about these issues usually have the technical savvy (or access to those who do) to easily circumvent restrictions imposed on device makers, and thus don't tend to think it's all that big a deal. Since the legislation is prospective, imposing restrictions on devices consumers do not yet own, tech mandates lack the sense of urgency created by criminalizing previously legal activity that fueled opposition to the DMCA.

Traditional foes of "big government" seem to take a pass on these unprecedented technology mandates. A lot of this can be chalked up to the power of the "intellectual property" meme, which equates the copyright protections with the protections we afford real property. "Intellectual property" is misleading—there are a lot of reasons to treat real property differently than copyrightable material—but it provides policymakers an intuitive handle on a complex issue. For legislators whose opposition to big government is rooted in a belief in strong private property rights, government mandates to protect intellectual property seem reasonable. As a result many conservative legislators who often find themselves opposed to Hollywood on cultural issues end up on their side when talk turns to flags and holes.

Looking Forward

Though the broadcast flag has remained on the content industry's legislative agenda four years after the D.C. Circuit struck down the FCC's broadcast flag rules, simply delaying the flag appears to have been enough to kill it. The content industries now broadcast nearly all of their high-value content in digital format, and the end of the transition to digital television has rendered useless the argument that the absence of high-value content will delay the rollout of digital television. As the installed base of non-flag-compliant digital tuners grows, subsequent flag mandates would simply come too late to have any realistic effect on the availability of DTV content online, undermining the flag's justification as an anti-infringement measure.[79] As these policy rationales fall away, the scope of the flag mandate—the requirement that all downstream devices be flag compliant—that doomed it in court may doom it in Congress too. Any legislation that would make obsolete the current wave of consumer electronics purchases—HDTVs, next-generation game consoles, and portable video platforms—is likely to be a political nonstarter.

Analog hole legislature and the audio broadcast flag will probably share its fate. The demise of DRM for digital music suggests that the terms of the debate may be shifting: the question is no longer who should implement DRM, but whether we should have DRM at all.

This is a highly volatile and dynamic domain of technology and public policy. The number of institutional, legal, and technical acronyms and buzzwords is daunting. But because these issues affect the daily behaviors and expectations of so many citizens, especially younger citizens, they represent one of the relatively few domains of technology policy about which many typical consumers care and choose to keep informed about. This theater of policy warfare engaging the content industries, the consumer electronics and online industries, and the public has witnessed many battles fought and is likely to witness many yet to come. Although we cannot predict the outcomes ahead, we have reviewed the historical background to the debate at the turn of the millennium in the United States and urge readers to—as they often say in the traditional media—stay tuned.

In many ways, the world of Digital Rights Management (DRM) has changed drastically in the two years since this chapter was first drafted. Most prominently, the use of DRM for music downloads is, as a practical matter, finished. Its demise was hastened by Amazon.com's decision to sell DRM-free MP3s[80] and Apple CEO Steve Jobs's impassioned denouncement of DRM,[81] both of which occurred in 2007.

However, DRM is still living and thriving in the video world. That fact was highlighted early in 2009 when newly elected U.S. President Barack Obama gave Britain's Prime Minister, Gordon Brown, a gift of 25 dozen movie DVDs. To the delight of DRM and DMCA opponents everywhere, it was discovered that the Prime Minister could not play the DVDs on his DVD player because they are "region encoded"—DRM that prohibits the playback of DVDs on DVD players from different regions of the world (thereby ensuring that people do not purchase lower-priced DVDs from other parts of the world).[82]

Nor have the content industry's efforts to mandate DRM ceased. Legislative efforts to give the FCC the power to reinstate the broadcast flag have arisen every year since the D.C. Circuit struck down the FCC's broadcast flag rules in 2005. And in 2008, the Motion Picture Association of America (MPAA) petitioned the FCC to allow it to engage in "selectable output control," ostensibly for the purpose of slightly closing the window between release of a movie on DVD and cable video-on-demand. Selectable output control would permit a content owner to shut off certain outputs on a consumer's television set, which in turn, would ensure that large numbers of television sets (particularly those with analog outputs) could not view those movies, whether or not they were willing to pay to view them.[83] Organizations like Public Knowledge and industry groups like the Consumer Electronics Association oppose the MPAA's request, and it remains pending at the agency.

NOTES

1. Microsoft, "Microsoft Security Glossary," December 19, 2005, retrieved January 8, 2007, from http://www.microsoft.com/security/glossary.mspx. This chapter uses *digital rights management* to refer to technical measures used to control content, though the term is not universally accepted. WIPO (see note 36) and many Europeans use the term *technical protection measures* (TPMs) to refer to such technologies, and some advocates believe that *digital rights management* is a misleading term for reasons we will outline subsequently. (For a sample of this debate see Margaret Radin, "DRM," June 15, 2005, mailing list e-mail, retrieved January 17, 2007, from http://www.interesting-people.org/archives/interesting-people/200506/msg00278.html.) Though *TPM* is perhaps more accurate, *DRM* is the term used by the public and in most U.S. policy debates, so that's what we'll use here.

2. Consider, for example the testimony at House Committee on the Judiciary, Subcommittee on Courts, the Internet and Intellectual Property, Consumer Benefits of Today's Digital Rights Management (DRM) Solutions, 107th Cong., 2nd Sess., 2002,

available at http://commdocs.house.gov/committees/judiciary/hju80031.000/ hju80031_0.HTM: "The ultimate victims of limited DRM options will be consumers, who will enjoy fewer opportunities to enjoy the many benefits of digitally distributed commercial content, or manage their own digital information securely, easily and inexpensively" (Testimony of Will Poole, Microsoft's New Media Platforms Division).

3. Retrieved from http://wiki.hydrogenaudio.org/index.php?title=MP3.

4. For a comparison of the restriction imposed by several popular online music services, see Electronic Frontier Foundation 2007. For iTunes, see Apple Computer, iTunes Store Authorization FAQ, retrieved January 8, 2006, from http://www.apple.com/support/itunes/store/burn/ and http://www.apple.com/support/itunes/musicstore/authorization/.

5. U.S. Const, Art. I, § 1: "To promote the Progress of Science and useful Arts, by securing for limited Times to Authors and Inventors the exclusive Right to their respective Writings and Discoveries."

6. Federal law is not the only law for governing creative works. State law may also apply to types of work not covered by federal copyright.

7. 17 USC § 106:

Subject to sections 107 through 122, the owner of copyright under this title has the exclusive rights to do and to authorize any of the following:

(1) to reproduce the copyrighted work in copies or phonorecords;
(2) to prepare derivative works based upon the copyrighted work;
(3) to distribute copies or phonorecords of the copyrighted work to the public by sale or other transfer of ownership, or by rental, lease, or lending;
(4) in the case of literary, musical, dramatic, and choreographic works, pantomimes, and motion pictures and other audiovisual works, to perform the copyrighted work publicly;
(5) in the case of literary, musical, dramatic, and choreographic works, pantomimes, and pictorial, graphic, or sculptural works, including the individual images of a motion picture or other audiovisual work, to display the copyrighted work publicly; and
(6) in the case of sound recordings, to perform the copyrighted work publicly by means of a digital audio transmission.

8. 17 USC § 109(a) provides in relevant part: "Notwithstanding the provisions of 106(3), the owner of a particular copy or phonorecord lawfully made under this title, or any person authorized by such owner, is entitled, without the authority of the Copyright owner, to sell or otherwise dispose of the possession of that copy or phonorecord."

9. 17 USC § 110(3).

10. 17 USC §107.

11. The most famous example of this is the Supreme Court's decision in *Sony Corp. of America v. Universal City Studios Inc.*, 464 U.S. 417 (1984), in which the Court held that use of a home video-recording machine to record television programs for later use was protected by fair use.

12. This narrative focuses on the music and to a lesser extent the motion picture industries, since they have most aggressively pursued government technology mandates. It is worth noting that the computer software industry's products have been digital and readily copied for nearly the entirety of the industry's existence. Faced with a user base with both the incentive and the skills to copy and share their prod-

ucts, software makers initially experimented with elaborate methods of DRM. After these methods proved ineffective, costly, and anathema to consumers, many software makers dropped DRM altogether, while others settled on a limited—and by no means piracy-proof—access control model that used technical support as an incentive for purchasing software.

13. Home Audio Recording Act: Hearings on S. 1739 Before the Commitee on the Judiciary and its Subcommitee on Patents, Copyrights and Trademarks, 99th Cong., 1st and 2nd Sess. (1985–86).

14. U.S. Senate, Committee of the Judiciary, Piracy and Counterfeiting Amendments Act of 1981. 97th Cong., 1st Sess., 1981, S. Rpt. 97-274.

15. William K. Knoedelseder Jr., "Compromise Reached on Digital Audio Tapes," *Los Angeles Times,* July 26, 1989, business section, 1.

16. *Cahn v. Sony Corp.,* No. 90 Civ. 4537 (S.D.N.Y. July 11, 1991).

17. Public Law No. 102-563, 17 USC 1001-10.

18. 17 U.S.C. §1002, Public Law No: 102-563.

19. 17 USC §1003-07, Public Law No: 102-563.

20. 17 USC 1001 5(B)(ii), U.S. Congress, House, Committee on Ways and Means, Audio Home Recording Act, 102nd Cong., 2nd Sess., 1992, H. Rpt. 102-873; Litman 2001, 60.

21. Borland 2001. In response to such attempts, Philips, creator of the compact disc, stated that its players would refuse to respect the copy protection, and that it would require such CDs to bear a warning label (Boutin 2002).

22. Napter FAQ: Subscribe to Napster, February 2, 2006, retrieved January 10, 2007, from http://www.napster.com/faq/subscribetonapster.html.

23. First exposed by Mark Russinovich on his blog (Russinovich 2005).

24. Andrew Edgecliffe-Johnson, "Sony BMG Settles Suits over 'Flawed' Music CDs," *Financial Times,* December 31, 2005, 19.

25. A title Johansen acquired for his work on—and eventual prosecution in Norway for—DeCSS, a program to strip the Content Scrambling System intended to prevent copying of DRM.

26. Rob Pegoraro, "RealPlayer's iPod-Compatible Update 'Stunned' Apple," *Washington Post,* August 8, 2004, F6. Real faces potential liability for this under the DMCA, but so far Apple has chosen not to litigate.

27. Preliminary indications are that they are not: at the time of writing, circumvention tools for AACS, the encryption used on both Blu-ray and HD-DVD, are available. (Blu-ray includes additional watermarking and encryption technologies.) "Companies Probe Possible High-def DVD Hack," Reuters, December 28, 2006. For a thorough discussion, see Felten 2007.

28. Dan Glickman of the Motion Picture Association of America (MPAA):

> Content owners use DRMs because it provides casual, honest users with guidelines for using and consuming content based on the usage rights that were acquired. Without the use of DRMs, honest consumers would have no guidelines and might eventually come to totally disregard copyright and therefore become a pirate, resulting in great harm to content creators.

BBC News, "Digital Film: Industry Answers," question 7, February 9, 2006, retrieved January 17, 2007, from http://news.bbc.co.uk/1/hi/entertainment/4691232.stm#7.

29. This relationship is at the root of many content industry statistics citing the harm caused by illegal downloading or tools that enable copying. This is obviously questionable: the songs that users download for free are not necessarily songs that they would have paid money to own. For a good critique of the relationship between unauthorized copies and purchasing in the context of the AHRA, see Mckuin 1993–94.

30. In fact, this is the only working group anyone remembers, since most felt that government intervention would be premature (Litman 2001, 97 n. 1).

31. White paper, 213–17. Intellectual Property and the National Information Infrastructure: The Report of the Working Group on Intellectual Property Rights, U.S. Patent and Trademark Office, Washington D.C., 1995. http://www.uspto.gov/web/offices/com/doc/ipnii/front.pdf.

32. Ibid., 230–34.

33. WIPO is a UN agency that develops international intellectual property standards and promotes intellectual property rights around the world.

34. WIPO Copyright Treaty, Article 11.

35. For a thorough analysis of the legislative history of the DMCA, including use of WIPO for "policy laundering," see Herman and Gandy 2005.

36. Eventually codified at 17 U.S.C. § 512(c).

37. *Mai Systems Corp. v. Peak Computer, INC.,* 991 F.2d 511 (9th Cir. 1993).

38. This term is legislative code for Macrovision, a proprietary copy protection technology that introduces pulses into the video output of playback devices that render copies of videos made with most VCRs unwatchable.

39. 17 U.S.C. § 1203.

40. 17 U.S.C. § 1204.

41. 17 U.S.C. § 1204(a) (1–2).

42. 17 U.S.C. § 1201(d).

43. 17 U.S.C. § 1201 (i).

44. 17 U.S.C. § 1201(h).

45. 17 U.S.C. § 1201(j).

46. 17 USC § 1201(g).

47. 17 U.S.C. §1201(f).

48. 17 U.S.C. § 1201(a)(1) Triennial review problems.

49. *Universal City Studios v. Reimerdes,* 111 F.Supp.2d 294.

50. In September 2003, the RIAA filed 261 lawsuits against online file sharers for copyright infringement, the first of more than 17,500 such suits through June 2006. Frank Ahrens, "Music Industry Sues Online Song Swappers; Trade Group Says First Batch of Lawsuits Targets 261 Major Offenders," *Washington Post,* September 9, 2003, A1; RIAA Watch, http://sharenomore.blogspot.com/, June 16, 2006, retrieved January 17, 2006 (tracking suits against file sharers based on RIAA press releases).

51. Despite the abject failure of CSS as an anticircumvention tool, it has done a remarkable job of preventing innovation in the DVD player market. For example, the absence of a DVD jukebox is likely due to the combination of the DMCA and the restrictions imposed by the CSS license (Slater 2007; Borland 2004).

52. Consumer Broadband and Digital Television Promotion Act, 107th Cong., 2nd Sess., S. 2048, hereinafter CBDTPA. The bill was actually a revision of an even more flawed previous draft bill, the Security Systems Standards Certification Act (SSSCA) The SSSCA covered even more devices, and included no provisions for fair use or consumer input on standards (Rosenblatt 2002).

53. Ibid., section 7.

54. Mike Musgrove, "Hollings Proposes Copyright Defense; Bill Would Require Electronic Products to Deter Piracy," *Washington Post*, March 22, 2002, E3.

55. Section 201 of the Telecommunications Act of 1996 directed the FCC to issue DTV licenses only to those currently holding television broadcast licenses, adding section 336 to the Communications Act of 1934.

56. 1997 S. 705; 105 S. 705.

57. Deficit Reduction Act of 2005 Pub.L. 109–171 modifying 309 of the Telecommunications Act of 1934.

58. See *In the Matter of Digital Broadcast Content Protection*, FCC 03-273, 18 FCC Rcd 23550, 23553 (November 4, 2003).

59. At the time, Viacom was the parent company of both the CBS broadcasting network and Paramount Pictures.

60. See Comments of Viacom, *In the Matter of Digital Broadcast Content Protection*, MM Docket No. 02-230 at 12 (December 6, 2002).

61. See *In the Matter of Digital Broadcast Content Protection*.

62. D.C. Circuit Court judge Harry Edwards noted this reach at oral argument when he said, "You're beyond transmission . . . I mean you're out there in the whole world regulating. . . . I mean, I suppose it will be washing machines next." *American Library Association v. FCC*, 406 F.3d 689 (D.C. Cir. 2005), Oral Argument Transcript at 31.

63. For a detailed analysis of the flaws of the FCC's certifications process, see Center for Democracy and Technology 2005.

64. Section 1201(c)(3) of the DMCA is an explicit rejection of this kind of technology mandate:

> (3) Nothing in this section shall require that the design of, or design and selection of parts and components for, a consumer electronics, telecommunications, or computing product provide for a response to any particular technological measure, so long as such part or component, or the product in which such part or component is integrated, does not otherwise fall within the prohibitions of subsection (a)(2) or (b)(1).

65. BitTorrent is a peer-to-peer file distribution protocol designed to simplify the distribution of large files by splitting them into smaller pieces that are distributed among a number of peers.

66. HDTV is the industry name for digital broadcasts of the higher resolutions (720p, 1080i, or 1080p) made possible by digital television.

67. Despite the fact that CSS was defeated years ago and circumvention tools are readily available online, DVD sales in 2005 were more than $16 billion. Ken Belson, "As DVD Sales Slow, Hollywood Hunts for a New Cash Cow," *New York Times*, June 13, 2006.

68. FCC Report and Order and Further Notice of Proposed Rulemaking, MB Docket No. 02-230, *In the Matter of Digital Broadcast Content Protection*, released November 4, 2003, 17.

69. *American Library Association v. FCC.* For more information on this case, see Public Knowledge, "Broadcast Flag Court Challenge," http://www.publicknowledge.org/issues/bfcase, retrieved January 17, 2007, from http://www.publicknowledge.org/issues/bfcase.

70. *American Library Association*, at 4.

71. Communications Act of 2006, H.R. 5252, 109th Congr., 2nd Sess.

72. See Digital Transition Content Security Act of 2005, H.R. 4569, 109th Congr., 1st Sess. This law is particularly troubling, since after passage of the DMCA the "analog hole" was the only legal way to make fair use excerpts of movies encoded on DVDs. See Letter from Marybeth Peters, Register of Copyrights, to James H. Billington, Librarian of Congress, 115 (October 27, 2003), available from http://www.copyright.gov/1201/docs/registers-recommendation.pdf.

73. Communications Opportunity, Promotion, and Enhancement Act of 2006: Report of the Senate Committee on Commerce, Science, and Transportation on H.R. 5252 Together with Additional Views.

74. Audio Broadcast Flag Licensing Act of 2006 H.R. 4861, 109th Congr., 2nd Sess.

75. Testimony of Gary J. Shapiro on behalf of the Consumer Electronics Association and the Home Recording Rights Coalition, "Protecting Copyright and Innovation in a Post-Grokster World," Senate Judiciary Committee, September 28, 2005.

76. Elizabeth Wasserman, "Security Code-Cracking, Professor Pulls 'How-to-Paper.'" *The Industry Standard*, April 26, 2001.

77. "[A]ny disclosure of information gained from participating in the Public Challenge would be outside the scope of activities permitted by the Agreement and could subject you and your research team to actions under the Digital Millennium Copyright Act ("DCMA")." http://www.cs.princeton.edu/sip/sdmi/riaaletter.html.

78. Retrieved from http://www.eff.org/cases/us-v-elcomsoft-sklyarov/faq.

79. This is increasingly problematic as broadcasters place popular content online for free.

80. Joshua Topolsky, "Amazon Launches DRM-Free 'Amazon MP3' Music Downloads," *Engadget*, September 25, 2007.

81. Steve Jobs, "Thoughts on Music," http://www.apple.com/hotnews/thoughtsonmusic/.

82. Carlo Longino, "Obama's Gift to British Prime Minister Rendered Useless by DRM," *Tech Dirt*, March 19, 2009, http://www.techdirt.com/articles/20090319/1337464182.shtml.

83. Retrieved from http://www.publicknowledge.org/issues/soc.

REFERENCES

Benkler, Yochai. 1999. "Free as the Air to Common Use: First Amendment Constraints on Enclosure of the Public Domain." *New York University Law Review* 74:354–446.
Benkler, Yochai. 2006. *The Wealth of Networks: How Social Production Transforms Markets and Freedom.* New Haven: Yale University Press.
Biddle, Peter, Paul England, Marcus Peinado, and Bryan Willman. 2002. "The Darknet and the Future of Content Distribution." Retrieved January 10, 2008, from http://crypto.stanford.edu/DRM2002/darknet5.doc.
Borland, John. 2001. "Protected CDs Quietly Slip into Stores." July 18. Retrieved January 10, 2007, from http://news.com.com/2100-1023-270164.html.
Borland, John. 2004. "Hollywood Allies Sue DVD Jukebox Maker." CNET, December 7. Retrieved April 6, 2009, from http://news.com.com/2100-1025_3-5482206.html.

Boutin, Paul. 2002. "Philips Burning on Protection." February 4. Retrieved January 10, 2007, from http://www.wired.com/news/politics/0,1283,50101,00.html.

Center for Democracy and Technology. 2003. "Implications of the Broadcast Flag: A Public Interest Primer (Version 2.0)." December. Retrieved April 6, 2009, from http://www.cdt.org/copyright/broadcastflag.pdf.

Center for Democracy and Technology. 2005. "Lessons of the FCC Broadcast Flag Process." September. Retrieved April 6, 2009, from http://cdt.org/copyright/20050919flaglessons.pdf.

Chiariglione, Leonard. 2000. "Open Letter to the Digital Community." September 6. Available from http://web.archive.org/web/20020924131633/http://www.sdmi.org/pr/OL_Sept_6_2000.htm.

Doctorow, Cory. 2004. "Microsoft Research DRM Talk." June 17. Retrieved January 10, 2007, from http://www.craphound.com/msftdrm.txt.

Electronic Frontier Foundation. 2006. "Unintended Consequences: Seven Years under the DMCA." April. Retrieved April 9, 2009, from http://www.eff.org/IP/DMCA/unintended_consequences.php.

Electronic Frontier Foundation. 2007. "The Customer Is Always Wrong: A User's Guide to DRM in Online Music." January 8. Retrieved April 6, 2009, from http://www.eff.org/IP/DRM/guide.

Elmer-Dewitt, Philip. 1993. "Take a Trip into the Future on the ELECTRONIC SUPERHIGHWAY." Time, April 12.

Felten, Ed. 2007. "AACS Decryption Code Released." Freedom to Tinker, January 8. Retrieved April 6, 2009, from http://www.freedom-to-tinker.com/?p=1104.

Godwin, Mike. n.d. "What Every Citizen Should Know about DRM, a.k.a. 'Digital Rights Management.'" Public Knowledge and New America Foundation, Washington, DC. Retrieved April 6, 2009, from http://www.publicknowledge.org/pdf/citizens_guide_to_drm.pdf.

Goldstein, Paul. 2003. Copyright's Highway: From Gutenberg to the Celestial Jukebox. Rev. ed. Stanford, CA: Stanford Law and Politics.

Herman, Bill D., and Oscar H. Gandy. 2005. "Catch 1201: A Legislative History and Content Analysis of the DMCA Exemption Proceedings." Retrieved April 6, 2009, from http://works.bepress.com/billdherman/1.

Information Infrastructure Task Force, Working Group on Intellectual Property Rights. 1995. Intellectual Property and the National Information Infrastructure. September. Retrieved April 6, 2009, from http://www.uspto.gov/web/offices/com/doc/ipnii/.

Kim, James. 2006. "Insider: The Truth about Battery Life." March 13. Retrieved January 8, 2008, from http://reviews.cnet.com/4520-6450_7-642771-1.html.

Kiss, Jemima. 2006. "@ Mipcom: Piracy Is a Business Model, Says Disney Co-chair Anne Sweeney." paidcontent.org, October 9. Retrieved January 10, 2007, from http://www.paidcontent.org/entry/mipcom-piracy-is-a-business-model-says-disney-co-chair-anne-sweeney/.

Lee, Timothy B. 2006. "Circumventing Competition: The Perverse Consequences of the Digital Millennium Copyright Act." Cato Institute Policy Analysis no. 564, March 21. Retrieved April 6, 2009, from http://www.cato.org/pubs/pas/pa564.pdf.

Lessig, Lawrence. 2004a. Free Culture: How Big Media Uses Technology and the Law to Lock Down Culture and Control Creativity. New York: Penguin.

Lessig, Lawrence. 2004b. "This Is the Constitution on DRM." June 24. Retrieved April 6, 2009, from http://www.lessig.org/blog/2004/06/this_is_the_constitution_on_dr.html.

Litman, Jessica. 2001. *Digital Copyright: Protecting Intellectual Property on the Internet.* Amherst, NY: Prometheus Books.

McCullagh, Declan. 2001. "Hollywood Loves Hollings' Bill." *Wired,* September 11. Retrieved April 6, 2009, from http://www.wired.com/news/politics/0,1283,46671,00.html.

Mckuin, Joel L. 1993–94. "Home Audio Taping of Copyrighted Works and the Audio Home Recording Act of 1992: A Critical Analysis." *Hastings Communications and Entertainment Law Journal* 16:311–48.

Oestreicher-Singer, Gal, and Arun Sundararajan. 2005. "Digital Rights and Wrongs." *SternBusiness,* Fall–Winter, 28–31.

Rosenblatt, Bill. 2002. "Consumer Broadband and Digital Television Promotion Act." DRM Watch, March 22. Retrieved April 6, 2009, from http://www.drmwatch.com/special/article.php/3095121.

Russinovich, Mark. 2005. "Sony Rootkits and Digital Rights Management Gone Too Far." October 31. Retrieved January 10, 2007, from http://blogs.technet.com/markrussinovich/archive/2005/10/31/sony-rootkits-and-digital-rights-management-gone-too-far.aspx.

Slater, Derek. 2006. "Windows Media DRM Apparently Cracked, and No One Cares." A Copyfighter's Musings, August 25. Retrieved January 10, 2007, from http://blogs.law.harvard.edu/cmusings/2006/08/25#a1889.

Slater, Derek. 2007. "CES 2007: In Search of the DVD Home Server." January 9. Retrieved April 6, 2009, from http://www.eff.org/deeplinks/archives/005064.php.

Contributors

PABLO J. BOCZKOWSKI is Associate Professor in the Program of Media, Technology, and Society at Northwestern University. His research examines transformations in the institutions and technologies of print culture in the digital age. His publications include the multi-award winning *Digitizing the News: Innovation in Online Newspapers* (MIT Press, 2004), the forthcoming *News at Work: Imitation in an Age of Information Abundance* (University of Chicago Press, 2010), and papers in numerous journals and edited volumes. He is currently writing up the results of recent studies about news, culture, and politics in Europe, Latin America, and the United States, and beginning to work on his next book, tentatively entitled *How Institutions Decay: What the Demise of Print Newspapers Tells Us About the Unravelling of Social Formations.*

JOHN CAREY is Professor in Communications and Media Management at Fordham Business School. For many years he has directed the telecommunications consulting firm Greystone Communications. His current research focuses on broadband telecommunication networks and interactive television. Publications include "Plato at the Keyboard: Telecommunications Technology and Education Policy," "How Communication Technologies Enter American Households," "How New Media Affect TV Viewing," and "Interactive Media." His B.A. is from Fordham University, and his M.A. and Ph.D. from Annenberg School for Communications, University of Pennsylvania.

PAUL N. EDWARDS is Associate Professor in the School of Information at the University of Michigan, where he writes and teaches on the history, politics, and culture of information technology and infrastructure.

Edwards is the author of *The Closed World: Computers and the Politics of Discourse in Cold War America* (MIT Press, 1996) and coeditor of *Changing the Atmosphere: Expert Knowledge and Environmental Governance* (MIT Press, 2001), as well as numerous articles, reports, and web sites. He founded the University of Michigan Science, Technology and Society Program and directed it from 2000 to 2003. With Gabrielle Hecht, Edwards is presently writing a book on the technopolitics of information infrastructure in South Africa. He is also leading the Monitoring, Modeling, and Memory Project (monmodmem.org), a three-year comparative study of large-scale cyberinfrastructure efforts in the earth and environmental sciences. Edwards' most recent book is *The World in a Machine: Computer Models, Data Networks, and Global Atmospheric Politics* (MIT Press, 2010).

AMITAI ETZIONI received his Ph.D. in sociology from the University of California, Berkeley, in 1958 and served as a Professor of Sociology at Columbia University for twenty years; part of that time as the Chairman of the department. He was a guest scholar at the Brookings Institution in 1978 before serving as a Senior Advisor to the White House on domestic affairs from 1979 to 1980. In 1980, Etzioni was named the first University Professor at The George Washington University, where he is the Director of the Institute for Communitarian Policy Studies. From 1987 to 1989 he served as the Thomas Henry Carroll Ford Foundation Professor at the Harvard Business School. Etzioni served as President of the American Sociological Association in 1994–95, and in 1989–90 was the founding president of the international Society for the Advancement of Socio-Economics. In 1990, he founded the Communitarian Network, a not-for-profit, nonpartisan organization dedicated to shoring up the moral, social, and political foundations of society. He was the editor of *The Responsive Community: Rights and Responsibilities,* the organization's quarterly journal, from 1991 to 2004 (in 1991, the press began referring to Etzioni as the "guru" of the communitarian movement). Etzioni is the author of more than twenty books, including *The Monochrome Society* (Princeton University Press, 2001), *The Limits of Privacy* (Basic Books, 1999), *The New Golden Rule* (Basic Books, 1996), which received the Simon Wiesenthal Center's 1997 Tolerance Book Award, *The Spirit of Community* (Crown Books, 1993), and *The Moral Dimension: Toward a New Economics* (Free Press, 1988). His most recent books include *My Brother's Keeper: A Memoir and a Message* (Rowman and Littlefield, 2003), *From Empire to Community: A New Approach to International Relations* (Palgrave Macmillan, 2004), *Security First: For a Muscular, Moral Foreign Policy* (Yale

University Press, 2007), and *New Common Ground: A New America, a New World* (Potomac Books, 2009).

Outside of academia, Etzioni's voice is frequently heard in the media. In 2001, Etzioni was named among the top one hundred American intellectuals as measured by academic citations in Richard Posner's book *Public Intellectuals*. In the same year Etzioni was awarded the John P. McGovern Award in Behavioral Sciences as well as the Officer's Cross of the Order of Merit of the Federal Republic of Germany. He was also the recipient of the Seventh James Wilbur Award for Extraordinary Contributions to the Appreciation and Advancement of Human Values by the Conference on Value Inquiry, as well as the Sociological Practice Association's Outstanding Contribution Award.

RICH LING is a sociologist at Telenor's research institute located near Oslo, Norway, and is also a Visiting Professor at the IT University of Copenhagen. He has also been the Pohs visiting professor of communication studies at the University of Michigan in Ann Arbor, Michigan, and now he holds an adjunct position in that department. He is the author of the book *New Tech, New Ties: How Mobile Communication Is Reshaping Social Cohesion* (MIT, 2008). He is also the author of a book on the social consequences of mobile telephony entitled *The Mobile Connection: The Cell Phone's Impact on Society* (Morgan Kaufmann, 2004) and along with Per E. Pederson the editor of the book *Mobile Communications: Re-negotiation of the Social Sphere* (Springer, 2005). Along with Scott Campbell he is the editor of *The Mobile Communication Research Series* and he is an associate editor for *The Information Society*.

Rich Ling received his Ph.D. in sociology from the University of Colorado, Boulder, in his native United States. Upon completion of his doctorate, he taught at the University of Wyoming in Laramie before going to Norway on a Marshall Foundation grant. Since that time he has worked at the Gruppen for Ressursstudier (the resource study group), and he has been a partner in a consulting firm, Ressurskonsult, which focused on studies of energy, technology, and society. For the past thirteen years, he has worked at Telenor R&D and has been active in researching issues associated with new information communication technology and society with a particular focus on mobile telephony. He has led projects in Norway and participated in projects at the European level.

Ling has published numerous articles, held posts at and lectured at universities in Europe and the United States, and has particpated in academic conferences in Europe, Asia, Africa, Australia, and in the United

States. He has been responsible for organizing scholarly meetings and editing both academic journals and proceedings from academic conferences. He has received recognition as an outstanding scholar from Rutgers University and Telenor (more recently with the Telenor research award for 250,000 Norske Kroner). His analysis has appeared in Norwegian newspapers. He has been interviewed on *The Discovery Channel, National Public Radio,* and Norwegian TV as well as for periodicals such as the *New York Times,* the *Economist,* the *Los Angeles Times, Der Speigel, Newsweek, Epoca (Brazil),* the *Toronto Globe and Mail,* and Norwegian publications such as *Aftenposten, VG,* and *Dagbladet.* He has also had photographs used on the cover of *Norsk Medietidsskrift* and as a part of the Ex Ungue Leonem exhibition in San Francisco at the Ampersand International Arts Gallery, January 2009.

W. RUSSELL NEUMAN is the John Derby Evans Professor of Media Technology in Communication Studies and Research Professor at the Institute for Social Research, University of Michigan. He recently returned from serving as a senior policy analyst in the White House Office of Science and Technology Policy, working in the areas of information technology, broadband policy, and technologies for border security. Coauthored books include *The Gordian Knot: Political Gridlock on the Information Highway* (MIT Press, 1997), *Affective Intelligence* (University of Chicago Press, 2000), and *The Affect Effect* (University of Chicago Press, 2007). Dr. Neuman taught at the University of Pennsylvania, where he directed the Information and Society Program of the Annenberg Public Policy Center. He also taught at Harvard and Yale and was one of the founding faculty of the MIT Media Laboratory. His Ph.D. is from the University of California, Berkeley, and his undergraduate degree is from Cornell University.

ELI NOAM has been Professor of Economics and Finance at the Columbia Business School since 1976. In 1990, after having served for three years as Commissioner with the New York State Public Service Commission, he returned to Columbia. He is the Director of the Columbia Institute for Tele-Information. CITI is a university-based research center focusing on strategy, management, and policy issues in telecommunications, computing, and electronic mass media. In addition to leading CITI's research activities, Noam initiated the M.B.A. concentration in the Management of Media, Communications, and Information at the Business School and the Virtual Institute of Information, an independent, web-based research facility. Besides over 300 articles in economics, legal, communications, and other journals on subjects such as communications, information, public choice, public finance, and general regulation, Professor Noam has authored, edited, and coedited some 25 books. His Harvard degrees include A.B. 1970 (Phi Beta Kappa, summa cum laude thesis); A.M., 1972; J.D. ,1975; Ph.D. in economics, 1975. He was awarded honorary doctorates from the University of Marseille and the University of Munich.

HARMEET SAWHNEY is Professor in the Department of Telecommunications at Indiana University and Editor-in-Chief of the highly influential journal *The Information Society.* He brings a broad and varied background that includes a B.S. in electrical engineering, an M.B.A., and a Ph.D. in communication (from the University of Texas, Austin) to the study of telecommunications policy issues. His research interests focus on areas such as telecommunications infrastructure planning and policy, rural telecommunications, and universal service. He has published numerous research articles in *Telecommunications Policy; Journal of Broadcasting and Electronic Media; Media, Culture, and Society;* and *Entrepreneurship and Regional Development.* As he puts it: "I like to work on the intersections of the profound and the pragmatic where complex reality disrupts the tidy logic of established thought and forces new ways of thinking. I was drawn toward Telecommunications because it offers many such points of intersection."

TIMOTHY SCHNEIDER is an associate at Pierce Atwood LLP, Portland, Maine. He received his J.D. from New York University School of Law in 2008 and his B.A., magna cum laude, in social studies from Harvard University in 2003. While a student at NYU he served as an intern at Public Knowledge in Washington, DC.

EVAN I. SCHWARTZ writes and speaks about invention and creativity. His latest book is *Finding Oz: How L. Frank Baum Discovered the Great American Story* (Houghton Mifflin, 2009). His previous book, *Juice: The Creative Fuel That Drives World-Class Inventors* (Harvard Business School Press, 2004), explores the mix of unconventional thinking patterns that are practiced by some of the world's most creative and successful inventors. He is also the author of *The Last Lone Inventor: A Tale of Genius, Deceit, and the Birth of Television* (HarperCollins, 2002), which tells the true story of Philo T. Farnsworth, the farm boy who invented electronic television in the 1920s. A *Discover* magazine top 10 science bestseller, the book follows Farnsworth's Depression-era battle against RCA tycoon and NBC founder David Sarnoff, and shows how their clash symbolized a turning point in the way innovation happens in our economy. *Fortune,* in the magazine's seventy-fifth anniversary issue (March 2005), named *The Last Lone Inventor* one of the seventy-five best business books of all time. The *New Yorker* called it "a wonderful tale, riveting and bittersweet." Schwartz is a former editor at *BusinessWeek,* where he was part of a team that won a National Magazine Award. He has also written for the *New York Times,* Wired, and MIT's *Technology Review.* He holds a bachelor of science degree from Union College in Schenectady, New York.

GIGI SOHN is the President and co-founder of Public Knowledge, a non-profit organization that addresses the public's stake in the convergence of communications policy and intellectual property law. Public Knowledge seeks to ensure that the three layers of our communications system— the physical infrastructure, the systems, and the content layer—promote fundamental democratic principles and cultural values including openness, access, and the capacity to create and compete. Sohn serves as the chief strategist, fund-raiser, and public face of Public Knowledge. She is frequently quoted in the *New York Times, Washington Post,* and *Wall Street Journal,* as well as in trade and local press. She has had articles published in the *Washington Post, Variety, CNET,* and *Legal Times.* In addition, she has appeared on numerous national and local cable, broadcast television, and radio programs, including the *Today Show, McNeil-Lehrer Report,* Fox News Channel, C-SPAN's *Washington Journal,* and National Public Radio's *All Things Considered* and *Morning Edition.* She is a Senior Fellow at the University of Melbourne Faculty of Law, Graduate Studies Program in Melbourne, Australia. In 2002 she was Adjunct Professor at Georgetown University, and in 2001 was Adjunct Professor at the Benjamin N. Cardozo School of Law, Yeshiva University, in New York City. Sohn previously served as a Project Specialist in the Ford Foundation's Media, Arts and Culture unit. In that capacity, she developed the strategic vision and oversaw grantmaking for the Foundation's first-ever media policy and technology portfolio. Prior to joining the Ford Foundation, she served as Executive Director of the Media Access Project (MAP), a Washington, DC–based public interest telecommunications law firm that represents citizens' rights before the Federal Communications Commission and the courts. In recognition of her work at MAP, President Clinton appointed her to serve as a member of his Advisory Committee on the Public Interest Obligations of Digital Television Broadcasters ("Gore Commission") in October 1997. In that same year, she was selected by *American Lawyer* magazine as one of the leading public sector lawyers in the country under the age of forty-five. She holds a B.S. in Broadcasting and Film, summa cum laude, from the Boston University College of Communication and a J.D. from the University of Pennsylvania Law School.

Index